BOB BLAIR'S PIPELINE

BOB BLAIR'S PIPELINE

The Business and Politics of Northern Energy Development Projects

FRANÇOIS BREGHA

James Lorimer & Company, Publishers
Toronto, 1979

ISBN 0-88862-280-5 cloth

Design: Brant Cowie

6 5 4 3 2 1 79 80 81 82 83 84 85

CANADIAN CATALOGUING IN PUBLICATION DATA

Bregha, François, 1952-
Bob Blair's pipeline

Includes index.
ISBN 0-88862-280-5

1. Petroleum–Alaska–Pipelines. 2. Gas, Natural –Alaska–Pipelines. 3. Petroleum–Canada, Northern–Pipelines. 4. Gas, Natural–Canada, Northern–Pipelines. 5. Blair, Bob. I. Title.

TN879.5.B74 388.5'0971 C79-094536-3

James Lorimer & Company, Publishers
Egerton Ryerson Memorial Building
35 Britain Street,
Toronto, Ontario
M5A 1R7

Printed and bound in Canada

Bob Blair photo courtesy of John Schreiner.

This work was published with the assistance of a grant from the Social Science Federation of Canada using funds provided by the Social Sciences and Humanities Council of Canada.

Contents

PREFACE

The pipeline story is the story of pipeline builders and the political context in which they work. Even as the complex interplay between business interests, governments, regulatory agencies and government commissions continues, the Alaska Highway natural gas pipeline faces an uncertain future, stalled by bureaucratic inertia in the United States and haunted by the inability of its sponsors to raise the capital needed for its construction.

In this book, I have chronicled ten years of government policy towards Arctic pipelines. The decade of the Seventies witnessed more than its share of spectacular and unexpected developments: the emergence of Foothills' Alaska Highway proposal and the collapse of Canadian Arctic Gas' Mackenzie Valley scheme; the sudden expectation of domestic natural gas shortages in the mid-Seventies and the equally sudden rise of a gas surplus. The most startling development, and one that raises serious questions as to whether the national interest is being served, concerns Foothills' evolution from promoter of a Mackenzie pipeline to serve Canadian needs to, first, sponsor of an Alaska Highway pipeline to serve American needs and, now, advocate of large new Canadian gas exports to the United States.

Foothills' Bob Blair argued vigorously in the early Seventies for an all-Canadian Mackenzie Valley pipeline to serve domestic needs on the grounds that it would best serve the national interest. In 1976, however, he swung Foothills behind the Alaska Highway project to carry Alaska natural gas. He became a key figure in the plan to construct an enormous and very expensive pipeline that will carry American gas across Canadian soil to United States markets.

There are certain to be just as many dramatic turns in the history of Arctic pipeline projects in the Eighties as there were in the decade covered by this book. I have therefore resisted the temptation of trying to predict what may happen in the next few years except to say that the Alaska Highway pipeline will be built and that it will need government financial help.

Until the American government agrees to assist in the pipeline's financing, however, the struggle of its sponsors to keep their project alive promises to be very interesting indeed.

The task of writing this book would have proved immensely more difficult had it not been for the assistance of the Canadian Wildlife Federation and the Canadian Arctic Resources Committee. I am deeply grateful to both for their generous help and owe a large personal debt to their executive directors, Ken Brynaert and Murray Coolican.

During the course of my research, I benefited also from the advice and encouragement of numerous individuals who agreed to review and criticize my work. I want to single out particularly Helen Henderson, John Pepperell, John Robinson and Bruce Willson. To them and the many others who helped me unravel the strands of the pipeline story, I extend a heartfelt thanks.

I want to thank also Sue Belair and Ann Ray who typed the various drafts of my manuscript. Their contribution, too, was invaluable. I, of course, assume full responsibility for any mistakes.

F.B.
August 1979

CHAPTER ONE

THE ISSUES AND THE PLAYERS

On February 8, 1968, Atlantic Richfield, a large independent American oil company, discovered an elephant at Prudhoe Bay on the north coast of Alaska. An elephant, in the vernacular of the oil industry, is a very large oil field containing at least a billion barrels of oil. It took a second well and six more months before the full size of the Prudhoe Bay discovery was known, but by July 1968 it became clear that on the inhospitable North Slope of Alaska lay the biggest oil and gas field in North America: 9.6 billion barrels of oil and 26 trillion cubic feet of gas, enough energy to meet all of Canada's needs for eleven years at current rates of consumption.

Even at the depressed oil and gas prices of the late 1960s, Prudhoe Bay represented a bonanza worth many billions of dollars. The several oil companies that shared an interest in the discovery therefore began immediately to examine how Prudhoe Bay oil and gas could be brought to market as quickly and cheaply as possible. Because Canada lies between Alaska and the rest of the United States, it was a natural route for any pipeline that would connect Prudhoe Bay to the American mid-west.

Pipelines, it must be understood, are more than arteries of steel connecting distant oil or gas wells to market. They are instruments of industrial strategy with far-reaching implications for the regions they serve. By acting as a stimulus to economic diversification or accelerating the concentration of industrial activity, they can affect the growth and pattern of growth of an economy. Their ownership, capacity, cost, routing and destination all become, as a result, matters of the utmost importance to a nation. The pioneering nature of the northern pipelines magnified their importance even further: not only would the unprecedented scale of these projects multiply their potential costs and benefits several-fold, but the pipelines would govern in Prudhoe Bay the exploitation of one of the world's largest oil and gas fields while they would play a determining role in the development of Canada's own potentially oil and gas rich Beaufort Sea and Mackenzie Delta.

The Canadian government crossed its Rubicon early, in 1970, when it decided to encourage the construction of both an oil and a gas pipeline from Prudhoe Bay up the Mackenzie Valley to American markets. The United States, however, chose to build the oil line to the south coast of Alaska and use tankers to deliver Alaskan oil to California. This is the story of how the gas line decision was made.

THE AMERICAN CONNECTION

The decision to build the Alaska Highway gas pipeline was unquestionably one of the most important Canada took in the 1970s. What makes it so unique is not only the size of the project—at least $14 billion—but even more unique is its bi-national nature. The Alaska Highway pipeline will link the energy destinies of Canada and the United States more closely than ever before. If the connecting Dempster pipeline to carry Canadian gas from the Mackenzie Delta is built, Canadian and American gas will be flowing in a single pipeline, giving each country an unprecedented say in the management of the other's resources. The interdependence of both countries in energy matters is already very high: Canada exports substantial quantities of both oil and gas to the United States and imports American coal; Canadian pipelines cross American territory; the electricity grids of the two countries are closely integrated; the Canadian oil industry is largely American-owned. The construction of a pipeline that will carry a vital strategic resource from one part of the US across Canadian land to another part of the US will not fail to give the United States an even greater stake in Canada's energy policy.

The pipeline decision itself illustrated the interdependence of the two countries. In order to reach optimal decisions in their respective interests, both Canada and the United States had to co-ordinate their policies closely. The preferred route to carry Prudhoe Bay gas lay in Canada and required therefore a Canadian decision for the United States to gain the greatest benefits from its Alaskan reserves. If Canada, on the other hand, wanted to develop its own gas in the Mackenzie Delta—and in the mid-1970s it appeared it would have to do so to forestall domestic shortages—it had to build a pipeline jointly with the United States since the Delta reserves were too small in themselves to justify a pipeline to market.

Each country was therefore in a position to determine the range of transportation alternatives for the other's frontier gas. This mutual dependence inevitably meant that the pipeline issue would be resolved as much on its own merits as on the ability of Canada and the US to bargain most effectively. The pipeline decision then must be judged not only in terms of the benefits and costs it will bring to each country but also on the distribution of these costs and benefits.

The United States, of course, stood to benefit most from the pipeline's construction. From the date Prudhoe Bay was discovered until the Canadian and American governments agreed to build the Alaska Highway pipeline, it was an American demand for gas that constituted first and foremost the driving force behind the proposals to develop the northern frontier. Both the Mackenzie Valley and Alaska Highway pipelines were conceived to serve American gas consumers. While they might also tap the Mackenzie Delta, this was not a prerequisite to their viability and was almost incidental to their prime purpose.

Nevertheless, Canada did not fare as well as might have been expected in the pipeline negotiations with the United States. The Alaska Highway pipeline was approved within an American-designed timetable and will be built according to a schedule which maximizes its benefits to the United States. Canada will earn few of the benefits which its position as the land-bridge between Alaska and American consumers should have entitled it to collect.

Once Canada had embraced pipeline construction as its vision of northern development in the early Seventies, it implicitly accepted the risks inherent in marrying the Canadian and American interests. The measure of these risks was to be found in those areas where the aims of the two countries might be expected to diverge, such as the optimal pace of development and the attendant probability that the more powerful American interest would prevail. A substantial amount of socio-economic, environmental and engineering design work remained to be done on the Alaska Highway pipeline after it had received approval; this was an indication that the Canadian government had committed itself to a project in the absence of a rigorous evaluation of its costs and benefits.

A decision in favour of another pipeline would have been based on similarly inadequate information. In 1977, when the pipeline decision was made, there were four alternatives to develop the Prudhoe Bay and Mackenzie Delta reserves:

1) the Canadian Arctic Gas Pipeline to tap both Alaskan and Canadian reserves via a Mackenzie Valley pipeline;
2) the Foothills "Maple Leaf" project to carry Delta gas only to domestic markets along the Mackenzie Valley;
3) the Foothills (Yukon) proposal—sponsored by the same companies supporting the Maple Leaf project—to transport Prudhoe Bay gas along the Alaska Highway to American markets; a Dempster pipeline from the Delta to Whitehorse, on the Alaska Highway main-line, may be built later;
4) the "all-American" El Paso project which bypassed Canada entirely and would have carried Prudhoe Bay gas to the south coast of Alaska where it would have been liquefied and shipped by tanker to California.

All these projects were extremely large, implying the expenditure of several billion dollars, and they all relied to varying degrees on the application of new or upgraded technology. All would be built, at least in part, through inhospitable terrain under difficult climatic and logistical conditions and were as a result susceptible to extensive cost overruns. They were also for the most part mutually exclusive, either because they tapped the same reserves or because the construction of one precluded the need for or viability of the others. Finally most of them would cause large environmental and social impacts.

The Maple Leaf pipeline was uneconomic and never became a serious contender. El Paso was costly and delivered gas to the American Midwest where it was most needed by a circuitous route. The choice effectively therefore was between Arctic Gas and Foothills (Yukon). Until the very end, Arctic Gas had substantial advantages over its rival: it was more powerful, wealthier, had been formed earlier, had the most industry support and, at one time, the strongest political support as well. The Alaska Highway pipeline, conceived at the eleventh hour, was chosen nevertheless because it offered the prospects of fewer cost overruns, less environmental and social impacts and did not seem to require government financial assistance to be built.

Foothills' victory was also the victory of its main sponsor, Alberta Gas Trunk Lines (AGTL). Above all, it was the victory of AGTL's president and chief executive officer, Bob Blair.

BOB BLAIR

Sidney Robert Blair is a man of unique vision. A self-proclaimed nationalist, Blair has dedicated himself to the creation of Canadian-owned and western-based industries, a pursuit that has brought him into conflict with both the eastern business establishment and some of Canada's largest foreign-owned oil companies. Blair wastes little affection for these companies (several of which sponsored Arctic Gas). It is said that when Petro-Canada, the Crown-owned oil company, assembled a consortium of companies in the mid-Seventies to sponsor the transportation of liquefied natural gas from the High Arctic by ice-breaking tanker (the so-called Arctic Pilot Project), Blair refused to join until Petrocan first dismissed the major oil companies it had already invited to participate.

Blair traces some of his nationalism to the years he spent at the Choate School in Connecticut, an exclusive institution which counts the Rockefellers and the Mellons among its alumni:

> I have quite a lot of the same attitudes Americans have about the US and I transpose them to Canada. It's much like what they say about Arabs—the most nationalistic are the ones that went to Stanford and UCLA, because they took home some of that American enthusiasm for business working in the national direction.[1]

Before he joined AGTL, his ten years with Alberta and Southern, a wholly-owned subsidiary of Pacific Gas and Electric of San Francisco, was another experience which strengthened Blair's resolve to "work in the national direction." Blair, though, admits candidly that he is nationalistic only "relative to Canadian business, which is probably the least nationalistic business community any place. If I took my attitudes to the US or Great Britain, I wouldn't be extreme at all."[2]

What truly sets Blair apart from his peers, however, is his extraordinary political acumen. Blair's political instincts are so finely honed that they seem to be second nature. Blair exhibits a rare talent for capturing the mood of the time and tailoring his projects accordingly. His aggressive drive to diversify AGTL's operations, for example, fitted perfectly with Alberta's desire in the early Seventies to strengthen its industrial base. His sponsorship of no fewer than five different frontier pipeline proposals over a period of six years demonstrated even more clearly his willingness to shift with the prevailing wind. This pattern of behaviour has led one observer to remark that "if the National Energy Board gives prizes for versatility, there's no doubt at all that it has been treated to a virtuoso performance."[3] Yet, despite this implied criticism, there can be little question that AGTL's unique talent to anticipate changing circumstances constituted the key to its success in winning the northern pipeline application.

AGTL's readiness to accommodate competing interests is perhaps best revealed in Blair's speeches. One must guard, however, against being seduced by the rhetoric they often exhibit. Although his humanistic concerns are real, they have also proved their business value. Blair can be self-serving as well as pious: his testimony before the National Energy Board in December 1976 that no Mackenzie pipeline should be built until after a settlement of land claims was gratuitous, as it put the Arctic Gas project in jeopardy without endangering the Alaska Highway application. It is similarly difficult to judge other Foothills commitments about environmental safeguards and the protection of the native people made in the heat of regulatory battle when it was to each pipeline company's advantage to promise more than its competitor. Certainly, if any conflicts arise between Foothills' public posture and the stringencies of the Pipeline Agreement between Canada and the United States which obliges Foothills to build a pipeline along a predetermined route, within an explicit timetable and for a cost already agreed to, they will be resolved to the benefit of the latter.

Blair's style is best seen in the way AGTL deals with the public. The company does not have a public relations department, and queries about speeches or press releases go directly to senior officials, including Blair himself. At the height of the battle against Arctic Gas, AGTL and Foothills chose not to compete with their rival for media attention and advertising space. Instead, they paid $31,000 to a journalist, Don M. Peacock, to write a book, *People, Peregrines and Arctic Pipelines*, about the issues the northern pipeline raised[4] (Foothills made money on the book). Foothills also engaged at that time a well-known public opinion polling firm, Goldfarb Consultants, to conduct, in the words of the company, "policy research on the attitudes of the public at large, media, politicians and civil servants".[5] The cost, $337,750, was steep, but the insights Foothills must have gained were undoubtedly worth more.

Having worked personally in either field engineering or construction management for each of the main gas and oil pipelines in Canada, Blair brought with him an extensive knowledge of the industry when he joined Alberta Gas Trunk in 1969. In the ten years under his tutelage, the company has prospered mightily.

THE COMPANIES

In 1970, AGTL was but a provincial transmission utility whose potential for growth appeared unexciting. By the time the Alaska Highway pipeline is completed, AGTL will have become one of Canada's largest corporations, controlling assets in excess of $7 billion in pipelines, manufacturing and petrochemical projects. AGTL's spectacular growth has been accompanied by an equally impressive increase in operating revenue which rose five-fold between 1974 and 1978, and profits which more than quadrupled over the same period. In mid-1979, the two-billion-dollar-plus AGTL empire included 6,640 miles of transmission line; majority interests in two valve manufacturing companies; 10% of the Interprovincial Steel and Pipe Corp. of Regina (IPSCO); a 50% ownership of Alberta Gas Chemicals, the operator of two world scale methanol plants in south-east Alberta; 100% ownership in Alberta Gas Ethylene, one of Canada's largest petrochemical projects; control of Husky Oil, a medium-sized integrated oil company; and 50% ownership of Pan Alberta, the most active purchaser of gas in Alberta today. AGTL was furthermore involved in promoting the Quebec and Maritimes pipeline to eastern Canada, the Arctic Pilot Project jointly with Petrocan and, with Westcoast Transmission, the construction of an oil pipeline along the Alaska Highway.

AGTL's partner in Foothills, Westcoast, is often overlooked in the publicity that surrounds the Alaska Highway pipeline. A smaller and less diversified company than AGTL, Westcoast also adopts a lower profile as a matter of corporate policy. But appearances can be deceiving: Westcoast is one of Canada's largest corporations, with assets at the end of 1978 of close to a billion dollars. For the company, the most exciting growth still lies ahead: the construction of the Alaska Highway pipeline will multiply Westcoast's assets three-fold and could make the company British Columbia's largest.

Edwin Phillips, Westcoast's able and unassuming president, was overshadowed during the pipeline debate by the more charismatic Blair, although he too played a key role in developing the Alaska Highway pipeline. Like

Blair, Phillips worked for an American subsidiary before entering the gas transmission business. His experience, however, did not transform him into an economic nationalist and, on the contrary, made him appreciate the benefits of foreign investment: "I learned through this period it was a serious mistake to attach a nationality to the dollars that come to Canada, as long as they created good Canadian jobs".[6] An Americanophile, Phillips was instrumental in persuading Blair to sponsor the Alaska Highway pipeline after Blair had committed himself to the Maple Leaf project.

Until 1978, Westcoast's largest shareholder was Pacific Petroleum, a subsidiary of Phillips Petroleum of Oklahoma. Petro-Canada's purchase of Pacific Pete in the fall of 1978 gave the crown corporation 31% of Westcoast's shares and thus a potentially important say in the future of both the Alaska Highway and Dempster pipelines.

Impressive though the assets of its sponsors are, Foothills was no match for the corporate muscle of its rival, Canadian Arctic Gas Pipeline Limited (whose acronym, CAPGL, is pronounced "CAG-pull"). CAGPL represented the establishment in the Canadian oil and gas industry. It counted in its ranks Canada's largest oil company, Imperial Oil (total assets at the end of 1978: $3.8 billion) and two other subsidiaries of the world's seven sisters, Gulf and Shell; Canada's biggest gas pipeline, TransCanada PipeLines; and several very large American gas transmission companies, almost all of which were bigger than either Westcoast or AGTL.

CAGPL's chairman was William (Bill) P. Wilder, the former president of Wood Gundy, Canada's pre-eminent investment firm. A product of the Harvard Business School, Wilder helped finance some of Canada's largest energy projects during his years at Wood Gundy, such as TransCanada PipeLines and the Churchill Falls hydro-electric development. A blunt man, Wilder is an uncomfortable public figure and the task of chief Arctic Gas spokesman during the years of its existence therefore fell upon the shoulders of Vernon L. Horte, the consortium's president. Born in Alberta, Horte worked as a gas engineer before becoming vice-president and then president of TransCanada. Articulate and aggressive, Horte was an adversary of Blair's stature.

The rest of CAGPL's senior staff was also remarkable. It included Bob Beattie, the former senior deputy governor of the Bank of Canada, Bob Ward, the former Lieutenant Governor of Alaska and John Yarnell, group vice-president of Consolidated Bathurst. These were all influential men, with extensive contacts in financial circles, the oil and gas industry and government. Top Arctic Gas executives indeed enjoyed easy and frequent access to Cabinet ministers and senior civil servants. Partly as a result, they won the open endorsement of the Canadian government in the early Seventies. CAGPL's cause was helped further a few years later when the threat of domestic shortages prompted a long list of organizations and companies to support the early construction of the Mackenzie pipeline. Among them were trade unions such as the International Brotherhood of Teamsters; business associations such as the Board of Trade of Metropolitan Toronto and the Calgary Chamber of Commerce; large corporations such as the Steel Company of Canada, Noranda Mines, Falconbridge, Abitibi Paper and Du Pont of Canada; and governments such as the Ontario and Quebec governments and the Legislative Assembly of the Northwest Territories. No enterprise in Canadian history, with the possible exception of the Canadian Pacific Railway, had ever marshalled such a formidable list of allies.

Foothills and Arctic Gas epitomized the confrontation between David and Goliath, East and West, nationalists and continentalists. Foothills made the case for the Maple Leaf pipeline in spite of all economic arguments, Arctic Gas the case for a joint Mackenzie pipeline with the United States exclusively on economic grounds. In February 1974, Wilder would begin an article in *Maclean's* by asking: "What price nationalism?" Blair, on the other hand, asked: "Why dedicate a north-south corridor to foreign use and control?"

THE ISSUES

But if Foothills and Arctic Gas offered a study in contrasts, the fact that one rather than the other will build the northern pipeline is only of secondary importance since the issues both projects raised were very similar. The Mackenzie pipeline lost because it had become anachronistic, a solution whose time had passed; the Alaska Highway line won because it represented the artful compromise so typical of the Canadian tradition. Generically, however, the two stood at the centre of a web of issues which, in spite of years of public hearings, innumerable studies and the expenditure of hundreds of millions of dollars, still remain largely unresolved. It will be in this light that the pipeline decision will have to be judged in retrospect. William Kilbourn's description of the controversy which surrounded the construction of the Trans-Canada pipeline in the mid 1950s has a strong contemporary relevance that time has not eroded:

> Any account of its long struggle to be born inevitably raises most of the classic issues in Canada's survival as a nation; American economic influence and the nature of Canadian-American relations; the debate between north-south continentalism and east-west nationalism, the question of transportation and national unity, of energy and national growth, of control over natural resources and their exploitation; the latent conflict between western producer and eastern consumer; dominion-provincial relations; the problem of public versus private enterprise and the compromise of the Crown corporation; the connections between business and politicians, and the role of regulatory bodies between them; the rights of Parliament; and the place of popular feelings,

> pressure groups and the press in the difficult matter of making decisions on complex issues of great national importance.[7]

To this long list the northern pipeline added the tension between environmental concerns and economic imperatives; the value to be placed on the cultural survival of the native people and the settlement of their land claims; and the direction of long term energy policy and the pace of northern development.

Not only was the majority of these issues not resolved after the pipeline decision; several had not even been addressed. The government's failure to confront them at this time will make their future resolution more difficult and curtail the range of energy options open to this country.

The government's record over the northern pipeline does not inspire confidence that future pipeline applications will be dealt with more openly and more responsibly. The Pipeline Agreement with the United States implies that Canada has already committed itself to the construction of a Dempster pipeline to the Mackenzie Delta in the same manner it had committed itself earlier to the construction of a Mackenzie pipeline, that is, before any studies on the desirability or feasibility of the project have been concluded.

Already the effects of the government's northern pipeline policy are being felt in one area of crucial importance to this country's future. After having resisted and seemingly arrested the continental pull in energy policy in the early 1970s, Canada has now been seduced anew by the deceptive attractiveness of co-operative energy ventures with the United States. Oil swaps, gas exports, a closer integration of the electricity grid, the benefits of a common oil storage program and the possibility of building an oil pipeline paralleling the Alaska Highway line to carry American oil were all discussed or implemented in the months immediately following the pipeline decision. The reassuring government pronouncements that enlightened self-interest would guide all these joint endeavours cannot disguise the reality that, taken together, these projects spell continentalism by another name.

Canada's reborn inclination towards closer energy ties with its neighbour will not fail to yield significant economic benefits in the short term. Cumulatively, however, these incremental decisions—many perhaps inconsequential in themselves—impose the risk that Canada's future policy latitude will be whittled away as this country's interest becomes irreversibly identified with that of the United States. These are the broader opportunity costs of the present pattern of energy development. They may be the Pipeline Agreement's longest lasting legacy.

CHAPTER TWO

PIPELINE PLANNING

For several years after the Prudhoe Bay discovery, the construction of an overland pipeline through Canada to carry North Slope gas seemed a virtual certainty. Although it is possible to liquefy gas to transport it by ship, this is a costly and inefficient method of transportation. For that reason pipelines have always remained the preferred way of delivering gas to market.

A gas pipeline, however, would have to await the construction of an oil line. Both oil and gas are found together at Prudhoe Bay, but it is the oil that is the more important of the two: roughly two-thirds of the energy Prudhoe Bay contains is in the form of oil. Alaskan state law requires that oil recovery be maximized; in the initial years of production, gas would have to be reinjected into the field to maintain reservoir pressure and push oil to the surface. As increasing quantities of oil were withdrawn, it would then become feasible to start producing gas without endangering ultimate oil recovery. In 1968 and 1969, therefore, the attention of industry and government was focused on the problems of oil transportation. It was only after industry had settled on a route to carry the oil to market that gas transportation itself became an issue.

From the beginning there existed two main alternatives to deliver Prudhoe Bay oil: a pipeline through Canada up the Mackenzie Valley and into Alberta to US Midwest markets; and a pipeline across Alaska to Valdez on the Gulf of Alaska from which the oil would be shipped to California by tanker. A third alternative, transportation by ice-breaking tankers from the Beaufort Sea through the Northwest Passage to the American East Coast, was considered and rejected.

It took the oil companies which controlled the bulk of Prudhoe Bay reserves—Humble (now Exxon), Atlantic Richfield (ARCO) and later British Petroleum/Sohio—only a few months to indicate their preference for the trans-Alaskan route. The reasons for this preference were straightforward: a pipeline through Alaska would be shorter, cheaper and could be built more quickly than one through Canada.[1] In July 1968, nevertheless, the presidents of these companies met J.J. Greene, the Canadian Minister of Energy, Mines and Resources, in Ottawa to discuss the possibility of a Mackenzie oil pipeline. The Trudeau government was only three months old at the time. It was brimming with confidence after having scored a convincing election victory in June. In 1968, foreign ownership had become a major public issue with the release in January of a Privy Council office report on the structure of the Canadian industry (the *Watkins Report*). The oil companies were told that a Mackenzie pipeline would have to have majority Canadian control.

This condition strengthened the resolve of the Prudhoe Bay producers to stay in Alaska. In late July, Humble transferred one of its top engineers to Anchorage to begin studies on a pipeline route from Prudhoe Bay to Valdez. In October, Humble, ARCO and British Petroleum formed the Trans-Alaska Pipeline System (TAPS) which would later become known formally as the Alyeska Pipeline Service Company.

The visit of the oil company presidents to Ottawa in July had shown that Canada too would be affected by the development of Alaskan oil. In government and industry circles, the discovery at Prudhoe Bay was perceived as both an opportunity and a threat.[2] On the one hand, it was felt that the presence of large hydrocarbon reserves on the North Slope of Alaska would provide a welcome impetus to the development of Canada's North. The possible overland transportation of Prudhoe Bay oil to American markets might furthermore result in an increase in Canadian oil exports, particularly if it stimulated the exploitation of the reserves which were thought to exist in the Mackenzie Delta. This optimism was tempered by the apprehension that Alaskan oil might well displace Canadian exports and make the United States self-sufficient in oil. The loss of the American market would exacerbate the domestic over-capacity in the oil industry and deal a severe blow to Alberta's economy.

If in retrospect the basis for the government's hopes and fears appears disingenuous, it is important to recall that a decade ago Canada's petroleum reserves appeared practically inexhaustible. In a world of surpluses and declining real prices, government and industry agreed that the chief problem confronting Canadian energy policy was to find sufficient markets for domestic production.

THE TASK FORCE ON NORTHERN OIL DEVELOPMENT

The government reacted to the Prudhoe Bay discovery by creating in December 1968 the Task Force on Northern Oil Development (TFNOD), a high-level committee of senior civil servants composed of the deputy ministers of Energy, Mines and Resources (EMR), Transport (MOT), Indian and

Northern Affairs (DINA) and the chairman of the National Energy Board (NEB).* The task force's purpose was to formulate the government's response to the challenge posed by the development of the Alaskan reserves. Through its terms of reference, the task force was officially charged with assessing the feasibility of building an oil pipeline from Prudhoe Bay to the lower United States, alternatives to the overland transportation of Alaskan oil, the effect of the North Slope reserves on North American oil supply and demand and the economic costs and benefits of the various policy alternatives open to the government.

The task force very quickly outgrew its original mandate to become a tireless advocate of Mackenzie Valley oil and gas pipelines. Secret task force memoranda make it clear that TFNOD was transformed from an early date into "a transmission belt for industry initiatives requiring speedy approval by Cabinet".[3]

Three points deserve emphasis here. First, the task force centralized the formation of the government's northern and energy policy into the hands of a few individuals who, operating in secrecy, wielded an enormous influence for four years over matters which affected all Canadians. Second, the task force's pursuit of a Mackenzie Valley oil pipeline was undertaken unencumbered by any studies of the likely environmental, economic or social impacts of the projects. Third, the National Energy Board, the agency responsible for regulating the Canadian gas industry, which would hear any applications to build northern pipelines, was at the very centre of the team promoting their construction within government.

The NEB chaired the task force's pipeline and marketing committees and was represented on the economic impact and socio-environmental committees. In July 1968, the then board chairman, Robert Howland, had attended the meeting between Greene and the Prudhoe Bay producers. In the following years, the board continued to monitor closely the progress of the various pipeline application groups and to advise Cabinet on northern pipeline issues. By participating in the formation of government policy, the NEB provided valuable technical expertise to TFNOD's work. As a result of this participation also, it became exposed directly to the government's plans for northern development. When hearings on the northern pipeline would be called, the NEB would not only be ready, it would also be expected to render a decision which reflected the work the task force had conducted.

Because the construction of an oil pipeline had to precede that of a gas pipeline, the task force directed its first efforts towards winning the oil pipeline for Canada. These efforts failed but not before they had compromised Canada to such an extent vis-a-vis the United States that they made the refusal to accommodate the overland transportation of Prudhoe Bay gas un-

* The deputy minister of the Environment was to join the task force after that department's creation in 1971.

thinkable. The government's decision in 1977 to approve the construction of the Alaska Highway gas pipeline was pre-ordained to a large extent by the commitments it had made at the beginning of the decade to build a Mackenzie Valley oil line.

By February 1969, the three main Prudhoe Bay producers had firmly committed themselves to a trans-Alaska oil pipeline. Neither this announcement nor the companies' prompt purchase of steel pipe to build the line seemed to deter the task force from its self-appointed mission. On the contrary, it was buoyed by the formation in May of a consortium of various Canadian and American oil companies, Mackenzie Valley Pipeline Research Ltd., to study the feasibility of an overland oil pipeline through Canada. More good news came in June when two more groups of companies announced plans to assess various routes for the transportation of Prudhoe Bay gas through Canada.

The pace was clearly accelerating but neither the task force nor the government was in control of events. No other issue reveals more painfully the government's unpreparedness in coping with the issues raised by northern petroleum development than the challenge to Canadian sovereignty which was posed by the sea trials of the American supertanker *SS Manhattan* in 1969 and 1970.[4]

THE SOVEREIGNTY CRISIS

In late 1968, Humble had announced that it would test the waters of the Northwest Passage to determine the feasibility of shipping Prudhoe Bay oil by tanker to the American East Coast. At that time, Humble believed there might be enough oil in Prudhoe Bay to warrant both a trans-Alaska pipeline and tanker shipments to the New England states. The US Coast Guard decision to escort the *Manhattan*, without asking for Canadian permission, directly impugned Canada's claim over the waters of the Arctic archipelago and demanded an uncompromising response if Canada was to retain control of development in the Arctic. The government's reaction, however, was typically timid.

After a request that the American government apply for permission to send a Coast Guard vessel through the Northwest Passage was ignored, Ottawa decided to assert its sovereignty by co-operating with the United States and becoming part of the *Manhattan* project.

Publicly, Ottawa maintained that there was no challenge to Canada's jurisdiction over Arctic waters. In September, Mitchell Sharp, the Secretary of State for External Affairs, wrote in a newspaper article that "it is wholly misleading... to portray the *Manhattan* passage as a test of Canada's sovereignty in the Arctic. The issue simply does not arise." The US State Department was not duped by this rhetoric. When the crunch had come, Canada had vacillated.

Another occasion to intimidate Canada presented itself in early 1970. In February, the US Cabinet Task Force on Oil Import Control recommended that the United States reach a continental energy pact with Canada. In order to pressure Canada into such an agreement, President Nixon announced on March 10 a substantial reduction in the Canadian oil import quota. This reduction immediately reawakened Canada's fears that it might lose the American oil market. Significantly, it was imposed as Canada was developing a strategy to respond to the second *Manhattan* voyage.*

Although the sovereignty crisis ended inconclusively and a showdown was averted when the *Manhattan* trials were abandoned later that year, Ottawa had been made acutely aware of Canada's vulnerability to trade retaliation. The government felt it necessary in the months ahead, therefore, to placate the United States. This it tried to do by giving what was effectively approval in principle to a Mackenzie pipeline and vastly increasing Canadian gas exports.

THE PROMOTION OF A MACKENZIE PIPELINE

In April 1970, TFNOD, in its second progress report to Cabinet, had recommended a policy of "passive promotion" towards northern pipelines. In the absence of more detailed information about industry plans and their impact on Canada, the task force had been wary of advising Cabinet to make any definitive commitments.

Only a month later, however, it was felt that this strategy would no longer suffice: the government was coming under growing industry pressure to endorse a pipeline. An application was expected in 1972 at the very latest and a number of senior officials believed that "the Canadian Government owed it to industry to set out its philosophical stance".[5] In the aftermath of the confrontation with the US, furthermore, it was clear that positive action regarding the overland transportation of Prudhoe Bay oil and gas would help to improve bilateral relations. To give approval in principle to the construction of northern pipelines, however, would be a serious step to take and was perceived as such.[6]

On May 12, 1970, therefore, at the initiative of Gerry Stoner, the deputy minister of Transport, representatives of DINA, EMR, MOT, the NEB, the Department of Finance, the Privy Council Office (PCO), the Northern Transportation Company (a Crown corporation) and the yet-to-be-born Canada Development Corporation assembled to discuss some of the policy questions raised by the Mackenzie pipeline. Chairing the meeting was Marshall Crowe, deputy secretary to the Cabinet, who was to become the chairman of the National Energy Board four years later. The consensus which emerged that

* The first one had ended in failure after the *Manhattan* had been unable to sail through McClure Strait and had been forced to pass though the Prince of Wales Strait and within Canada's three mile territorial limit.

day was that the construction of a Mackenzie pipeline would indeed be in the national interest. There was a rumour of a great oil discovery in the Mackenzie Delta. An application to build a Mackenzie Valley gas pipeline was expected soon. The meeting agreed that it was in Canada's best interest to plan for a pipeline now before development pressures became overwhelming. Besides, recent technological developments in the transportation of liquefied natural gas made a tanker alternative to an overland pipeline a distinct possibility in the NEB's opinion. Canada could therefore lose a gas pipeline if it did not move quickly.

It is noteworthy that the consensus in favour of pipeline construction was reached in the absence of any knowledge of what the environmental impact of such a project might be. Nor were the economic implications of building one or more pipelines known. The first evaluation of a pipeline's macroeconomic effects would not be complete for another two years. A pipeline meant development and it was simply felt that its economic benefits would greatly outweigh its costs. Finally, the decision to encourage the construction of a Mackenzie pipeline was made without any reference to the native people or their land claims. Typically, Parliament had had no say in the decision.

The May meeting constituted a decisive milestone in the government's policy towards northern pipelines. Three months later, it led to the promulgation of the Preliminary Guidelines for Northern Pipelines which listed the conditions under which the government was prepared to accept the construction of northern pipelines. These guidelines provided the industry with the assurance it needed to proceed with its studies. Indeed, already in June, Alberta Gas Trunk Line, one of Canada's largest gas transmission companies, had announced its plans to study the feasibility of building a Mackenzie Valley gas pipeline (later to become the Gas Arctic Project Study Group); a month later, a competitive group, the Northwest Project Study Group, was incorporated. In the context of Canadian-American relations at the time, the publication of the guidelines reaffirmed Canada's willingness to co-operate with the United States in the delivery of Alaskan oil and gas. Once given, this was not a commitment from which the government would be able to withdraw easily.

GAS EXPORTS

The second thrust of Canada's conciliatory policy towards the US over the summer of 1970 was to approve on the recommendation of the National Energy Board a 50% increase in long term natural gas exports. This raised Canada's export commitments to one third of all then proven reserves. The government's purpose, in approving these exports, had been stated in May by J.J. Greene, Minister of Energy, Mines and Resources. Before a meeting of the Independent Petroleum Association of America in Denver, Greene had declared that

> ... Canadian gas will be available to supplement United States supplies only if our petroleum industry as a whole receives the incentives of progressive growth and assured stability of access to export markets for oil and natural gas liquids.[7]

Canada's strategy of inducing the United States to accept greater oil exports by promising additional natural gas supplies was both myopic and reckless. The government's policy of producing reserves as fast as possible was rooted in the erroneous conviction, nurtured by the oil industry, that Canada had virtually unlimited reserves of oil and gas which would be easily discovered if industry were only given sufficient incentives to explore for them.[8] The pursuit of this policy was all the more indefensible in light of the fact that, in April 1970, TFNOD had already noted a growing gap between future American oil supply and demand. In other words, by promoting increased oil and gas exports, the government was giving away an increasingly valuable bargaining lever in its relations with the United States. It is an indication of the fool's paradise in which Canadian policy-makers were living that Greene pointed out with satisfaction the day he announced the export of 6.3 trillion cubic feet of gas that the United States had agreed to a modest 10% increase in Canadian oil imports.

Cabinet's approval of the gas export and its publication of the pipeline guidelines were complementary components of the northerns policy it was promoting. The two decisions were linked and both were aimed at accelerating the pace of northern development. Although Cabinet did not appreciate it at the time, its decision would, only five years later, make the early exploitation of the North appear absolutely essential. The effective result of the increase in exports was to overcommit Canadian reserves to the American market and thus force growing future domestic requirements to be met from gas discoveries rather than existing stocks of gas in the ground. Intended as a lever to win greater access to the American oil market, the gas exports became, in light of the apprehended shortages which they precipitated, the most important factor militating in favour of the expeditious construction of a Mackenzie pipeline. Canada's policy of appeasement towards the United States over the summer of 1970 was to prove onerous indeed.

NEW GOVERNMENT OVERTURES

The pipeline guidelines and the export decision had set Canada firmly on the path of accelerated northern development. In early 1971, the delays encountered by the trans-Alaska pipeline were to give the government's promotion of a Mackenzie Valley oil pipeline a renewed impetus. Since April 1970, all progress on the Alyeska pipeline had come to a halt. The project was tied up in the courts because its right-of-way application had not complied with the US Mineral Leasing Act. Furthermore, additional engineering work was raising fundamental questions about Alyeska's intentions of burying the pipeline for most of its route. As time went by and the stalemate continued, the Canadian alternative began to look more attractive in the United States.

On March 2, Greene visited American energy officials in Washington to press Canada's case personally. The government explained Greene's trip and statements made by various ministers in favour of a Mackenzie oil pipeline at the time by professing concern over the environmental threat posed by the movement of oil tankers off the coast of British Columbia. This was a hollow concern: the government did not appear similarly preoccupied by the dangers associated with the proposed construction of deepwater oil ports on Canada's East Coast; nor, in the absence of an environmental evaluation of the effects of a pipeline, was it in a position to argue that a Mackenzie route was a superior environmental alternative to tanker traffic.

As has already been noted, however, the dearth of baseline ecological data about the Mackenzie Valley had not fettered the government's initial enthusiasm for northern pipelines. Now that the trans-Alaska pipeline appeared in trouble as a result of opposition from American and Canadian environmentalists, this was not the time for pusillanimous worries about potential environmental dangers in the Northwest Territories. On March 10, 1971, Jean Chretien, Minister of Indian and Northern Affairs, reaffirmed the government's position before an audience of oilmen in Dallas:

> We in Canada would welcome the building of such a gas pipeline through our country and would do everything that is reasonable to facilitate this particular development.
>
> With respect to an oil pipeline, it would appear that we are facing a somewhat different situation. An oil pipeline would also be acceptable. In other words, if it is felt desirable to build an oil pipeline from Prudhoe Bay direct to the mid-continent market, then a right of way through Canada, I am sure, can and will be made available.[9]

Two days later Greene was to remark that the government was "in a position to move with considerable expedition"[10] if an application to build a pipeline were submitted. The Prudhoe Bay producers, however, remained firm in their preference for the trans-Alaska route. At a meeting on March 24, Greene and Chretien were told by the presidents of ARCO, BP, Humble, Mobil, Phillips, Union and Amerada Hess that none of these companies intended to apply for a Mackenzie oil pipeline. There was little more that the government could do for the time being: it had already accepted that a Mackenzie pipeline could be built without full knowledge of its environmental effects; it had also promised quick approval for its construction, a powerful inducement to both the oil industry and the American government in light of the uncertainty then facing the trans-Alaska pipeline. Having established the framework for development and set up the rules under which a pipeline would be acceptable, the government felt that the initiative now belonged to industry.

If no progress was being made on the Mackenzie Valley oil pipeline, the Task Force on Northern Oil Development was comforted nevertheless by the fact that the trans-Alaska pipeline remained stalled; Cabinet was also pleased by, and had indeed encouraged, the beginning of merger talks between Gas Arctic and Northwest, the two groups of companies competing to build the Mackenzie Valley gas pipeline.

By fall, however, the government had become increasingly impatient at the slow progress being made. On October 28, the Interdepartmental Committee on Oil, the chief energy policy-making body within government, advised Cabinet to make a further overture to the United States. In a memorandum, it recommended "that the Secretary of State for External Affairs communicate with the United States and advise publicly that we were seeking the opportunity of discussing the Canadian alternative with US government officials".[11] The committee advanced this recommendation in full knowledge of stiff American demands relating to a trans-Canadian pipeline. On March 9, the Canadian embassy in Washington had sent a note to the Department of External Affairs outlining the views of American officials on the Mackenzie pipeline:

> In this context, one hears the frequent comment that the corporate interests could scarcely be expected to pursue the Canadian alternative in the absence of an inter-governmental agreement sufficiently definitive to permit the companies to plan realistically. At the same time, there is recognition that the oil and gas potential of Canada's northern reaches would have to be given consideration in any bilateral agreement.[12]

In other words, not only did the United States seek a treaty to protect its interests if a Mackenzie pipeline were built, it also wanted access to Canada's northern reserves. In these circumstances, Cabinet's continued promotion of the oil pipeline implied at least a willingness to negotiate the American demand if not indeed acquiescence to the US position. Very soon after, in May 1972, Cabinet was going to bring this policy to its logical conclusion by offering the United States a *de facto* continental energy pact.

Only a few days after the Interdepartmental Committee on Oil's recommendation, a bombshell came: The National Energy Board turned down new gas export applications because Canada no longer enjoyed an exportable surplus and indeed faced a projected deficit of 1.1 trillion cubic feet according to the board's export formula. The NEB report was the first indication that Canada was approaching the limits of its gas reserves. The rate of discovery in Alberta had fallen, and by November 1971, the date of the NEB report, only one discovery of gas had been made in the Mackenzie Delta, by Imperial Oil.

Four months later, Imperial was to sign agreements with two American pipeline companies, giving them first call on the first 10 trillion cubic feet of gas Imperial would find, in return for which both companies agreed to advance interest-free loans for further exploration. Although it is true that the export of this gas would have to be subject to NEB approval, these agreements nevertheless constituted an important prior claim to the Delta reserves, especially since the American consumer would have shouldered part of the risk of making any discovery. Canada's control over its northern reserves was slipping before they had even been found.

In spite of the warning contained in the NEB denial of new exports, TFNOD continued blithely to pursue its old policies. The NEB restriction on further exports was considered an irritating obstacle that "must and will" be removed by the development of frontier supplies.[13] In April 1972, when Jack Austin, a former Vancouver mining promoter who had become the deputy minister of Energy and the task force's chairman, wrote these words, Canada's energy policy was still based on the premise of exporting as much as possible.

THE MACKENZIE HIGHWAY

A few days earlier, Cabinet's hopes for a Mackenzie Valley oil pipeline had just been rekindled as the result of a visit on March 30 by Greene's successor to the post of Minister of Energy, Mines and Resources, Donald Macdonald, to the American Secretary of the Interior, Rogers Morton. During their meeting, Morton had asked for more information about Canada's interest in the Mackenzie route. Cabinet interpreted this request as an indication that the US might be wavering and would hence be amenable to persuasion. Sensing an opportunity, Cabinet looked for a new argument, one which might tip the balance once and for all in favour of the Canadian alternative. It found this argument in the offer to build an all-weather highway in the Mackenzie Valley.

On April 28, 1972, at a pre-election rally in Edmonton, Trudeau announced that the government would undertake the highway's construction that very summer:

> The route will be carefully selected so that it will be indispensable when oil or gas pipelines are built along the Mackenzie Valley. It will be built ahead of any pipeline and will therefore offer considerable cost savings to them during the construction period.[14]

Trudeau's announcement was a shock. Only two weeks before, Digby Hunt, the assistant deputy minister of Indian and Northern Affairs, had testified before a House of Commons committee that the northward extension of the highway from Fort Simpson was "... not included in the present (departmental) estimates, and at the moment provision is not contemplated for the following year."[15] The highway decision, it was clear, had been taken in haste. Its purpose was equally transparent: to influence the United States in favour of the Mackenzie pipeline.

Macdonald lost no time in bringing the significance of Trudeau's announcement to Morton's attention. The imminent application to the US Department of the Interior by the Prudhoe Bay producers for a right-of-way through Alaska added to the urgency of delivering Canada's views promptly. In a letter to Morton on May 4, Macdonald claimed that

> such a road will, on our judgement, substantially ease the construction of a pipeline. This decision is, I think, a significant new factor which affects the balance of advantage between alternative routes.

Macdonald's letter was remarkable for its single-minded marshalling of arguments in favour of a Mackenzie pipeline. First, he noted that a Mackenzie line would increase the energy security of the United States. "Furthermore, this security of supply", he added, "could be further enhanced during the interim period of northern pipeline construction by extra Canadian crude..." Only eight and a half months later, Macdonald would be forced to impose controls on oil exports in order to protect domestic requirements. There could have been no more damning proof of the ignorance in which the government was formulating its energy policy in the early Seventies.

Second, Macdonald argued that

> in considering the environmental impact of oil pipelining in northern Canada, it should not be overlooked that there are current proposals being studied by gas transmission and distribution companies for a gas pipeline from Alaska to the continental United States. If these proposals are successful, there will be environmental disturbance in any event.

This was an extraordinary argument to present. An oil pipeline would give rise to environmental hazards that would be substantially different from those posed by a gas pipeline. Prudhoe Bay oil is viscous and must be heated to flow. A heated oil pipeline created the danger that the permafrost—the permanently frozen ground which underlies much of Canada's north—would melt, resulting in large-scale environmental degradation. Furthermore, the construction of two pipelines in the same corridor would lead to cumulative impacts that would compound each other. In May 1972, the government was still in no position to assess the environmental effects of one, let alone two, pipelines in the Mackenzie Valley.

Third, Macdonald repeated in his letter the assurance given earlier by Greene "... there should be no reason why regulatory and governmental consideration could not be given in an expeditious manner commencing with an application filed by the end of the year".

Although Macdonald did not mention it in his letter, the government at that time also dropped its requirement of majority Canadian ownership for an oil pipeline. The government's commitment to the pipeline was such that it overrode even the mildest conditions.

In spite of Macdonald's last minute intervention, Ottawa's efforts to see Alaskan oil delivered through Canada failed. Macdonald's letter had promised too much and American energy officials were openly skeptical of Ottawa's ability to deliver on some of its claims. They knew that Canada had not done its homework and could not be counted on therefore to back up its assurances. More importantly, it had been clear for some time that the oil pipeline decision was going to be a political one. There were strong pressures on the American government to retain the transportation of Prudhoe Bay oil under exclusive American jurisdiction. Powerful lobbies such as the US Merchant Marine preferred the trans-Alaska route. Congressional elections were due in the fall. In June, the Department of the Interior officially approved the Alyeska pipeline application. In December, Mackenzie Valley Pipeline Research folded. The Canadian government would now turn its attention to the gas pipeline.

In order to win the Mackenzie Valley oil pipeline, the government had been prepared to build a highway, increase oil exports, accept an unknown degree of environmental degradation and promise the US prompt regulatory approval. What was the purpose of these concessions? Simply put, their purpose was to promote development, open up the North and foster economic growth. These goals were held to be intrinsically desirable. It did not matter that they could not be quantified, that their contribution to an industrial strategy was assumed rather than demonstrated, that they did not meet the aspirations of the native people and that they benefited mostly American oil companies. It was sufficient that a market for oil and gas existed and that these resources themselves were thought to exist.

THE GOVERNMENT'S OFFICIAL POLICY

If, behind the scenes, the government continued to promote the construction of one or more Mackenzie pipelines during the first half of 1972, in public its posture was suitably more restrained. The government's official position on northern development was presented early in 1972 in a policy statement called *Canada's North 1970-1980.* This document, parenthetically, had been ready since July 1971. At the time, however, Cabinet had decided to withhold its publication because it felt that "it would only create more dissent among the northern people".[16] The native people had never been consulted and were on record as opposing large scale development before the settlement of their land claims. The acceleration in the pace of petroleum activity (in 1972 Inuvik was the fifth busiest airport in Canada) forced the government's hand, and on March 28, it finally released *Canada's North 1970-1980.*

This was an admirable statement of policy. After proclaiming that "the needs of the people in the North are more important than resource development", *Canada's North 1970-1980* ranked the government's first three priorities in the North as follows:

1) "To provide for a higher standard of living, quality of life and equality of opportunity for northern residents by methods which are compatible with their own preferences and aspirations.
2) "To maintain and enhance the northern environment with due consideration to economic and social development.
3) "To encourage viable economic development...".

How closely did the government's actions correspond to its stated policy? In July 1972, TFNOD recommended that a land claim settlement with the native people of the Territories not be a prerequisite to pipeline construction. Cabinet agreed. It was the announcement, however, only one month after the release of *Canada's North 1970-1980* that the Mackenzie highway would be built, without any prior environmental assessment, that best revealed the government's disregard for its enunciated policy. The fact is that Cabinet's dedication to a pipeline overrode all other concerns. *Canada's North 1970-1980* must be seen in retrospect not as a guide to government policy, but as an instrument to placate an increasingly alarmed public.

The summer of 1972 would mark the last occasion when TFNOD would be able to report optimistically on the progress of its work and the prospects for an early start on a Mackenzie pipeline. By the fall, the premises under which it had been proceeding since 1968 had been sharply challenged. TFNOD's economic impact committee had prepared an evaluation of the impact on the Canadian economy of a Mackenzie Valley gas pipeline and its conclusions were sobering:

> A northern pipeline will not make a major long-term contribution to the Canadian economy in terms of employment or personal income. Furthermore, it will be of specific benefit to the United States. ... The construction and operation of a northern gas pipeline, even if it were to carry a substantial proportion of Canadian gas, would likely prove to be a mixed blessing to Canada.[17]

A further brake on TFNOD's promotion of a Mackenzie pipeline came with the October election which the Liberals won narrowly with a plurality of only two seats. The survival of their minority government would depend on the New Democratic Party who made one of its conditions for parliamentary support the "setting aside of the Mackenzie pipeline". Another shock was the release in December of a National Energy Board report on the potential limitations of Canadian petroleum supplies which noted that domestic oil production would no longer be able to meet total demand after 1973. The same month, a Cabinet directive temporarily halted work on the Mackenzie highway because of unexpected construction difficulties and native opposition.

Occurring in quick succession, these events had forced TFNOD to come to grips with a much different environment from that in which it had functioned until then. As the Mackenzie pipeline came to attract growing opposition, the task force would gradually lose its effectiveness and would eventually be disbanded. Its duties would be taken over by the Interdepartmental Committee on Oil.

By 1973 the Mackenzie pipeline had turned into a lightning rod for all those who were critical of the government's northern development policy. Public interest groups such as Pollution Probe and the Canadian Arctic Resources Committee were increasingly effective in questioning the dubious assumptions under which the government was proceeding; economic nationalists led by the Committee for an Independent Canada articulated a latent public concern about the pace and purpose of resource exploitation in the Arctic; most importantly, the native people were now organized and united in their resistance to development prior to the settlement of their claims. In April 1973, the Northwest Territories Indian Brotherhood won a restraining order from the Territorial Court freezing the development of lands in the Mackenzie Valley. Although the freeze was to come into effect only after all avenues of appeal had been exhausted (the government succeeded in having the ruling overturned three years later), the native people had won an important psychological victory. The court-ordered halt on behalf of the Cree Indians of James Bay to the massive hydroelectric project in September 1973, even though it lasted only a week, constituted another unmistakable warning to the government. Even in the absence of future legal challenges, the rules of the game had changed and a new note of uncertainty now existed.

This opposition happened to coincide, of course, with a time when the retention of power had become the government's paramount concern. Until it regained a majority in Parliament, its plans for pipeline development would have to be largely held in abeyance. Nevertheless, the government's record constituted a powerful commitment to the continued development of the North, and its behaviour would have to be influenced by the expectations it had aroused. If it had been forced to abandon its role as active promoter, it would not, nor did it wish to, reverse the progress that had been realized over the previous four years. It understood that it would have to respond to the formal filing of a pipeline application in light of the undertakings it had given. Publicly, however, the government felt it important to restore confidence in its stewardship in light of growing public skepticism. This is why the government could not be seen as imposing its choice on the National Energy Board and would now have to maintain a more circumspect posture as the date for regulatory hearings approached. If the NEB could publicly retain its independence, its decision in favour of the pipeline could be used to vindicate the government's northern policy. Only twice in the next year would the government reaffirm publicly its support for a Mackenzie pipeline and then only in response to events in the United States.

Canada was fortunate in obtaining the reprieve that it did. The government's unquestioning dedication to a Mackenzie pipeline had led it to propose ruinous concessions to the United States whose implications it patently did not understand. In its series of initiatives culminating with Macdonald's letter to Morton in May 1972, the government had shown itself eager to perpetuate Canada's role as a resource hinterland to the US. The construction of one or more Mackenzie pipelines under the conditions the government seemed blithely prepared to accept would have entailed ominous consequences for Canada's sovereignty by sacrificing an important measure of control over northern resources. Canada's economic structure would have been skewed further by the massive injection of capital into resource extraction. Patterns of trade with the United States would also have been affected. Eric Kierans was perhaps the most eloquent exponent of the dangers of similar capital intensive developments:

> If we build the pipeline, Canada could well revert to being a resource-based nation and we would be pushers of oil, gas and other resources, comparable to the hewers of wood and drawers of water image of Canada a century ago.... The pipeline could lead to a kind of industrial suicide.[18]

The point which warrants most emphasis here is that the government did not abandon its pursuit of a Mackenzie Valley oil pipeline because it was concerned about the economic or political implications of the project; or because insufficient environmental research had been carried out; or because the native people opposed it; or because its own conduct clashed with its stated northern policy. On the contrary, it gave up its efforts only in the face of the unshakable determination of the Prudhoe Bay producers and the American government to build the trans-Alaska pipeline instead. Its resolve to promote the Mackenzie Valley natural gas pipeline was similarly single-minded in the early years of the decade. It is against this background that we must see the events which followed.

CHAPTER THREE

CANADA'S PROJECT OF THE CENTURY

In the early 1970s, the Mackenzie Valley corridor seemed to exert an hypnotic effect on the Liberal government. The corridor was to hold not only a gas pipeline and a highway but also eventually an oil pipeline, electrical transmission facilities and a communications network. When Trudeau announced the construction of the Mackenzie Valley Highway in April 1972, he declared:

> A transportation system is the key to rational development in the North. This northern transportation system is mind-boggling in its size. But then so was the very concept of a continent-wide fur trade 100 years ago. It's expensive too, but so was the Canadian Pacific Railway a century ago. Is it too big a project for Canada? Only in the view of those who have lost faith in what Canada is all about.[1]

Trudeau's speech was a powerful appeal to the Canadian mythology of nation-building. In his remarks, Trudeau was marrying Diefenbaker's Northern Vision and its policy of "roads to resources" with Macdonald's successful unification of a young Canadian dominion through a transcontinental railroad.

The analogy that Trudeau and his cabinet colleagues drew at the time between the CPR and the Mackenzie Valley pipeline was more apt than they perhaps realized.[2] In the nineteenth century, the CPR had helped to open up a vast unexploited region of the country; it had enjoyed the overt and close collaboration of the government; indeed, the government had even extended financial guarantees to the CPR bonds; railway construction had begun before a land claim settlement with the native people of the Prairies and had met with their strong opposition; in spite of the treaties that were subsequently signed, the native people had not prospered as a result of the white man's intrusion and, on the contrary, had been made marginal to the new economic order.

These precedents offered alarming parallels with the situation prevailing in the Mackenzie Valley a hundred years later. Here too, the government was proposing a new transportation system with profound economic implications for the region and the country as a whole. Here too, the government had allied itself to powerful business interests to advocate one concept of northern development that paid little heed to the native people.

The concrete manifestation of the alliance between the government and industry was to be found in the birth of Canadian Arctic Gas Study Limited (CAGSL), a large consortium of oil and gas companies promoting the construction of the Mackenzie Valley gas pipeline. Until 1972, there had been two rival groups of companies to build the gas pipeline. In 1972, government pressure helped to persuade them to merge into one corporate entity.

THE BIRTH OF CANADIAN ARCTIC GAS

These two groups, the Northwest Project Study Group and the Gas Arctic Systems Study Group, had been headed by TransCanada Pipelines and Alberta Gas Trunk Line respectively, the two largest gas transmission companies in Canada. Both had been incorporated in the summer of 1970 although Northwest was the older of the two, having begun studies of a Mackenzie gas pipeline in 1969. AGTL had at first applied for membership in this group. When its overtures were rebuffed, it established the Trunk North project to pursue its own research in the transportation of northern gas. For AGTL, a Mackenzie pipeline represented more than just an interesting business opportunity. It could not afford to be left out of the studies other companies were undertaking. Alberta gas reserves would eventually decline and become depleted, putting AGTL out of business. Prudhoe Bay gas thus offered an attractive long-term supply which would offset the inevitable reduction in Alberta deliveries. But a Mackenzie pipeline also constituted a threat: being a high-pressure, large-diameter pipeline, it would offer transportation savings which AGTL's own lower-pressure, and hence less efficient, pipeline system would be unable to match. In order to protect its interests, therefore, AGTL had to ensure both that frontier gas would flow through Alberta and that it would flow under its control so that its monopoly over gas transportation in the province would not be undermined.

In December 1970, Trunk North was joined by three large American transmission companies, Columbia Gas System, Northern Natural Gas and Texas Eastern Transmission and, as a result, changed its name to the Gas Arctic Systems Study Group. Canadian National Railways—a crown corporation whose executive vice-president was Blair's brother-in-law—and Pacific Lighting Gas Development of Los Angeles became Gas Arctic members in 1971.

The Northwest Project Study Group had incorporated itself in July 1970 as a consortium of one Canadian company, Trans Canada Pipelines, and five

American ones, Michigan Wisconsin Pipeline, Natural Gas Pipeline of America, Atlantic Richfield, Standard Oil of Ohio (which had recently merged with British Petroleum) and Humble Oil and Refining (Exxon). Only a month later, the federal government issued the Northern Pipeline Guidelines, stipulating the conditions under which an oil and a gas pipeline would be built in the Mackenzie Valley. These guidelines stated that the government would approve the construction of only one trunk gas pipeline. The pressure was on to force Northwest and Gas Arctic to merge. As J.J. Greene put it after the guidelines' release, "We are saying to them, 'Get together boys and find a common corridor for only one of you is going to be in the ball game.'"[3]

The issues that were keeping Gas Arctic and Northwest apart could be reduced to three major areas of disagreement: routing, ownership and the use of AGTL facilities. In other words, would the pipeline cross Alberta to serve both the California and American Midwest markets or would it largely bypass the province to go directly to the Midwest? Would the line be Canadian-owned, as Gas Arctic insisted, or would its ownership depend on the nationality of its sponsor companies, which was Northwest's position? If the pipeline did go through Alberta, would it use AGTL facilities or an entirely new system? Although these differences were significant and could not easily be reconciled, equally powerful forces were pushing the two companies towards union. Through the publication of the pipeline guidelines and in private, the government was encouraging the two competing applicants to merge. The cost of designing such a long pipeline through unknown terrain was already high and the duplication of effort would only result in higher costs; finally, competing applications implied protracted adversary hearings before the National Energy Board which would also be expensive.

Merger discussions therefore began in August 1971. They culminated ten months later on June 8, 1972, in Houston, where the terms of an agreement were finally reached. The forced marriage, however, was doomed from the start. AGTL had joined partly against its will, at the prodding of its American partners. For their part, the Northwest group of companies, far from wishing to accommodate this maverick, hoped to neutralize it within a larger consortium. A reluctant bride until the end, Blair instructed the lawyer who drafted the terms of the agreement to ensure that they allowed any company to withdraw without penalty.

The Northwest/Gas Arctic merger yielded a quick government response. The Task Force on Northern Oil Development recognized that the 1970 pipeline guidelines were too imprecise to provide satisfactory guidance to industry in its planning and would have to be expanded. This seemed particularly necessary in the case of the environmental and social guidelines. Acting in haste, the Cabinet was able to table the Expanded Guidelines for Northern Pipelines in the House of Commons on June 28, 1972, three weeks after Arctic Gas had been formed. It was no coincidence that these guidelines proposed the same transportation corridor in the Territories for which Arctic Gas had already announced its intention to apply. References to an Alaska Highway corridor in earlier drafts of the guidelines had been deleted. The government did not just want a northern pipeline: it wanted a Mackenzie pipeline which could carry any gas that would be found in the Mackenzie Delta.

ARCTIC GAS: THE POWER

The government rejoiced at the Northwest/Gas Arctic merger. It did not understand the implications of the enormous concentration of economic power that Arctic Gas represented. At its zenith the Arctic Gas consortium comprised no less than twenty-seven member companies, and, although this membership fluctuated over the years, it never dropped below fifteen. At all times, the majority of these companies were American-owned or controlled.

Who were these companies? In March 1974, when Arctic Gas finally submitted its application to build the Mackenzie pipeline, the three largest owners of Prudhoe Bay gas, Atlantic Richfield, British Petroleum and Exxon, as well as the prospective producers of Mackenzie Delta gas, Imperial Oil, Gulf and Shell, were all members; so were three of the four main Canadian gas transmission companies, TransCanada Pipelines, Alberta Gas Trunk Line and Alberta Natural Gas (Westcoast Transmission was the sole exception); the largest gas distribution utilities whose sales accounted for 85% of the Canadian market—Canadian Utilities, Union Gas, Consumers' Gas and Northern and Central Gas—were also represented; finally, several of the largest American transmission companies which would purchase Prudhoe Bay gas and, they hoped, Mackenzie Delta gas also belonged to Arctic Gas.

The presence of three other companies in the consortium was particularly noteworthy. The participation of Canadian National Realties and Canadian Pacific Investments was significant, because the construction of a railroad to the Arctic was thought for a time to constitute an attractive alternative to a pipeline. CN and CP's participation in the Arctic Gas consortium preempted the thorough examination of this option. The third company deserving special mention was the government-controlled Canada Development Corporation, because its presence within CAG implied that the government not only supported the construction of the pipeline but was also prepared to invest in it.

The creation of CAGSL carried profound political consequences. By eliminating competition, it reduced the number of policy options to one, thereby sharply curtailing the government's control over northern development. The common front presented by the oil and gas industry implied that development would proceed on the industry's own terms or not at all. By late 1974, the steady deterioration in the Canadian natural gas supply outlook would

---

Canadian Arctic Gas Pipeline Ltd.
Corporate Membership (March 1974)

1. Participant Group A
   —Colorado Interstate Gas
   —Columbia Gas Transmission
   —Michigan Wisconsin Pipeline
   —Natural Gas Pipeline Company of America
   —Northern Natural Gas
   —Pacific Lighting Gas Development
   —Panhandle Eastern PipeLine
   —Texas Eastern Transmission

2. Participant Group B
   —Alberta Gas Trunk Line
   —Alberta Natural Gas
   —Canada Development Corporation
   —Canadian National Realties
   —Canadian Pacific Investments
   —Canadian Utilities
   —Consumers' Gas
   —Pembina Pipe Line
   —Polaris Pipe Lines
   —TransCanada PipeLines
   —Union Gas

3. Participant Group C
   —Atlantic Richfield
   —BP/SOHIO
   —Canadian Superior Oil
   —Exxon
   —Gulf Oil Canada
   —Imperial Oil
   —Numac Oil and Gas
   —Shell Canada

---

make CAG's arguments more persuasive still. Even if, in 1972, the government had been inclined towards imposing stringent conditions on pipeline construction, the threat of domestic shortages would two years later preclude such consideration.

Its large membership was at once CAG's chief asset and its main liability. It was an asset because it meant more money to spend for engineering and environmental studies and made the consortium extraordinarily powerful. It was a liability because it made consensus difficult to reach. The companies that joined Arctic Gas did so only because they agreed that the Mackenzie Valley represented the best route for the transportation of Prudhoe Bay and Mackenzie Delta gas. Their common interest did not extend further than the delivery of frontier gas as cheaply as possible. Each of them therefore jealously protected its autonomy within the consortium. CAG's chairman and president, Bill Wilder and Vern Horte, were asked to report to a management committee every month and their discretionary authority was always limited. In order to protect the minority interests of each of its companies, the consortium was divided into three groups: US Distributors, Canadian Distributors and Prospective Producers. A majority vote in each group was required for all important decisions. This cumbersome management structure gave a small number of companies in each of these groups a virtual veto over these decisions which injected a fatal rigidity in CAG's plans. As time elapsed and conditions changed, CAG's inability to react quickly became a major handicap.

THE ENERGY CRISIS

Arctic Gas gained considerable momentum in late 1973 as a result of the traumatic readjustment in Canadian and American energy policy following the energy crisis. As an instinctive reaction to the Arab oil embargo, both governments made self-sufficiency in oil by 1980 the cornerstone of their new energy policies. An integral component of the American "Project Independence" was to be the early development of the Alaskan oil and gas reserves. Taking advantage of the new public mood, the Nixon administration moved swiftly to certify the Alyeska oil pipeline whose construction had been held up in court for three years. On November 12, 1973, the US Congress passed the Trans Alaska Pipeline Authorization Act which was signed into law four days later. With an eye to the future, section 301 of the act authorized the President to enter into negotiations with Canada to determine

(a) the willingness of the Government of Canada to permit the construction of pipelines or other transportation systems across Canadian territory for the transport of natural gas and oil from Alaska's North Slope to markets in the United States... ;

(b) the need for intergovernmental understandings, agreements or treaties to protect the interests of the Governments of Canada and the United States and any party or parties involved with the construction, operation and maintenance of pipelines or other transportation systems for the transport of such natural gas or oil;

(c) the terms and conditions under which pipelines or other transportation systems could be constructed across Canadian territory.

The Canadian government's response was contained in Prime Minister Trudeau's speech on energy policy delivered in the House of Commons on December 6, 1973. Although the purpose of the speech was to outline the government's measures to cope with the oil crisis, the reference to the Mackenzie pipeline was obviously intended for an American audience:

> A major development is the proposed gas pipeline up the Mackenzie Valley to move Alaskan gas to United States markets and at the same time, to make it possible to move Canadian northern gas to Canadian markets. While this project must, of course, be submitted to the usual regulatory proceedings and cannot go ahead until it has been approved by responsible Canadian authorities, the government believes that it would be in the public interest to facilitate early construction by any means which do not require the lowering of environmental standards or the neglect of Indian rights and interests.
>
> At this point, I might just say that I can see no reason why Canada could not give suitable undertakings as to the movement, without any discriminatory impediment, of Alaskan gas through a pipeline across Canada to United States markets provided all public interest and regulatory conditions are met in the building and operation of the pipeline. An undertaking of this sort would of course be reciprocal, with the same assurance being given to Canada regarding our oil and gas shipments through the United States.

The government's position in favour of the early construction of a Mackenzie pipeline was reiterated publicly four days later by Finance Minister John Turner in a major speech before top American businessmen in New York, by Indian and Northern Affairs Minister Jean Chretien in Yellowknife in January and by the Canadian ambassador to Washington, Marcel Cadieux, in March 1974.

To Arctic Gas, these expressions of government support were "encouraging" but they were not enough. Unless the government translated its support quickly into formal regulatory approval, Arctic Gas feared that the United States would turn to a competitor, the rival "all-American" El Paso proposal. El Paso wanted to bypass Canada completely and build a pipeline parallel to the Trans-Alaska oil pipeline. The gas would be liquefied at a terminal on the south coast of Alaska and delivered by tanker to California. Although this was an expensive scheme, it held the advantage of being entirely within American jurisdiction. Regulatory delays in Canada, Arctic Gas therefore warned, would inevitably push the US towards El Paso.

On the surface this was a powerful argument. Unless there were very large discoveries in the Mackenzie Delta to warrant a multi-billion dollar investment in a new delivery system, a Mackenzie pipeline could be built

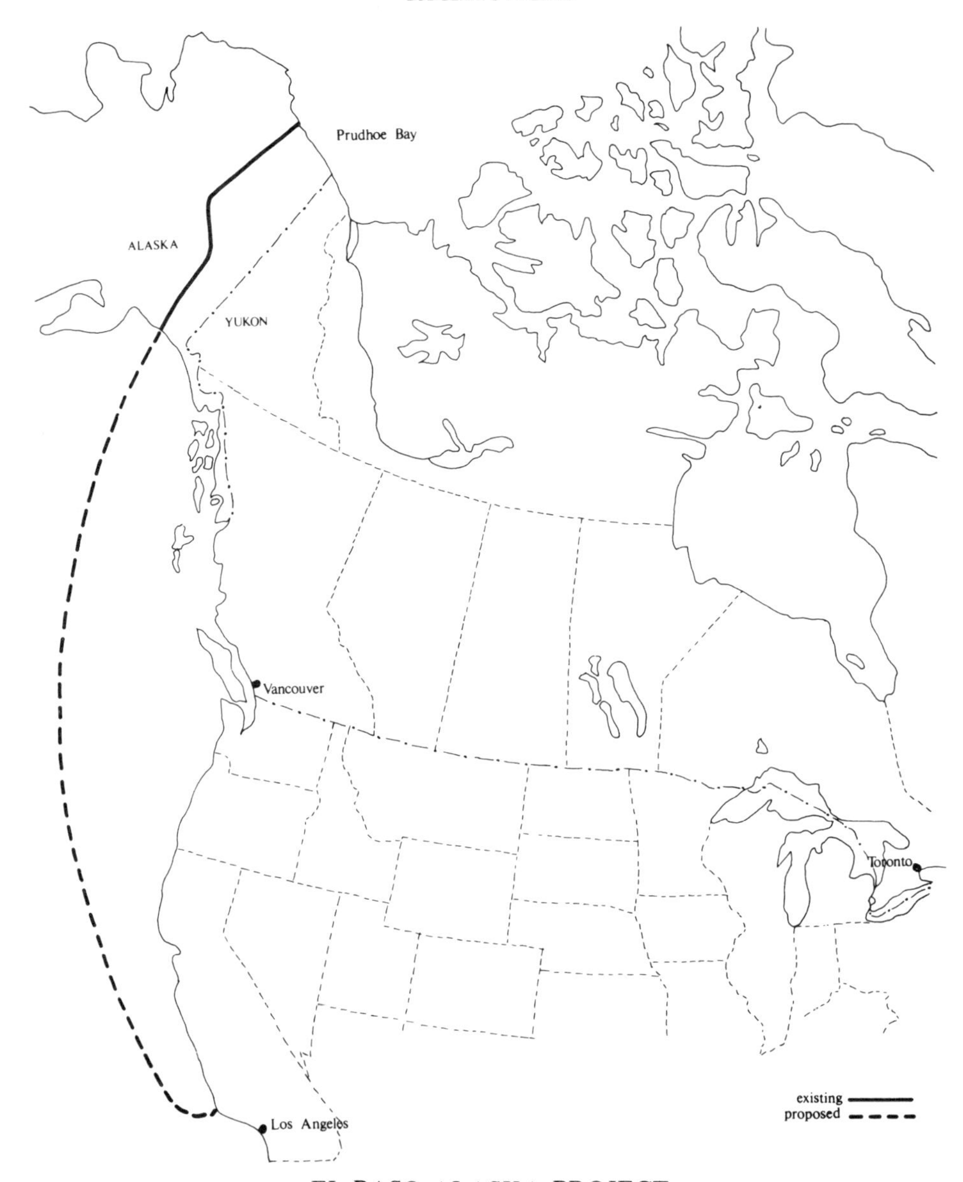

EL PASO ALASKA PROJECT

only if it transported Alaskan gas as well. There was not enough gas in the Mackenzie Delta alone, and, if Canada wanted to avert threatening domestic shortages, it would have to "piggy-back" its Delta reserves on the much larger Alaskan ones.

This argument, however, was seriously flawed. First, it minimized the many undisputed benefits to the US of an overland pipeline through Canada—benefits that Arctic Gas was emphasizing in the United States. Second, it assumed that Canada's substantial gas exports to the US were inviolable and could not be renegotiated if domestic shortages were to arise. American approval of El Paso, when shortages in Canada loomed, would have driven Canada to abrogate its exports, at least in part, an obviously self-defeating policy for the United States. Finally, as will be seen below, the date when Canada might have needed frontier gas was itself a contentious issue.

Nevertheless, Arctic Gas had considerable success in convincing the Canadian government of the threat posed by El Paso. In January 1973, Bill Wilder, CAG chairman, claimed: "Were the United States to be faced with excessive delay in obtaining Alaskan gas by means of a pipeline across Canada, it could well turn to alternative means of obtaining that Alaskan gas." Exactly a year later, Jean Chrétien, the Minister of Indian and Northern Affairs would acknowledge:

> The government has been influenced by the possibility that a failure to act in a positive manner towards this project could lead to acceptance by the US government of the El Paso alternative for Prudhoe Bay gas, that of its liquefication and transportation by tanker from Valdez. This in turn could mean that Canadians would not have access to Mackenzie Delta gas when they need it. The key to meeting Canada's gas needs in the next decade involves a joint pipeline along the Mackenzie Valley.[4]

ARCTIC GAS: THE PROJECT

On March 21, 1974, Canadian Arctic Gas Study Ltd., now formally renamed Canadian Arctic Gas Pipeline Ltd., finally filed its applications before the National Energy Board for a certificate of public convenience and necessity and with the Department of Indian and Northern Affairs for a right-of-way permit to cross federal lands. The same day, Alaskan Arctic Gas Pipeline Ltd., CAG's sister company in the United States, filed a companion application before the US Federal Power Commission to build the Alaskan portion of the Mackenzie gas pipeline. The documentation Arctic Gas submitted in support of its project was in keeping with the enormous enterprise it was proposing: although the application itself was incomplete—only those sections dealing with engineering, environmental and social matters were ready—it nonetheless covered some 7,000 pages and weighed fifty pounds. Stacked on the floor, it reached the waist of an average-sized person.

From its conception, the Arctic Gas project invited the application of superlatives to describe it: it would be the longest pipeline ever built, 5,400 miles when all connecting facilities in the United States were included; once fully powered, it would carry 4.5 billion cubic feet of gas a day (bcfd), more than the entire daily Canadian gas consumption; it would be the most expensive project ever undertaken by private enterprise, costing an estimated $5.7 billion at the time, an investment equivalent to that in all operating gas pipelines in Canada. This was an underestimate since it applied to a pipeline that started nowhere and went nowhere. It did not include the costs of gathering and processing the gas at Prudhoe Bay and the Mackenzie Delta, nor the cost of the pipelines that would have to be built in the continental United States to deliver the gas.

The Arctic Gas application called originally for the construction of two supply laterals from Prudhoe Bay and the Mackenzie Delta. The western branch carrying 2.25 bcfd of Alaska gas was to follow the coast of the Beaufort Sea, although a more southern route through the interior of the Yukon remained under study. The coastal route would have crossed the Arctic National Wildlife Range in Alaska, one of the last remaining wilderness areas in the US, and for that reason generated a great deal of opposition from American environmental groups.

The eastern supply lateral, carrying an equivalent volume of Canadian gas, would have met the Prudhoe Bay line near Inuvik where the two gas streams would have been combined in a single 48-inch high pressure trunk line to Caroline, Alberta. From Caroline, the pipeline would have bifurcated into two delivery laterals, one western leg to California and one eastern leg to Illinois. The eastern leg would have interconnected at the Saskatchewan-Alberta border with TransCanada Pipelines to allow for the transportation of Mackenzie Delta gas to Canadian markets.

Although the project evolved over time to provide a more direct access to Prudhoe Bay gas across the Mackenzie Delta, to allow the delivery of gas to Westcoast Transmission in northeast British Columbia and adopt other route changes, the basic system configuration remained remarkably consistent to the end. From the beginning, Arctic Gas was committed to the one route that linked both Prudhoe Bay and the Mackenzie Delta to southern markets in the most economically efficient manner. That route lay in the Mackenzie Valley. The Canadian companies in Arctic Gas had no interest in a longer pipeline through the southern Yukon along the Alaska Highway which would necessitate a costly connection to the Delta.

Although the pipeline's gigantic proportions had captured the imagination of the government, the pipeline's very size also raised a dilemma: since the domestic market was too small to absorb but a fraction of the initial volume of gas projected to be available from the Mackenzie Delta, a substantial portion of that gas would have to be exported at first, likely on long-term contracts. Reducing the pipeline's throughput—which would have solved this problem—was not possible for economic reasons. The pipeline's cost was such that it would have to operate at close to capacity to be financially viable; a smaller throughput would also have meant higher transportation costs, a result the United States would have been sure to object to. The pipeline was therefore an all or nothing proposition.

Because the potential of the Mackenzie Delta had once been thought to be large, the news in September 1973 that only 7 trillion cubic feet of gas had been discovered—a volume which would have met Canadian demand for

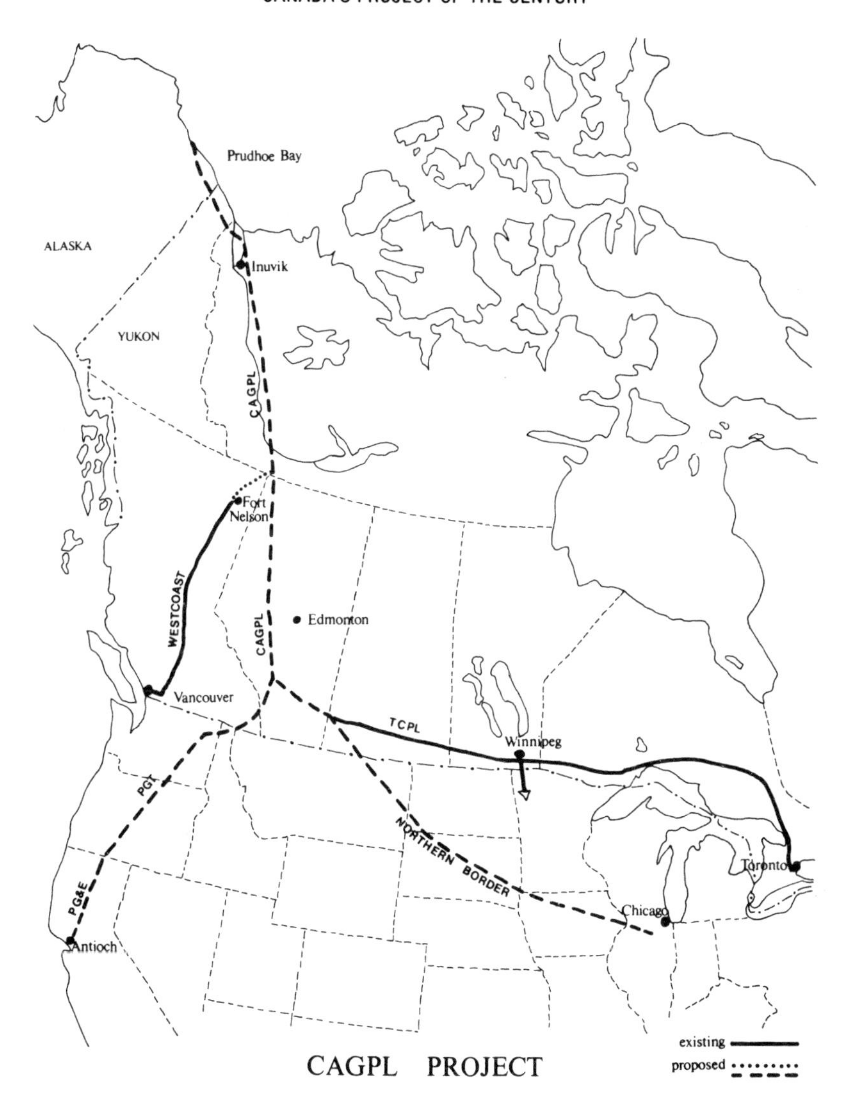

CAGPL PROJECT

only five years—caught many by surprise. The risk that Canada might overcommit itself to the export of frontier gas by building a Mackenzie pipeline, just as it had apparently overcommitted itself to the export of conventional reserves in 1970, could not be discounted. In its application, however, Arctic Gas had indicated that companion export applications would be filed later.

That these export applications might be very substantial had been implied by Bill Wilder in January 1973 at a public debate on the Mackenzie pipeline:

> You have to really have a large foreign or export component in the throughput of a pipeline in order to finance it and to make it economi-

> cally viable—just to get it started. If it takes 15 to 20 trillion cubic feet to get to the US market initially to finance the pipeline, the balance that's available is going to last many, many years.[5]

Coming at a time when the three largest exploration companies in the Mackenzie Delta, Imperial Oil, the Gulf/Mobil partnership and Shell, had already negotiated or were in the process of negotiating contracts with American purchasers for the sale of 23 trillion cubic feet of Delta gas—a volume equivalent to half the reserves known to exist in Alberta—Wilder's statement only reinforced the impression that CAG's purpose was to exploit the North quickly and for American profit.

The Arctic Gas pipeline raised other concerns as well. Pipeline construction through Canada's North would entail much more than simply laying down a string of pipe into a ditch. It entailed the construction of snow roads, wharfs, camps, stockpile sites, air-strips, gravel mining operations—in short, a huge infrastructure. The pipeline's existence itself would give rise to other activities: it would accelerate the pace of petroleum exploration in the Mackenzie Delta and Beaufort Sea and could lead eventually to the laying of a second pipeline.

All these activities would exert environmental impacts. The pipeline itself would have to be built in the cold and darkness of winter to keep the disturbance to the tundra to a minimum. The pipeline's route through the northern Yukon would have crossed the calving range of the Porcupine Caribou herd, one of the last great herds on the North American continent. Many biologists feared that the activities associated with the construction and operation of a pipeline and ancillary developments would reduce the herd's size. Similar concerns were expressed for various species of migratory water fowl that use the northern Yukon as a staging area.

CAG's plan to cross the Mackenzie Delta, rather than circumvent it as it had initially proposed, could have given rise to other impacts. The Mackenzie Delta is the only major delta in North America which feeds the Arctic ocean with warm water and nutrients. It is therefore an exceptionally rich biological area and CAG's proposal raised serious environmental implications for both fish and whale populations.

Although it was there concerns that attracted public attention, the technical problems that the Mackenzie pipeline would have faced were no less severe. Many of these stemmed from the presence of permafrost over the northern portions of the route. In order to prevent thawing, Arctic Gas had decided at an early date to chill its gas and operate the pipeline at a temperature below freezing. However, in zones of discontinuous permafrost—those areas where pockets of permafrost are found in unfrozen soils—there was a risk that a pipeline would form a frost bulb over time which would heave and perhaps fracture the line. The alternative of warming the gas could have led to the thawing and settling of these permafrost islands, another possible cause of pipe rupture. One solution to the permafrost problem would have consisted of elevating the pipeline as Alyeska would do for its oil line. But this was a very expensive solution and therefore one to avoid if at all possible.

On top of the inevitable environmental impacts, a Mackenzie pipeline would also have given rise to potentially severe socio-economic impacts. The native people of the Mackenzie Valley were opposed to a pipeline until their land claims were settled. They feared that a pipeline would accentuate the boom-bust cycle of the northern development and lead to the influx of thousands of construction workers to the North. Native people who might obtain pipeline work would be employed mostly in unskilled positions. Once the pipeline was built, most of these jobs would disappear. The native people were therefore afraid that a pipeline would further erode their culture and disrupt their traditional economy based on hunting and trapping.

By the date Arctic Gas submitted its application to the NEB, public concern over the pipeline's environmental and social impacts had become widespread. Heading a minority government, the Trudeau Cabinet was highly susceptible to mounting public criticism over its pipeline policy. Now that Arctic Gas was approaching regulatory hearings, a new problem had become evident. The National Energy Board only had very limited environmental and socio-economic expertise and it was increasingly clear that the board would not be able to review the pipeline's impact in the North without a large infusion of new staff. In anticipation of the Mackenzie pipeline hearings, the board had indeed drafted a memorandum to Cabinet in 1972 requesting that it be given formal jurisdiction over the environmental assessment of a Mackenzie pipeline. Chretien, however, had opposed this request on the grounds that consideration of the pipeline's impact in the Territories was the exclusive responsibility of his Department of Indian and Northern Affairs.

In January 1973, Cabinet decided that DINA would hold public hearings to assess the pipeline's environmental impact. There seemed to be several political advantages to such a procedure: it would meet the spirit of the government's 1972 statement on northern policy. It would allow public input in the refinement of the northern pipeline guidelines. It would depoliticize the volatile environmental and social issues by offering the pipeline critics a forum in which to channel their efforts. Finally, the hearings would assuage the New Democratic Party which was critical of the government's northern development policy and at that time held the balance of power in Parliament.

THE BERGER INQUIRY

Thus was born the Mackenzie Valley Pipeline Inquiry, headed by Judge Thomas R. Berger of the British Columbia Supreme Court. Berger was an excellent if unexpected candidate for the job. His work on behalf of the

Nishga Indians of British Columbia had led to a landmark Supreme Court decision in 1973 on the question of aboriginal rights. Although the Supreme Court narrowly rejected Berger's arguments on a technicality, the judgement became the main legal basis for the assertion of native rights in Canada. A man with an intimate appreciation of native questions, Berger was obviously well qualified to head an inquiry on the environmental and socio-economic impacts of a Mackenzie Valley pipeline.

His appointment, however, surprised many. Before becoming a judge, Berger had been a politician. He had sat as a New Democratic Party Member of Parliament in the House of Commons in 1962-63. He had served in the British Columbia legislature for three years and had even been elected leader of the provincial NDP in 1969. The government's appointment of a man with a different political philosophy to examine a sensitive area of public policy would have been unlikely under normal circumstances. When Berger was named in March 1974, however, the government was still in a minority in Parliament, having to rely on a day-to-day basis on the NDP's support. As it had anticipated, Berger's appointment pleased the NDP.

Berger was given terms of reference which at first seemed quite narrow. He was asked:

> to inquire into and report upon the terms and conditions that should be imposed in respect of a right-of-way that might be granted across Crown lands for the purposes of the proposed Mackenzie Valley pipeline having regard to (a) the social, environmental and economic impact regionally of the construction, operation and subsequent abandonment of the proposed pipeline in the Yukon and Northwest Territories, and (b) any proposals to meet the specific environmental and social concerns set out in the expanded guidelines for northern pipelines....

In other words, Berger was to recommend stipulations which would mitigate a gas pipeline's impact. But he was also to take into consideration the northern pipeline guidelines which envisioned the creation of a Mackenzie Valley corridor comprising a highway and an oil pipeline as well as a gas line. Berger, if he chose to, could therefore interpret his terms of reference quite broadly. The first indication that he might do so came when he issued preliminary rulings on the conduct of the inquiry in July 1974. At that time, he stated that he felt "bound to consider the economic and social impact of the construction of an oil pipeline and to consider the combined effect of the construction of a gas pipeline and an oil pipeline in the corridor." This was a logical position to take given the history of government pipeline policy, but it was also one the government had arguably not expected when it had drafted Berger's terms of reference.

In his preliminary rulings Berger made other important decisions. He asked that all relevant studies in the hands of government, Arctic Gas and other organizations be submitted to the inquiry. He stated his intention to examine the ramifications of building a pipeline on gas exploration in the Mackenzie Delta and Beaufort Sea. He announced that he would hold his hearings using two formats: there would be formal hearings where experts presenting technical evidence would be cross-examined; there would also be community hearings, informal in nature, to allow the people living in the Mackenzie Valley to state their concerns directly to Berger himself. Finally, Berger declared he would give anyone with an interest in the Mackenzie Valley pipeline a chance to be heard. "I will not diminish anyone's right to be heard, nor will I curtail this inquiry so as to improve Arctic Gas's position in relation to the El Paso proposal in the United States." In light of Chretien's speech only six months earlier in favour of a quick approval of a Mackenzie pipeline, this was a tough and uncompromising position. Berger was serving notice that he would not tolerate any government interference.

The pressures Berger faced were enormous. For all intents and purposes, the government had already approved the construction of a Mackenzie Valley gas pipeline. It was anxious to formalize that approval quickly and indeed asked Berger to report back with all reasonable dispatch, suggesting a date of January 1, 1975. Berger therefore had to fight hard to overcome the public's cynicism that had surrounded his appointment. During the summer of 1974 he travelled extensively in the North with his family to experience the land first hand. He also visited Alaska to learn more about the problems of building a large pipeline in a northern environment. He went to Washington to familiarize himself with the procedures the United States had established under the National Environmental Policy Act for the preparation of environmental impact statements.

In the fall Berger released further rulings covering the procedures he intended to adopt in running his inquiry. He announced that his own commission lawyers would be responsible for obtaining the testimony from government and other witnesses necessary to ensure the inquiry's completeness. This was a major departure from established Canadian practice where an inquiry usually is limited to the evidence interveners choose to call. Berger also arranged to fund major interest groups, such as the Northwest Territories Chamber of Commerce, the NWT Association of Municipalities and native and environmental organizations, so they could present their cases more effectively. Furthermore, Berger ensured that the CBC would broadcast daily summaries of the hearings in all the native languages of the Mackenzie Valley so that the native people would be able to follow his inquiry.

Arctic Gas was unhappy with Berger's rulings. It was also concerned with Berger's background as an Indian rights lawyer. Nevertheless, in early 1974 it had few reasons to worry. The construction of the Mackenzie Valley pipeline seemed virtually assured. The government had repeatedly voiced its support for such a project, most recently in Chretien's speech in Yellowknife in January. It had published guidelines to assist the pipeline company in its in its planning and had begun to build the Mackenzie highway to lend logistical support to the pipeline's construction. It had helped to assemble a consortium to sponsor this venture and had even invested in it through the Canada Development Corporation. Furthermore, it had promised expeditious regulatory approval to the applicant before the application had even been filed.

THE MAPLE LEAF PIPELINE

In 1974, neither El Paso's intention to file a competing application before the US Federal Power Commission nor the appointment of a special inquiry to review the environmental and social impacts of the Mackenzie pipeline seemed to challenge CAG's progress towards certification by Canadian and American authorities; the presence of a recalcitrant within its ranks was cause for even less concern. The consortium had been the product of a shotgun marriage between two competing groups of companies which necessity rather than agreement had brought together. From the start, it had proved to be an acrimonious union marred by differences over the routing, financing and ownership of the project.

Alberta Gas Trunk Line was the consortium member most dissatisfied with CAG's evolution. Friction between AGTL and the other members of the Gas Arctic/Northwest Project Study Group developed at an early stage when the engineering firm Northwest had retained for its own project began to report directly to CAG's technical committee, thereby bypassing the Arctic Gas staff headed by a former AGTL man. Already, in the fall of 1972, AGTL complained that cost studies on various route proposals south of the 60th parallel did not include estimates for expanding its existing pipelines in Alberta. In light of the foreseeable decline in Alberta gas production, AGTL wanted to carry northern gas to keep its system operating at full capacity. It opposed the construction of a new large diameter pipeline in Alberta, preferring to accommodate the flow of frontier gas by "looping" its operating system. (Looping is the twinning of existing pipelines in order to increase capacity.) The other Arctic Gas companies, however, were skeptical of the economics of such a proposal. They were also leery of giving AGTL so much control over the transportation of their gas.

This matter came to a head at a management committee meeting in June 1973 at which AGTL and CNR argued in favour of a trans-Alberta route against Exxon and "Mich-Wich" (Michigan-Wisconsin) which preferred a more direct route to Emerson, on the Manitoba-Minnesota border. AGTL succeeded in imposing its views and keeping alive the concept of using spare capacity in its system for the transportation of frontier gas. At the same meeting, however, CAG decided to adopt only one corporate vehicle to implement its project rather than the regional ownership approach which AGTL had favoured. AGTL, of course, had argued for regional ownership in order to maintain maximum control over the Arctic Gas line in Alberta.

When it became obvious that Arctic Gas would not accommodate it, AGTL began to conduct its own "contingency" study on the feasibility of building a Canadian-only pipeline. In May 1974, AGTL announced to CAG's management committee that it was analysing the viability of a 42-inch pipeline to the Mackenzie Delta only. In a letter to Alberta's Premier Peter Lougheed, Blair declared that he had lost the "confidence that the present internationally controlled project proposal of Canadian Arctic Gas Study Ltd. will be able to succeed or that it is the right proposal at all."[6]

In September 1974, AGTL withdrew from the consortium. It was immediately joined by Westcoast Transmission, British Columbia's gas transportation utility, in the sponsorship of a new Mackenzie pipeline, the self-styled "Maple Leaf" project. Like most of the major natural gas transmission companies in North America, Westcoast had also examined how Prudhoe Bay gas could be delivered to market. Westcoast, indeed, had been one of the first companies to become involved in such studies. In 1969, it had joined four American companies—Bechtel, Southern California Edison, Pacific Lighting and El Paso—to form Mountain Pacific, a pipeline designed originally to move Alaskan gas to the US Pacific coast along the Rocky Mountain Trench.

Mountain Pacific did not prosper. In 1971, Pacific Lighting left to become a member of Gas Arctic. Another blow came in 1973 when El Paso withdrew to pursue its all-American alternative across Alaska. El Paso's departure followed a US Supreme Court-ordered divestiture of its pipeline facilities in the US Pacific Northwest which it would have used to deliver Prudhoe Bay gas. Ironically, the company which was formed as a result, the Northwest Pipeline Corporation, would sponsor the Alaska Highway Pipeline jointly with AGTL and Westcoast only three years later. By early 1974, Mountain Pacific was moribund. It had studied various transportation routes for the delivery of Prudhoe Bay gas, including one along the Alaska Highway, but had not succeeded in attracting strong corporate support.

Westcoast could have followed the rest of the Canadian and American gas industry by joining Arctic Gas but it did not. During that period, Westcoast indeed turned down repeated invitations from Arctic Gas. It did not believe Arctic Gas would succeed in crossing the inhospitable North Slope of Alaska and the Yukon, a region Mountain Pacific had avoided in designing its pipeline system. Most of all, it opposed CAG's decision to bypass existing pipelines in Alberta and British Columbia and build a thousand miles of new right-of-way in those provinces. Like AGTL, Westcoast thought that maximum advantage should be taken of already operating pipelines.

Mountain Pacific's collapse in 1974 coincided with a fundamental transformation in Canada's gas supply outlook. Domestic shortages were now forecast before the end of the decade. Westcoast was more affected than most by the deteriorating situation because some fields which supplied its system had unexpectedly experienced production difficulties, forcing it to

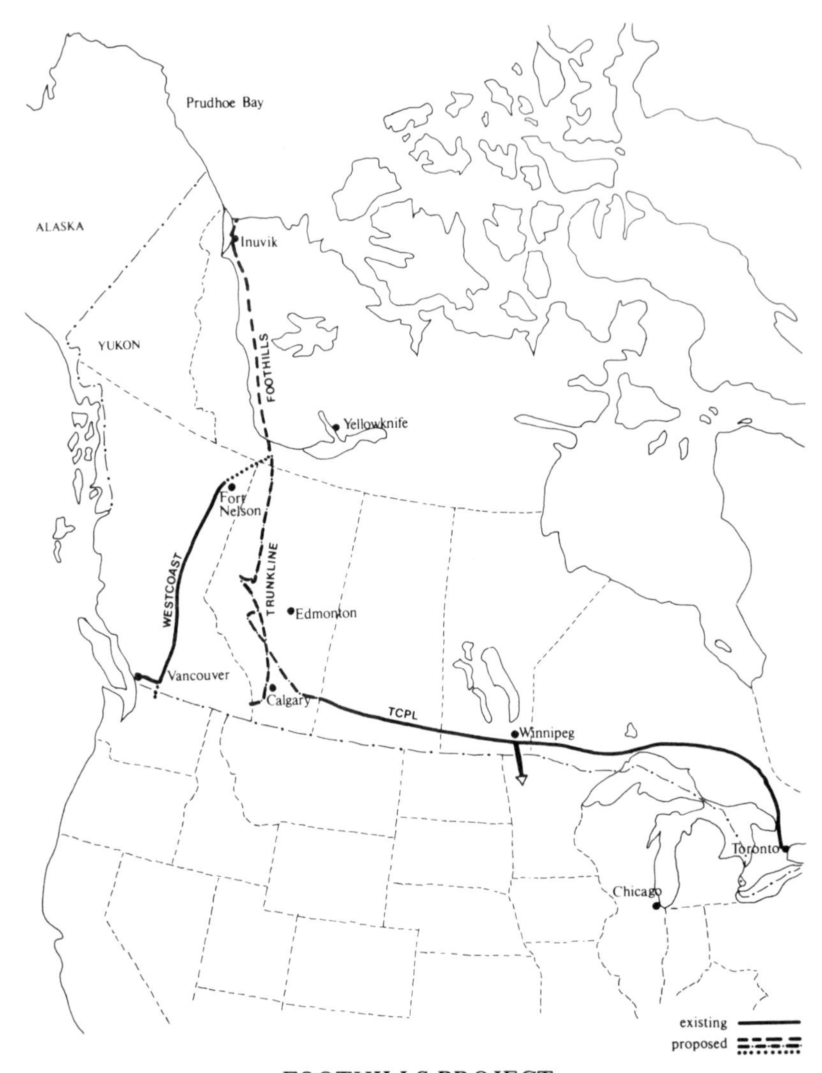

FOOTHILLS PROJECT

curtail deliveries to its customers. Almost overnight Westcoast was forced to readjust its priorities from moving Alaska gas to California to moving Mackenzie Delta gas to its customers.

Westcoast's awakening interest in a Mackenzie pipeline occurred at the same time that AGTL was growing increasingly disenchanted with Arctic Gas. As Blair dithered during the summer of 1974 on whether to leave CAG, Westcoast's chairman, Kelly Gibson, suggested the two companies form their own partnership to build a Mackenzie pipeline. For Westcoast this would be the last chance to become involved in the management of a frontier project. Gibson recalls what happened:

> We in Westcoast had stayed out of it. I could see there was a lot of fussing going on in there. Of course, when you get two bright and determined guys like Bob Blair and Vern Horte wrestling one another there is bound to be some problems. But then I also thought the wrong people were in it, that it ought to be a Canadian pipeliners' project. Well, there were three of us—ourselves, Bob and TransCanada. I thought I'd talk with Bob first to see if we could get together. I told him I thought he ought to pull out right away, that we could do it. Three or four days later he pulled out. People from back east used to ask me about Bob. They'd say, "Kelly, what are you doing business with that guy Blair for?" But I would just tell them that they didn't understand. Part of the problem was that Lougheed wasn't too popular back east just then, and every time some people, Don Macdonald for instance, would look at Bob, they'd see Peter.[7]

This was a real handicap. It took AGTL several years to overcome the suspicion that it was being used by Alberta in the battle over resource revenue that was then going on between the province and Ottawa.

Westcoast and AGTL resuscitated a dormant company, Foothills Pipe Lines, to serve as the project's corporate parent, 80% of its shares going to AGTL, 20% to Westcoast. On March 27, 1975, five months after AGTL had left CAG, Foothills filed its own application to build a Mackenzie pipeline. The cover of the application and that of every supporting document was adorned with a small maple leaf, an unsubtle allusion to CAG's American parentage. Foothills' nationalism, however carefully cultivated for public consumption, would prove somewhat hollow upon closer inspection. AGTL had left Arctic Gas, not because it opposed the trans-shipment of Prudhoe Bay gas across Canada, or indeed the export of Mackenzie Delta gas, but rather because it objected to these being the governing concepts behind the CAG application. Foothills had no compunction in its early days about offering to transport Prudhoe Bay gas and also considered the export of substantial volumes of Delta gas. These two proposals were subsequently dropped.

In keeping with the precedent Arctic Gas had set, the evidence Foothills submitted in support of its application was voluminous: the several sets of technical documents delivered to Ottawa by air charter a month after the application was filed weighed three tons. In preparing its case, Foothills had been able to rely on some of the documentation to which AGTL had had access during its membership in the Arctic Gas consortium and to which it had retained proprietary rights in spite of its break from the consortium. Blair's caution in 1972 in insuring that his company would be able to leave Arctic Gas without suffering any penalty was now paying off.

The pipeline Foothills proposed to build was a 42-inch trunk line from the Mackenzie Delta which would divide at the 60th Parallel into two branches to interconnect with Westcoast and AGTL. Both companies would carry the gas south by looping their pipelines to accommodate the flow of frontier gas. The whole system was scheduled to start operations in the fall of 1979, the date when domestic shortages were forecast to occur. For many years, Arctic Gas would deride Foothills' choice of a smaller pipeline by referring to it as a "spaghetti" pipeline.

Many of the features of the earlier Trunk North and Gas Arctic proposals were now incorporated in the Maple Leaf project: the insistence on Canadian ownership, the segmentation of management by region, the reliance on already operating pipelines, the conservative engineering design, the supply of gas to Mackenzie Valley communities—all accentuated the difference in approach between Arctic Gas and Foothills. The most fundamental difference between the two applications, of course, was that Foothills proposed to carry Canadian gas only. This, from the beginning, was the Achilles' heel of the Maple Leaf project. The modest volume of gas available in the Mackenzie Delta precluded the project's economic viability which is why Arctic Gas at first considered AGTL more as an irritant than a threat.

Foothills, however, had two major advantages over Arctic Gas. It was small, and it was willing to modify its project to answer its critics. At AGTL, Blair would boast that "we can make a decision in minutes on tens of thousands of dollars and hours on hundreds of thousands of dollars and in a day or two on some millions."[8] Blair used the same managerial style at Foothills. As a result of its streamlined operations, Foothills consistently adjusted to changing political conditions more quickly than its rival.

From the beginning, Foothills also stated its readiness to be flexible and accommodate competing interests. The willingness of Foothills' officials to listen was perhaps most evident in repeated visits Blair and his colleagues paid to the community hearings Berger held during the course of his inquiry.

Berger invited both Horte and Blair to go with him to some of the villages of the Mackenzie Valley. Blair went with Berger to Fort Good Hope, Norman Wells and Colville Lake. He was made aware of the depth of the opposition to the pipeline among the native people because he spent approximately a week in the communities with Berger. Horte, on the other hand, went for one morning to a hearing at Fort Providence and did not return to any other community hearing. Blair's visits were more than good public relations: they demonstrated a genuine interest in the concerns of the inhabitants in the Mackenzie Valley. They also allowed him to anticipate the recommendations of the Berger Inquiry two years later and helped to convince him that another route had to be found to carry Prudhoe Bay gas.

In 1974, however, AGTL's pursuit of its own frontier pipeline seemed truly quixotic. The Maple Leaf project was premised on an heroic assumption, the discovery of large reserves in the Mackenzie Delta which would by themselves sustain the pipeline's throughput without necessitating the joint transportation of Prudhoe Bay gas. Nor was this the only handicap besetting the AGTL proposal. By not connecting the Alaska reserves, the Maple Leaf project constituted a potential embarrassment to the Canadian government which had stated its support so unequivocally in the past for a pipeline which would serve both domestic and American needs. Although, strictly speaking, Canadian regulatory approval of Maple Leaf would not deny the US access to their gas, the overland route for the delivery of Prudhoe Bay gas was clearly superior to the alternative proposed by El Paso: it would deliver more gas to the United States more cheaply and more directly. As a result of this exclusively domestic orientation and the Canadian government's compromised position, AGTL found itself at a substantial disadvantage to Arctic Gas in Washington whose choice of a transportation route for Alaskan gas would exert a determining influence over the Canadian decision.

CHAPTER FOUR

SETTING THE STAGE

Although by the end of 1974, two new protagonists, Foothills and El Paso, had formally joined Arctic Gas in the fray, they were hardly competing as equals. Foothills, in particular, was dwarfed by its rival, its precarious position made even more vulnerable by the slowdown in exploratory activity in the Mackenzie Delta. The Delta was proving a major disappointment in spite of the expenditure of hundreds of millions of dollars in drilling and seismic work. Indeed, a reassessment of the reserves already discovered would show that they were smaller than had originally been estimated. Although the Maple Leaf project was endowed with considerable romantic appeal—Blair appeared on the cover of *Weekend Magazine* as a knight in shining armour— it was simply not viable on the basis of the proven reserves in the Delta. Foothills' fate depended on the exploratory success of Imperial, Gulf and Shell, the three major companies which were active in the Delta and which, of course, also belonged to Arctic Gas.

In the United States, CAG's other rival, El Paso, had filed its application before the Federal Power Commission in late September—less than two weeks after AGTL had left Arctic Gas. El Paso had improbably rested its case on the "dire consequences" the US would suffer if it trans-shipped its Alaskan gas across Canada. The chauvinism in El Paso's rhetoric could ill disguise the fundamental disadvantages of its project: high costs and a circuitous route to the American Midwest. Although a competitor to be reckoned with, El Paso never achieved the same broad base of support in the US that Arctic Gas garnered so conspicuously.

In spite of AGTL's defection and the loss of a handful of other members from its consortium, Arctic Gas had gained further momentum in 1974. The multiple repercussions of the energy crisis and the growing evidence of impending gas shortages in Canada suggested that frontier gas should be developed quickly, even if the Delta reserves were small. Indeed, because they were so small, Arctic Gas argued that, if Canada did not take advantage of the unique opportunity of building a joint Mackenzie pipeline with the United States, the development of the Delta would be postponed indefinitely with disastrous consequences for Canadian gas consumers.

THE POLITICS OF CONCILIATION

The revolution in world oil prices initiated in the fall of 1973 by the Organization of Petroleum Exporting Countries (OPEC) had profound repercussions on Canadian-American relations. To protect the Canadian consumer against rapidly escalating prices, the government imposed a domestic price freeze and began levying an export tax on the sale of oil to the United States. The imposition of this surcharge aroused the ire of many congressmen. One Republican senator, Richard Schweicker, even went so far as to charge Canada with "un-American conduct"[1].

To make matters worse, this was the time when production difficulties in some fields in British Columbia had forced Canada to reduce its gas exports to the United States. To keep the gas export price in line with that of alternate fuels, however, British Columbia's exports had almost doubled in price. These actions were providing ideal ammunition to El Paso. Canada's alleged unreliability became a prime selling factor in the presentation of its project.

Canada's protective reaction to the energy crisis seriously antagonized the United States. In January 1974, Donald Macdonald, the Minister of Energy, Mines and Resources, went on a much-needed fence-mending visit to Washington. At the top of the agenda was Canada's oil export tax whose monthly increases in line with every OPEC price hike were considered a major irritant in Canadian-American relations. Other energy issues were also discussed. Macdonald reaffirmed Canada's willingness, expressed in Trudeau's December 1973 speech on energy policy, to negotiate a pipeline treaty to provide for the free passage of Prudhoe Bay gas on Canadian soil. He also indicated that, although Canadian oil exports would continue to decline as a result of the steady drop in Alberta reserves, a short-term increase in gas exports was a possibility, but only if a Mackenzie pipeline was built.[2] As the United States was suffering a worsening gas deficit, an increase in Canadian gas exports was an attractive proposition, a fact of which Ottawa was not unmindful.

The defeat of the minority Liberal government over its May 1974 budget and the subsequent election campaign were to postpone future discussions at the ministerial level until the fall. In early October, with the Liberals back firmly in power, Macdonald returned to Washington to assure American officials that the negotiation of a pipeline treaty remained a high priority for Canada. At a conference held by the American Enterprise Institute, Macdonald made it clear to his business audience that Canada was still in favour of a joint Mackenzie pipeline with the United States although gas exports were now out of the question due to the worsening domestic supply outlook:

"There are obvious economies to be obtained for Canadian gas and gas users if our gas is travelling through a conduit which is also carrying larger volumes to the United States".[3] In spite of the recent unveiling of the Maple Leaf project and its appeal to Canadian nationalism, Macdonald was stating in his speech that the Canadian government would base its pipeline decision on hard-headed economics. The release of an American government energy document only a few days after Macdonald's visit, hinting at a quick resolution of the pipeline issue, must have confirmed to Ottawa the appropriateness of Macdonald's message.

Macdonald's conciliatory visits succeeded in defusing much of the United States' earlier displeasure over Canada's oil and gas export policy. It was thus in an improved atmosphere that the two countries began their negotiations over a transit pipeline treaty on November 1, 1974. These negotiations ostensibly were to yield rules to govern the treatment of Canadian pipelines crossing American territory and the possible future construction of American pipelines through Canada. However, as Canadian pipelines had operated in the US for many years without any need for such a treaty, it was clear that the negotiations were aimed at a Mackenzie pipeline. This, in any event, was the American view. Julius Katz, the US deputy assistant Secretary of State admitted readily that "the basic objectives of these negotiations were to facilitate the construction of a natural gas pipeline across Canada if it were deemed to be in the US national interest"[4]. Among the three companies competing at the time to transport frontier gas to market, the only one which stood to benefit from the signing of a transit pipeline treaty, of course, was Arctic Gas, even though the negotiations themselves did not address a Mackenzie pipeline specifically.

Canada's interest in a transit pipeline treaty had changed radically between the time Trudeau had first offered to discuss such an agreement in December 1973 and the date the negotiations began in November 1974. In 1973, a Mackenzie pipeline was still seen as meeting an American need almost exclusively. By late 1974, the worsening prognosis of the domestic natural gas situation was becoming an increasing cause for concern. This was a fundamental transformation in the context in which Arctic Gas was evolving. If Canada, too, needed access to frontier gas, it could no longer afford to irritate the United States by imposing export taxes, for example. On the contrary, it would have to accommodate future American concerns and take them explicitly into account in formulating policy. This greatly decreased Canada's leverage because, if the US had an alternative to Arctic Gas in El Paso, Canada did not.

The National Energy Board hearings on natural gas supply and demand which began in Calgary in November 1974 would reveal just how quickly Canada had moved from a position of surplus to one of deficit.

THE NEB GAS HEARINGS

At the end of 1974, only four years after the government had approved a 50% increase in long-term natural gas exports to the United States, shortages were looming in domestic markets. To determine the production levels that could be achieved (in industry parlance, this is called deliverability) from the conventional supply areas in the western provinces constituted therefore the single most important task facing the government at this critical juncture in natural gas policy. As the result of the accelerated depletion of the western reserves, Canada was confronted with the possible need to develop frontier gas. Such development raised several fundamental policy questions: which frontier area should be tapped first, the Mackenzie Delta or the Arctic islands where important gas discoveries had also been made? What would be the economic implications of rising gas costs on natural gas demand? industrial consumers competing in foreign markets? government revenues? How would Canada's gas export policy and the growth of a domestic petrochemical industry be affected? As the Canadian energy economy was already closely integrated with the American, it was relevant to ask yet another question: would a northern pipeline lead to greater continental integration and what would be the consequences of such an eventuality?

To reach an answer to some of these questions was ostensibly the task which the National Energy Board undertook during the course of its hearings on the supply of and demand for natural gas which were held from November 1974 to the beginning of March 1975. This marked the first time in its history that the board was inviting public submissions on gas supply and demand independently of an export or a pipeline application; the gas hearings thereby constituted an implicit admission that past practices were no longer adequate to ensure the proper development of domestic natural gas reserves. In a very real sense, the whole history of Canadian natural gas policy was on trial before these hearings. It thus came as an enormous paradox that the body which had to bear most of the blame for past errors was now sitting as its own judge, devising solutions to remedy its mistakes and formulating recommendations which, if adopted, would set the course of natural gas policy for years to come.

Created in 1959 to establish a greater measure of public control over the activities of the Canadian oil and gas industry, the National Energy Board had become instead the "Trojan horse" used by that industry to influence government policy. Throughout the 1960's, the NEB had demonstrated an alarming propensity to accept uncritically industry arguments in favour of increased exports.[5] The inescapable consequence of this behaviour was now evident in the threat of domestic shortages. Through its actions, the NEB had precipitated the very problem it had been created to avoid.

The effect of the 1970 export decison had been to force the satisfaction of future domestic requirements to depend substantially on the discovery of new reserves rather than on existing stocks of natural gas. It was inevitable therefore that any downturn in the rate of addition to supply or any unexpected jump in demand—both of which happened—would upset the delicate balance between the two and induce premature shortages. Thus, not only were Canada's exports clearly excessive but, because they represented firm contractual obligations, they constituted in effect a first charge on production; Canadian requirements had to be met from what was left over, a situation to which the NEB was forced to admit, much to its discomfiture.

If Canada's overcommitment to the export market was the main reason in 1974 why domestic shortages seemed inevitable, there can be little question that the jurisdictional confrontation which occurred at the time between Alberta and the federal government over an entirely different issue—oil prices—exacerbated the problem created by the 1970 export decision. The quadrupling in world oil prices wrought by OPEC in late 1973 and early 1974 had produced an enormous windfall, one that both Alberta and Ottawa tried to appropriate simultaneously by increasing royalties and taxes on the oil industry. Caught in the middle, the industry reacted by cutting back exploration and development programmes and threatening to leave the country. Although its profits had risen dramatically as a result of the rapid rise in oil prices, Alberta and the federal government's conflicting tax policies had made the United States a more attractive country in which to invest. Drilling rigs fled in droves.

Alberta and the federal government eventually reached a compromise and restored their generous treatment of the industry. Their year-long confrontation, however, had been achieved at a cost. Oil and gas exploration had slowed down, reserve additions had lagged and the need for frontier gas had been accentuated. Those in Ottawa who believed that Alberta's influence over Canadian energy policy had to be curtailed saw in the early development of frontier gas the means by which this goal could be achieved. The steep rise in international energy prices constituted an additional incentive to develop the Mackenzie Delta which the government, in 1974, still hoped would generate substantial revenue.

It is necessary to emphasize that the transformation in the domestic natural gas outlook had been both abrupt and totally unexpected. In March 1973, for example, the vice-chairman of the National Energy Board, Mr. D.M. Fraser, had stated that he saw *proven* reserves in the western provinces (therefore making no allowance for future discoveries) as "... being ample to cover Canadian deliverability requirements up to the end of the Eighties or into the early Nineties".[6] This judgement had been restated in June of the same year in the federal government's *An Energy Policy for Canada*: "The present volume of reserves is sufficient to meet export commitments and growing Canadian demands in the areas now served through the 1980s".[7]

These statements, of course, merely echoed earlier industry assurances that Canada enjoyed bountiful supplies of gas. The belief that there was no urgency in building a Mackenzie pipeline had been reinforced further by the position held by CAG until 1974 that a large portion of the Delta gas it would carry would have to be exported, at least initially.

The National Energy Board gas hearings, therefore, fulfilled two quite distinct objectives: they updated estimates of domestic requirements and deliverability; more importantly, perhaps, they gave the industry a forum in which to explain why a Mackenzie pipeline now had to be built as quickly as possible.

For Arctic Gas in particular, the value of these hearings could not be overestimated. The public hearings of regulatory agencies, it has long been observed[8], often serve as highly visible rituals to legitimize the demands of industry. The NEB's formal, court-like, hearing process invites public confidence in its outcome. The submission of elaborate technical briefs and the cross-examination of witnesses constitute important symbols which give wide credibility to the board's findings even when almost all the evidence comes from the oil and gas industry itself.

This evidence, in the case of the gas hearings, came in the form of universally gloomy forecasts, a not altogether surprising bias given the profit squeeze the industry was feeling as a result of Alberta and the federal government's battle over resource revenues. The NEB accepted these forecasts and concluded in its report at the end of the hearings that domestic gas shortages were imminent. By agreeing with industry and CAG's assessment of the situation, the NEB did more than just corroborate their estimates of supply and demand: it imprinted them with a seal of authority and gave them wide public acceptance. The Mackenzie pipeline had received an incalculable boost.

The NEB's conclusion had never been in doubt. It had been dictated to a very large extent by the hearings' very frame of reference based on a "business-as-usual" approach (a term used by the board). The board's orientation towards the status quo meant that the industry-favoured policies of the past—aggressive exploration and the rapid exploitation of known reserves (in this case, the Mackenzie Delta)—would again be advocated as the solution to future shortages. Inevitably, the possible contribution of energy conservation to alleviate these shortages was grossly underestimated. The board's traditional reliance on industry-supplied information continued to be reinforced therefore by a dependency on an industry-provided philosophy of development as well.

That dependency was reflected in a confidential memorandum to his colleagues that Geoffrey Edge, one of the three board members sitting on the gas panel, wrote in December 1974, half-way through the hearings: "The prospects for avoiding a shortage in the 1970's seem remote.... Surely the hearing has brought into focus the urgent need for frontier gas by as early a date as is practicable?"[9] In his memorandum, Edge was not prejudging the issue as he was stating the logical conclusion that the board's restricted view of the range of gas policy options was inviting. If that view had been broadened to recognize the profound impact the rapid rise in energy prices was having in stimulating exploration and inducing conservation, Edge's conclusion would have been radically different. An economist at the University of British Columbia, Dr. John Helliwell, had reached a result startlingly divergent from that of industry. He claimed on the basis of a computer model of supply and demand that gas production from conventional areas would be able to meet domestic requirements plus committed exports until the late 1980s[10]. Using industry-supplied data, Helliwell contended furthermore that the forecasts presented by most gas companies to the NEB hearings were unnecessarily pessimistic and, when adjusted to reflect more realistic assumptions, indicated that a substantial deliverability potential could be developed in western Canada.

Helliwell was in a minority of one. His credibility in the eyes of both the NEB and industry was limited because he was an academic with no industry experience. The board summarily dismissed his analysis. Helliwell was right but it would take two more years before the soundness of his argument would be recognized.

THE GAS REPORT'S IMPACT

On July 16, 1975, Donald Macdonald tabled the NEB report in the House of Commons. In his statement accompanying the report, Macdonald declared that

> it is clear from the information presented that there will have to be some curtailment of our export contracts and that growth of demand in Canada will have to be restrained until frontier supplies of gas are available.

The NEB's gas report had a profound effect on government policy: it transformed the Mackenzie pipeline from being a merely desirable project into one of compelling necessity. Its conclusions left the government with precious little discretion. Ottawa, of course, was the author of its own misfortune. In 1970, it had approved the NEB's recommendation to increase gas exports, in part because it had wanted to entice the United States to accept more Canadian oil. Now that both fuels were running short, it had to live with the consequences.

What could the government do? A unilateral reduction in gas exports to prevent domestic shortages invited certain American retaliation. The United States had already expressed its anger at the rise in gas export prices which it considered discriminatory and a breach of Canada's contractual commitments. In a leak to *The Globe and Mail*, senior State Department officials had indeed warned Canada explicitly about retaliatory measures in the event the flow of gas was interrupted.[11] At the very least, Canada could expect the negotiations over the pipeline treaty to be suspended, thereby putting the construction of a joint Mackenzie pipeline into jeopardy. The rededication of Canada's exports to domestic markets was thus likely to be counter-productive in the long run if it precluded the timely development of frontier reserves.

Although Arctic Gas had gained the most from the NEB report, it also stood paradoxically to lose the most if the government used the report to reduce exports to the United States, as Macdonald had indicated it would do. If the prospect of American retaliation was inhibiting, the political costs of allowing domestic shortages to materialize while exports were met in full were too great to be acceptable. The pressure on the government to protect Canadian consumers was immense and Ottawa's temptation accordingly to force the US to bear the brunt of any shortfall very high.

Arctic Gas was only too aware of its vulnerability. In January 1975 the Arctic Gas management committee had expressed its concern that "... the NEB might recommend curtailment under existing export commitments, which would do great harm to the financing prospects of the project."[12] CAG's plan, therefore, was to propose that "... in the event of an apprehended Canadian gas shortage, the Canadian authorities meet with their counterparts in the United States to analyze the situation before taking any action."

This is what the government decided to do. It informed the US of the NEB's conclusions and their implications in advance to avoid a repetition of the American backlash that had followed the imposition of the oil export surcharge in the fall of 1973. Ottawa also decided to phase in the scheduled increase in the export price of gas more slowly, in contrast with the policy it had followed with respect to the oil export tax. In July, Macdonald and the US federal energy administrator, Frank Zarb, met in Ottawa to discuss methods of allocating cutbacks between the two countries. On the domestic front, the government took two initiatives: it agreed to Alberta's demand for higher prices on the condition that they be raised more gradually; this, the government hoped, would induce conservation and stimulate exploration; in case shortages did arise, the government began to develop measures to ration supplies.

These policies, it needs stressing, were only palliatives aimed at minimizing the impact of shortages; they were not designed to preclude the need for the development of frontier gas which the government thought offered the only long-run solution to Canada's natural gas problem. There was no ambiguity in Ottawa about the fact that a frontier pipeline would have to be built and that it would have to be built soon. Here too, however, the government's choice was limited: it was not for Ottawa to decide which frontier basin should be tapped first—the Mackenzie Delta or the Arctic islands—nor indeed what route the pipeline would follow. These were decisions which had already been made by private companies although they would undoubtedly exert an enormous impact on Canadian energy policy and northern development. The government's role, an important one, was to facilitate the pipeline's construction by providing baseline environmental data, logistical support, a code of conduct, which, if adhered to, would legitimize the pipeline company's actions and, of course, also grant prompt regulatory approval. In 1975, the government's choice was effectively restricted to only one applicant, Arctic Gas, since Foothills remained a commercially non-viable proposition in the absence of larger reserves in the Mackenzie Delta. This gave Arctic Gas a strong bargaining position to argue not only for an expeditious government decision in its favour but also for the application of lenient terms and conditions on the construction of its pipeline.

Arctic Gas, of course, was aware of the leverage it enjoyed. It had pressed in the past for an early decision. At the end of 1974, for example, Bill Wilder had met privately with both Marshall Crowe, who had recently been appointed chairman of the National Energy Board, and Jim Coutts, Trudeau's principal secretary, to discuss the desirability of hurrying Canadian regulatory procedure. At that time, Arctic Gas also requested another form of governmental assistance. In separate meetings with John Turner, the Minister of Finance, and Simon Reisman, his deputy, Wilder raised the need for financial backstopping.

Arctic Gas wanted both the Canadian and American governments to guarantee that its debt would be repaid in the event it could not meet its financial obligations. This was a highly contentious request. It inevitably raised the question of whether a project which had failed the private market test was economic. Did the fact that Arctic Gas could not finance its project not indicate that more attractive alternatives to an investment in a Mackenzie pipeline existed and that public assistance therefore would constitute a misallocation of resources? And even though the pipeline would benefit Canada too, why should the government assist a project which would carry American gas mostly?

These were difficult questions. If the government agreed to backstop a Mackenzie pipeline, it could not expect to place an upper limit to its liability. Once pipeline construction had begun, the government would be in no position to refuse Arctic Gas money if private investors refused to commit more funds to the project. Cost overruns were a virtual certainty and the probability that the government would actually end up paying for part of the pipeline could therefore not be dismissed. There was an extraordinary irony, of course, in the fact that Arctic Gas, a consortium composed in part of companies whose denunciations of government interference were legendary, should nevertheless ask the same to bear a portion of the risks associated with its project. But then the government's vigorous campaign in favour of a Mackenzie pipeline was inviting such demands.

THE PIPELINE HEARINGS

The NEB gas hearings had served as a logical prelude to hearings on the Arctic Gas and Foothills applications. They had established the urgency of connecting frontier gas to market and hence of beginning the formal regulatory review of a Mackenzie pipeline as quickly as possible.

In spite of its public exhortations for greater haste, Arctic Gas itself had to bear a large portion of the responsibility for the fact that the National Energy Board hearings on the Mackenzie pipeline began only in October 1975. The length of the gas hearings and Foothills' intention to file a competing application, it is true, had entailed delays of their own. Nevertheless, the NEB had had to wait for CAG to supplement its incomplete application of March 1974 before it could call hearings. In November 1974, Arctic Gas had submitted its financing plan and cost estimates; these were followed in January 1975 by studies of the deliverability of Mackenzie Delta gas and the impact of the project on the Canadian economy. As part of its normal regulatory procedure, the NEB had reviewed the application for deficiencies and asked Arctic Gas to remedy them. The material CAG filed in answer to the NEB's deficiency letters was almost as voluminous as the original application itself.

A similar procedure was followed for Foothills after it had presented its application in March 1975. In May, the board issued its first hearing order, and in July it held a "conference of counsels" to set the procedural rules for the hearings. In August, it announced that the hearings would begin on October 27, 1975.

The NEB, of course, was no stranger to the issues raised by the construction of a Mackenzie pipeline. In the early 1970s, it had played a conspicuous role on the Task Force on Northern Oil Development which had been at the time the focal point within government co-ordinating northern policy. Now in 1975, as a purportedly independent regulatory agency, the NEB was to adjudicate the merits of the very policy it had helped to promote through its membership in various government interdepartmental committees.

The NEB's intimate involvement in the decision-making process, which had led the government in the early 1970s to give approval in principle to the construction of the Mackenzie pipeline, was the concrete evidence of a practice which makes the board today still an integral component of the policy process. It has been noted that in the case of "pioneering" applications[13] involving the development of major new energy markets or sources of supply, the NEB has traditionally deferred to a policy decision by Cabinet before commencing hearings which then no longer concern themselves with the broad public interest of the application itself but rather with subsidiary matters such as engineering design and financing. The government then often uses the NEB decision to justify its prior endorsement of the project in question. This is a blatantly circular argument but it is a politically effective one nevertheless.

Although the board exerts broad discretionary authority over the applications that come before it, it was clear that, in the case of the Mackenzie pipeline, only one outcome was conceivable. The purpose of the hearings was not to decide whether or not to build a pipeline. This question had been answered affirmatively by the gas hearings. Nor was it to choose which applicant would build the pipeline as there was effectively only one which could do so. The scope of the northern pipeline hearings had thus been sharply reduced before they had even begun.

There were other factors which militated in favour of the NEB recommending the construction of the Mackenzie pipeline. Under the NEB Act, affirmative NEB decisions are subject to Cabinet confirmation whereas the board's rejection of an application, on the other hand, is final. The latter places the board in an understandably difficult position, since it forces it to assume full responsibility for a negative decision which may well alienate the industry it is regulating. In the case of the northern pipeline, where two consortia composed of North America's leading oil and gas companies had spent millions of dollars preparing their applications and exploration companies hundreds of millions in the Mackenzie Delta and Prudhoe Bay, the board would have placed itself in an untenable position by rejecting both proposals.

The common perspective which the NEB and industry have traditionally espoused about the development of Canada's energy resources constituted yet another powerful factor which biased the board towards the Mackenzie pipeline. A study by the Law Reform Commission describes this consensus in the following terms:

> There seems to be little doubt... that board members' perspectives, perhaps largely shaped by experience and training, largely coincide with those of industry officials. All tend to view the rules of the game in very much the same way. There are no board members with overriding radical views of the public interest or humanist approaches to energy issues. The same unstated assumptions concerning energy development and use seem to be in the minds of both groups. Issues tend to be framed in technical terms with which both sides are comfortable. To a significant degree and perhaps of necessity, all speak the same industry dialect.[14]

The commonality of values between the board and the industry has been recognized explicitly in the past even by board members. In 1972 when he was still NEB chairman, Dr. R.D. Howland said before a government and industry gathering on the construction of Arctic pipelines that:

> there is no doubt that pipelines can be built in the North and that such

> pipelines can be rendered safe to the environment and compatible with major social objectives and programs. There is a danger, however, of the pipelines being priced out of the market if industry is compelled to meet standards which entail unrealistically high-cost components. Thus the guidelines (the Northern Pipeline Guidelines issued on August 13, 1970) must be translated into regulations and specific conditions which are realistic and operable. This will require extensive dialogue between industry and government.[15]

The facility with which Dr. Howland prejudged the desirability and environmental and social acceptability of northern pipelines—still few studies on the impacts of a pipeline were available at the time—is remarkable in itself. His concern that government regulations not price pipelines out of the market must also be noted as it implies that he saw this solicitude as an integral part of the board's functions.

THE CROWE CASE

When the National Energy Board opened its hearings on the Mackenzie Valley pipeline applications in October 1975, their outcome was virtually pre-ordained. Their sole remaining purpose seemed to be the formal consecration of Canadian Arctic Gas as the government's choice to build the northern pipeline. The feeling that the board would legitimize a policy agreed to, rather than probe alternatives to it, was reinforced by the presence of Marshall Crowe on the panel which was to hear the pipeline applications.

Crowe had been appointed chairman of the National Energy Board two years earlier at a time when there had been considerable friction between the board and the Department of Energy, Mines and Resources. Crowe's predecessor, Bob Howland, had difficulties getting along with Donald Macdonald, then the Energy Minister, and when he realized that his term would not be renewed, he resigned. The government had hoped that Crowe, a civil servant with a long and distinguished career, would put an end to the animosity between the NEB and EMR and help carry out the government's energy policy through a difficult time.

Crowe had been intimately involved in the planning for a Mackenzie pipeline from an early date. In the early 1970s, he had worked in senior positions in the Privy Council Office, the government's inner-most sanctum. In May 1970, Crowe, who had risen to the post of deputy secretary to the Cabinet, chaired a meeting of top-level government officials which led to what was effectively Cabinet approval in principle of a Mackenzie pipeline. (See Chapter Two)

In November 1971, Crowe left the Privy Council to become a director of the government-controlled Canada Development Corporation. A year later, as president, he led the CDC into the Canadian Arctic Gas Consortium. Only one week after the CDC had joined CAGSL, Crowe was named to its management committee. He attended seven meetings of the committee during his tenure with the CDC, including one in June 1973 which decided unanimously on the route the Arctic Gas project would follow and on the structure of its ownership. The CDC spent $1.2 million as its share of CAG's expenses during the year Crowe represented the company in the pipeline consortium.

Arctic Gas filed its application less than six months after Crowe left the CDC to assume his new duties as NEB chairman. After a year-long review of the deficiencies in the CAG submission, the NEB, in April 1975, named Crowe to the panel which would chair the Mackenzie Pipeline Hearings.

Arctic Gas realized the conundrum it faced immediately after Crowe's appointment to the NEB. If Crowe heard the pipeline applications, there was a risk that an NEB decision in CAG's favour would be challenged in court because of Crowe's former association with the project. In any event, this is what the three legal opinions CAG sought on the subject showed. The resulting uncertainty about the pipeline's fate—a court case might last many months—could well spell its doom if it pushed the United States to choose El Paso.

Arctic Gas therefore had to find a way of preventing such a legal challenge, preferably by persuading Crowe that he should not hear the pipeline applications himself. It was an open secret that several members of the Arctic Gas group of companies did not like Crowe and that the feeling was reciprocated. This then was another reason to have Crowe removed from the hearing panel.

During the fall of 1974, Wilder and Horte went to see Crowe on several occasions to inform him that there might be a reasonable apprehension of bias against him should he participate in the pipeline hearings. They showed him the legal opinions they had received. CAG's lawyers also wrote a formal letter to the NEB restating the reasons why Crowe should disqualify himself. Crowe refused to heed CAG's advice. In fact, he was outraged that his impartiality should be suspected. As far as he was concerned, he had only followed government policy by bringing the Canada Development Corporation into Arctic Gas. He was convinced that he was not biased. This, of course, was not the point. In the Canadian judicial system, justice must not only be done but also must be seen to be done. Even if Crowe was impartial, his year at the CDC dictated that he abstain from judging the pipeline applications.

For Arctic Gas, Crowe's intransigence was truly a "Catch 22" situation. If it accepted Crowe, it would almost certainly have to face a legal challenge in the future. If it objected to Crowe, it risked alienating the NEB and, not least of all, Crowe himself, whose continued role as the NEB's chairman and chief executive officer could some day influence the final outcome of the pipeline hearings.

To protect itself, Arctic Gas sought a legal ruling on the propriety of Crowe's membership on the panel. In doing so, it was careful not to allege that Crowe might be biased but merely that there might exist a reasonable apprehension that he was. By seeking such a ruling at the beginning of the hearings, Arctic Gas minimized its risks: at best, the issue would be resolved quickly and the regulatory process would not be delayed; at worst, the hearings would be held up slightly while the courts decided on the issue. In either case, the potential threat posed by Crowe's presence would be eliminated. After an exchange of correspondence with Arctic Gas, the NEB announced that Crowe would read a statement on the first day of the hearings reviewing his past role with the CDC. All interveners would be invited at that time to indicate whether they had any objections to Crowe's participation. If they did not do so then, it was unlikely that the courts would look favourably upon a challenge to the board's proceedings at a later stage.

The issue came to a head on October 27, the first day of the hearings. The board requested each intervener in turn to state his position. Arctic Gas, first in the order of precedence, said it had no objection. Neither did Foothills nor any industry intervener. Indeed, only five of eighty-nine parties recognized by the board objected, all of them public interest groups (among them were the Committee for Justice and Liberty, the Canadian Arctic Resources Committee, the Consumers' Association of Canada and the Workgroup on Canadian Energy Policy). The NEB accordingly referred the case to the Federal Court for a ruling and began to hear the pipeline applications pending the court's decision. On December 12, that decision was handed down: Crowe could continue to sit on the panel. CJL, CARC and the CAC appealed the ruling to the Supreme Court. The case was heard in early March 1976 and on the 11th, in a split judgement, the Supreme Court concluded that

> ... the participation of Mr. Crowe in the discussions and decisions leading to the application made by Canadian Arctic Gas Pipeline Limited for a certificate of public convenience and necessity... cannot but give rise to a reasonable apprehension, which reasonably well informed persons could properly have, of a biased appraisal and judgement of the issue to be determined...

Crowe was disqualified. The immediate effect of the decision was to abort the hearings. Although the NEB had finally suspended them when the Supreme Court had granted its leave to appeal the Federal Court decision, the hearings had nevertheless been well advanced by that date. They would now have to start over again, with a different panel, five and a half months after the first set of hearings had begun. As far as Arctic Gas was concerned, this was the worst possible outcome.

In retrospect, this delay was crucial in determining the fate of the Arctic Gas application. It allowed another competitor, the Alaska Highway consortium, to emerge and present its case. More importantly perhaps, it gave

Berger more time to conduct his hearings and scrutinize the Arctic Gas proposal. It is ironic that the initial success of the CAG gamble—Crowe's disqualification—carried with it the seeds of the consortium's eventual demise. Crowe never forgave Arctic Gas for the action it had initiated. Although his role in the NEB's final recommendation remains conjectural, his subsequent association with the sponsors of the Alaska Highway pipeline[16] has left much bitterness among former Arctic Gas executives.

The Crowe affair epitomized the conflict between the ostensible independence of the National Energy Board and its membership in the executive arm of government. Seldom had the incestuous nature of the government's decision-making process been so bluntly revealed. The real issue in this case—though not the legal one on which the Supreme Court ruled—was not whether Crowe would have been seen as favouring one pipeline applicant over another, as Arctic Gas had suggested. It was whether Crowe had prejudged the desirability of building a northern pipeline per se as a result of having participated in the formation of government policy during his years at the Privy Council Office and the Canada Development Corporation.

In an *Oilweek* interview shortly after his appointment to the NEB, Crowe had stated that he hoped "... the North will play a major role in supplying energy to Canada. The announced gas discoveries are important, as are the probable reserves. Development will not be too remote."[17] Ironically, his successor on the Northern Pipeline Panel, J.G. Stabback, expressed similar views before he assumed the chairmanship of the second set of NEB hearings. In 1975, he would say in a speech about Canadian energy policy that "a shortage of gas is likely to develop in the 1970s, but when gas from the Arctic is connected a large new supply will be available."[18] Although Stabback perhaps intended the statement to reflect nothing more than his optimism that development would take place, in 1975 Arctic Gas was the only project with the potential of developing the "large new supply" in the timeframe he had in mind.

The Mackenzie pipeline hearings' false start cast an enduring and pernicious shadow over the second set of NEB proceedings. The Supreme Court decision, besides affecting the constitution of the hearing panel, disjointed the Canadian and American decision-making timetables which until then had proceeded roughly in step. When the NEB resumed its hearings in April 1976, the US Federal Power Commission hearings had been in progress for almost a year. If Canada was to influence the American decision, the government was convinced that it would have to catch up to the more advanced American timetable. A lengthy regulatory delay in Canada, as Arctic Gas had repeatedly warned, might result in Canada losing the Mackenzie pipeline by default as the impatient Americans opted for El Paso, a project wholly under their jurisdiction. In order to make up the time it had "lost" as a result of the Supreme Court decision, the NEB was forced to accelerate its hearings several times until haste rather than method became the guiding principle in their conduct.

By early 1976, not only were the FPC hearings far ahead of the NEB's, but the US Congress furthermore seemed intent on legislating an early deadline to the American pipeline decision. In light of the NEB's forecast of imminent domestic gas shortages, the court challenge to Crowe and the multiplication of congressional bills aimed at expediting the American regulatory process, it is not surprising that the Canadian government too considered the legislation option in the late fall of 1975. This was an extremely distasteful solution politically. The "great pipeline debate" of 1956, during which the Liberals had forced Parliament to approve the construction of the then American-dominated TransCanada Pipeline, had after all contributed to the fall of the St. Laurent government a year later. The political costs of ramming an American pipeline through before the conclusion of the Berger and NEB hearings could not be foreseen in advance, and the government therefore wisely chose not to force the issue at the time.

Nevertheless, the problem of catching up to the United States remained a serious one. To compound it, a third pipeline application was now being prepared. This latest proposal bypassed the Mackenzie Valley to follow the Alaska highway across the southern Yukon instead. Its sponsor was Arctic Gas's rival, Foothills.

CHAPTER FIVE

THE NEW CONTENDER

Although Foothills had considered carrying Prudhoe Bay gas in its pipeline when it had first proposed the Maple Leaf project in September 1974, it did not give the plan much study. "It was a crazy idea," a former Foothills official now says. The simultaneous delivery of both Alaskan and Canadian gas would have required a system very much like CAG's, thereby eliminating Maple Leaf's main strengths (lower capital cost, earlier construction, avoidance of the inhospitable and environmentally-sensitive North Slope, use of operating pipelines). Blair, however, toyed with this "crazy idea" for almost a year before finally rejecting it. And with good reason: without Prudhoe Bay gas to fill it, the Maple Leaf pipeline was simply not viable.

This fact was becoming increasingly obvious. In 1975, no major gas discoveries were made in the Mackenzie Delta, and indeed, as a result of adjustments in previous estimates, the reserve picture remained unchanged for the second year in a row. Even the most optimistic assessment of these reserves yielded only half the "threshold" volume needed to make the Maple Leaf project economic. Foothills officials gamely continued to claim that this was enough to finance their pipeline, but their assurances were not taken seriously. It was axiomatic that a multi-billion dollar pipeline would not be financed merely on the expectation that there would eventually be enough gas to fill it. The reserves had to be discovered first. Because it would tap the large Prudhoe Bay field, Arctic Gas, of course, was not affected as seriously by the disappointing exploratory results in the Delta.

In the United States, meanwhile, the Federal Power Commission hearings under the chairmanship of Administrative Law Judge Nahum Litt were making steady progress and the record showed that Arctic Gas was proving the much superior alternative to El Paso for the delivery of Prudhoe Bay gas. This caused great concern among Foothills officials. It raised the possibility that CAG might win by default in the US, forcing AGTL into the same position it had feared in 1970 when it had first approached the Northwest Project

Study Group. If Arctic Gas won, AGTL would have to endure the substantial disruption in the natural gas service industry which the construction of a Mackenzie pipeline would entail. More importantly, it would have to accommodate itself to the threat posed by the existence of a high capacity express pipeline with a built-in cost-of-service advantage over its own lower pressure and, hence, less efficient pipeline system.

FOOTHILLS EXPLORES ALTERNATIVES

By the early fall of 1975, therefore, even before the beginning of the NEB hearings, a few senior Foothills officials were starting to feel that if they did not offer themselves as a stronger alternative to Arctic Gas in the United States than El Paso, the Maple Leaf project would be defeated in Canada regardless of its possible merits. The main problem with Maple Leaf, as they saw it, was that it did nothing for the US. This was a liability because they agreed the pipeline decision would be taken in Washington, not Ottawa. They firmly believed that if the US insisted on the construction of a joint Mackenzie pipeline, "... Canada would have a hard time withstanding that pressure".[1]

Foothills, however, was at a substantial strategic disadvantage to Arctic Gas in the United States because it sponsored no application of its own. Although it had won recognition as an intervener before the FPC, it had limited the presentation of its case to only two rather tenuous claims. The first of these was that, by keeping existing pipelines operating at full capacity, the Maple Leaf project would ensure that the transportation costs of Canadian gas already destined to American markets would not rise; the second was that Foothills would minimize the expected reduction in Canadian gas exports by building its pipeline before Arctic Gas. With so little gas in the Mackenzie Delta, these were singularly unconvincing arguments. If it still hoped to defeat Arctic Gas, Foothills would clearly have to devise a more compelling case against its rival.

It was the need to strengthen its precarious position that led Foothills in late 1975 to renew its interest in Westcoast's old Mountain Pacific Project to carry Prudhoe Bay gas along the Alaska Highway. Foothills had already updated some of the Mountain Pacific cost estimates that summer to use in cross-examination before the Berger Inquiry. Indeed, in attempting to demonstrate the superiority of the Alaska Highway corridor for the transportation of Alaskan gas, Foothills had tried to get Arctic Gas to switch over its route. "We tried to tell them this is a better route", Ron Rutherford, Foothills' former executive vice-president, recalls with a smile. In the summer of 1975, Foothills hoped that if it could establish the advantages of an Alaska Highway pipeline, Arctic Gas, whose primary interest was in carrying Prudhoe Bay gas, would abandon the Mackenzie Valley to the Maple Leaf project. It is extraordinarily ironic that this suicidal tactic failed. It did not take long for Foothills to realize how uncommonly fortunate it had been when CAG had refused to rise to the bait. Foothills instructed its lawyers before both Berger and the NEB that from then on they should under no circumstance attempt to shake CAG's blind commitment to a Mackenzie pipeline. Once it had decided to sponsor the Alaska Highway line itself, Foothills feared that its fate would be sealed the moment Arctic Gas decided to change the routing of its project.

If the Foothills cross-examination of Arctic Gas failed in its intended purpose, it nonetheless had a powerful impact on the Berger staff. Here was an alternative that seemed free from the engineering, environmental and social problems that were already becoming evident in the Arctic Gas proposal. The Berger Inquiry's examination of alternatives to a Mackenzie pipeline during the summer of 1975 would influence Berger's recommendations two years later.

At the beginning of October 1975, Blair and Westcoast's president, Edwin Phillips, met in Toronto with Senator Ted Stevens of Alaska to discuss the transportation of northern gas. A supporter of El Paso, Stevens was a natural ally in the fight against Arctic Gas. During that meeting, Phillips raised what was then known in the United States as the "Fairbanks route" for the delivery of Prudhoe Bay gas along the Alaska Highway. Phillips was an ardent advocate of that alternative. In a letter to Stevens a few days after the meeting, Phillips wrote:

> When I discuss the alternate route I must admit that my personal feelings come to the fore. From the time we started to study our initial plan to move Alaskan gas, called Mountain Pacific, I have felt very deeply that the United States should have the security of its own pipeline to the lower 48 states carrying exclusively Alaskan gas.[2]

In late 1975, the Fairbanks route was starting to receive increasing attention in the US. This attention was in large measure the result of the work conducted by the Federal Power Commission staff under the provisions of the National Environmental Policy Act (NEPA). The act, which has no Canadian equivalent, requires that all alternatives be evaluated before a decision is reached on a large project. In assessing the environmental impact of various methods of delivering Alaskan gas, the FPC staff paid particular attention to one alternative that Arctic Gas had once rejected for being too costly: the Fairbanks corridor. Indeed, as early as April 7, 1975, even before the FPC hearings had formally begun, the FPC staff had declared that an Alaska Highway pipeline "should not be written off". Seven months later, on November 21, the staff released its draft environmental impact statement, strongly endorsing the Fairbanks route as environmentally preferable to both Arctic Gas and El Paso. The proselytizing drive of the report, an intentional departure from the traditionally neutral tone of similar documents, commanded immediate attention.

The Fairbanks route received further attention in December 1975 when the US Department of the Interior issued a report to Congress on the transportation of Alaskan gas. This report, whose publication was required under the TransAlaska Pipeline Authorization Act, indicated that the economic benefits to the United States of building an Alaska Highway pipeline would be equivalent to those of building a Mackenzie Valley pipeline. Furthermore, on environmental grounds, the Department of the Interior concluded that the selection of a route paralleling existing transportation corridors (i.e., the Alyeska right-of-way and the Alaska Highway) would exert a lower environmental impact than the construction of a pipeline through unopened territory (the Arctic Wildlife Range and the Mackenzie Valley).

To those studying transportation alternatives for Prudhoe Bay gas, the Alaska Highway pipeline was proving itself increasingly worthy of closer examination. It was at this time that two US Senate committees decided to hold public hearings on the northern pipeline. Henry Jackson, as chairman of the Committee on Interior and Insular Affairs (now the Committee on Energy and Natural Resources), wielded considerable influence on American energy policy; in early 1976, Jackson was also aspiring to the Democratic presidential nomination, a fact which might have given him an additional incentive to keep a high public profile. His colleague from the State of Washington, Warren Magnuson, headed the Commerce Committee which, as part of its mandate, oversaw the work of the FPC and the implementation of American natural gas policy. He, too, therefore, was interested in the issues related to the transportation of Alaskan gas. The two committees wanted their hearings to explore three alternatives to Arctic Gas and El Paso:

1) an indefinite delay in the production of North Slope gas;
2) the conversion of the Prudhoe Bay gas reserves to methanol, a liquid which could then be transported in the Alyeska oil pipeline;
3) a new pipeline along the Alaska Highway which would take maximum advantage of the existing North American distribution system.

In January 1976, therefore, the two committees distributed a questionnaire entitled "Issues concerning the Transportation of Alaskan Natural Gas" which covered these alternatives as well as the wide range of energy, regulatory and bilateral issues raised by El Paso and Arctic Gas.

By coincidence, the chief economist to Jackson's committee at the time was Dr. Arlon Tussing whose extensive work on Alaskan oil and gas transportation issues had convinced him that, for a variety of reasons, neither Arctic Gas nor El Paso was desirable.

In the early 1970s, Tussing had argued strenuously against the Trans-Alaska oil pipeline on the ground that it would create an oil surplus on the US

West Coast which would necessitate the construction of a second pipeline to deliver that surplus from California to Midwest markets. Tussing had therefore favoured a pipeline through Canada. By early 1976, Tussing was being vindicated as oil industry forecasts started to show belatedly that California would indeed not be able to absorb the entire Alyeska throughput.

It is not surprising then that Tussing should have been highly skeptical of the El Paso proposal: not only was it costly and less reliable than an all-pipeline system, but it landed Prudhoe Bay gas in California where little of it was needed and required therefore the implementation of a complicated displacement scheme to deliver supplies to the Midwest. Tussing, however, did not accept Arctic Gas as the logical alternative. By crossing a vast wilderness with no existing infrastructure or construction history and relying on untried building techniques, Arctic Gas, Tussing believed, was highly vulnerable to cost overruns. The route to transport Prudhoe Bay gas did lie in Canada but along the Alaska Highway, not the Mackenzie Valley.

Tussing called Blair a couple of months before the Senate hearings were to begin to enquire about the methanol scheme (through Alberta Gas Chemicals, AGTL controls one of the biggest methanol production facilities in North America) and about AGTL's willingness to move Alaskan gas along the Fairbanks corridor. Blair was extremely receptive to Tussing's approach. He considered the matter important enough that he flew to Washington the next day to discuss both propositions further. During the meeting, he reminded Tussing of Westcoast's interest in the Mountain Pacific project and assured him that Foothills could develop a reliable cost estimate for the entire Alaska Highway system.

A few days later, however, Blair's initial enthusiasm seemed to wane. He called Tussing to complain that the generation of the numbers that had been requested would be expensive and that Foothills could justify the expenditure only if it received a formal request from Senators Jackson and Magnuson. Tussing then suggested a quid pro quo: Foothills would be invited to testify at the hearings on the Alaska Highway and methanol alternatives and would earn thereby the opportunity to promote the Maple Leaf project and attack Arctic Gas. Blair immediately accepted.

In spite of his acceptance, Blair was still concerned that his testimony about a pipeline to carry American gas across Canada would be interpreted as a betrayal of the lofty nationalist rhetoric Foothills had been using against Arctic Gas. Phillips, on the other hand, had no such qualms and was eager to take advantage of the Senate hearings to promote an Alaska Highway line. In his discussions with Blair over the issue, he used the argument that Tussing had given him in one of the several conversations the two men had during that period:

> It doesn't lessen Canadian independence, for a Canadian or a US firm, or a combination of them, to move Alaska gas *across* Canada. What Maple Leaf is about is the need for Canadians to decide when and how the

> Mackenzie is to be developed, and not a consortium of multinational oil companies and US banks.[3]

Blair ultimately accepted this argument but when he appeared on March 24, 1976 before the two committees, he was still far from convinced that Foothills should be drawn into proposing a second pipeline. In his testimony, Blair stated pointedly that "... we are not ourselves sponsoring or proposing a new project".[4] For greater emphasis, he added that, frankly, he would be more interested in investing $50 million to expand AGTL's petrochemical holdings than "... $250 million to express Alaska gas through Alberta.... The demands of capital investment as well as management and engineering-construction would quite outweigh the commercial gain in transmission business". In case any ambiguity remained, Blair went on to list five "cautionary provisions", or conditions, AGTL would seek before it would commit itself to transporting Alaskan gas. One of these was that the Canadian government make a decision in principle on "... whether to confer a long-term transmission service access for Alaska gas to US markets through routes crossing western Canada..." Another was that complementary methods of delivering Prudhoe Bay gas to market be approved so that "... Canadian companies shall not inherit complete responsibility for all future investment in providing and expanding transmission capacity for future gas production from the North Slope of Alaska."

Notwithstanding Blair's wariness, one month later the partnership to promote the Alaska Highway pipeline was firmly launched, with AGTL as an integral member. The Canadian sponsors, of course, included also Westcoast and a specially formed joint subsidiary, Foothills Pipe Lines (Yukon) Ltd. The American sponsor of this venture was a little-known pipeline company that was barely two years old at the time, the Northwest Pipeline Corporation. Northwest's corporate history,[5] a remarkably tumultuous one for such a young company, offers a fascinating insight into the character of its chairman and chief executive officer, John McMillian, which helps to explain how Northwest succeeded in winning the biggest prize in American regulatory history in spite of the overwhelming odds against it.

NORTHWEST PIPELINE

What was Northwest?

Northwest was born in February 1974, following seventeen years of litigation regarding the largest court-ordered divestiture in the annals of American business. The loser of this epic battle was the large El Paso Natural Gas Company which, in 1957, had acquired a newly-built pipeline stretching from the San Juan Basin in New Mexico to the Pacific Northwest States. This takeover had effectively made El Paso the sole gas supplier of any size for the entire American West Coast market. El Paso's purchase of its competitor prompted the US Justice Department to file an antitrust suit. The case was to go to the Supreme Court on eight separate occasions before finally being settled.

It was in 1967 that John McMillian, a cigar-smoking Texan who still speaks with a drawl, decided to bid for Pacific Northwest. McMillian had just come back from having spent eight frustrating months and $300,000 of his own money drilling dry wells in New Guinea, and Pacific Northwest must have seemed a beckoning prospect. "It's a big asset," he was quoted as saying at the time. "It's not often that individuals can buy something like that."[6] Indeed not: at stake was not only a 3,100 mile transmission system but, of greater significance, several trillion cubic feet of natural gas reserves in both Canada and the United States which placed Pacific Northwest in an enviable position among the members of its industry. McMillian, however, had arrived too late to be recognized as one of the official bidders for the pipeline. Undaunted, he bought his way into a partnership with a company that was. Two years later, McMillian's gambit seemed to have failed when a rival, the Colorado Interstate Company, was designated as the purchaser of Pacific Northwest. In one of the many extraordinary reversals which marked the divestiture fight, McMillian's group won a reprieve when the Supreme Court was persuaded to hear new arguments on the case.

In order to bankroll his efforts, McMillian needed new allies (he would spend $3.5 million in his bid for Pacific Northwest).[7] In 1971, he forged a partnership, of which his own company, the Tipperary Corporation, owned 10%, the Gulf Interstate Company 15%, the Apco Oil Company and the Alaska Interstate Company thirty-seven and a half per cent each. It is a testimony to McMillian's forcefulness that he should have headed this new group in spite of being its smallest member.

Late the same year, McMillian's group found itself forced to fight on another front. El Paso, which by then had already resisted divestiture for fourteen years, succeeded in having a bill introduced in Congress which would have legalized its ownership of Pacific Northwest. The bill was only 350 words long but, as the *New York Times* noted, each word was worth one million dollars to El Paso, since Pacific Northwest's assets at the time were valued at some $340 million. Although El Paso won the support of a former opponent, Senator Warren Magnuson, and spent over $893,000 in lobbying costs, the bill was eventually killed. McMillian's group was still in the running.

In 1972, Colorado Interstate was again awarded Pacific Northwest. However, before the court decision became final, Colorado was bought out by another company, thereby losing its award. As a result of this unexpected turn of events, McMillian's group found itself chosen by default as the new owner of Pacific Northwest, six years after McMillian himself had started bidding for the company. "It was a great feeling," McMillian recalls today. "It showed me what could be done with 100% determination". Throughout all these years, observers agree, it had been McMillian's tenacity that had kept the effort alive and his partners together. It was natural therefore that he should become the Northwest Pipeline Corporation's first president.

The new company faced its first major test before it was even formally incorporated. In the fall of 1973, Westcoast, which delivers two-thirds of Northwest's gas supply, sharply reduced its exports following production difficulties in fields in Northeastern British Columbia. The need to find new supplies to meet the requirements of its system suddenly became, in McMillian's words, Northwest's "most important challenge". In May 1974, only three months after it had begun operations, Northwest entered into a joint venture with the Pacific Lighting Corporation of Los Angeles to take delivery of Prudhoe Bay gas from CAG at the BC-Idaho border. Although this venture, Pacific Interstate Transmission Associates (Arctic), was at first an integral component of the Arctic Gas project, Northwest never did join the Arctic Gas consortium. McMillian felt uncomfortable with Arctic Gas's management style; he was also reluctant to become involved in a project whose costs he could not control. Subsequently, he was to become increasingly skeptical about the project itself.

Northwest almost ceased to exist as an independent entity in only its second year of operations when Alaska Interstate, one of Northwest's owners, made a bid to buy out its partner, Apco, and gain control of the company. Interstate's takeover attempt had been sparked by a disagreement between McMillian and Interstate's chairman, O. Charles Honig, over company policy. In July 1975, Interstate launched its takeover bid by making a public offer to buy 48% of Apco's stock. That offer, if successful, would have given Interstate effective control over Northwest and the power to appoint new management. Reacting with anger, McMillian had Honig ejected from Northwest's board of directors at an emergency meeting and announced a counter-offer for Apco's stock. After what McMillian refers to euphemistically as "a spirited battle", Northwest's second counter-offer prevailed for a price almost double that which Apco's shares had commanded before the takeover fight.

It is worth noting parenthetically that Interstate was to charge Northwest later with violations of the US Securities and Exchange Act. Although the case never went to trial and these charges were therefore never adjudicated, the Delaware judge chairing the case did find that both companies had "failed accurately to apprise the market place with respect to specific facts" and that both had given out "misleading and incorrect information".

McMillian's dramatic victory once again had demonstrated his unyielding determination and his ability to react quickly and forcefully to a challenge. Now that he had strengthened his personal control over Northwest and had reorganized it into the Northwest Energy Company, McMillian was ready to confront an even bigger task: the acquisition of a long term supply of energy.

The need to find new gas supplies was becoming increasingly pressing in light of Westcoast's continued inability to deliver the gas Northwest needed. To make matters worse, one of Northwest's contracts with Westcoast, representing over 10% of its daily receipts, was scheduled to expire in 1981. To continue to meet the demands of its customers, Northwest would have to find a new long term source of supply before then.

The largest undeveloped gas reserve in the United States was of course in Alaska. The bulk of Prudhoe Bay gas, however, had already been committed to the Arctic Gas sponsors. The only significant volume that was still unsold at Prudhoe Bay was the gas which the State of Alaska itself would receive in lieu of royalties. In early 1976 Northwest began to negotiate with the state for a share of the three trillion cubic feet of royalty gas. As a strong supporter of El Paso's liquefied natural gas (LNG) proposal, Alaska, however, wanted to use its gas to help that project. As a condition of sale, therefore, Alaska demanded that Northwest endorse its old corporate parent, the same company McMillian had fought so vigorously for six years. This request forced Northwest to assess further the various methods of delivering Prudhoe Bay gas. It concluded that the El Paso proposal was an inefficient one. Arctic Gas, on the other hand, appeared to Northwest to be susceptible to lengthy delays which might prevent it from delivering gas when Northwest would need it. Exploring other alternatives, Northwest held informal discussions with Westcoast over the possible use of spare capacity in its system to ship Alaskan gas south. Westcoast responded to Northwest's expression of interest with enthusiasm.

At Westcoast's initiative, a meeting was held in Vancouver on March 15, 1976, to discuss the Fairbanks route. Ironically, Westcoast had already approached other American companies about the possibility of sponsoring an Alaska Highway pipeline. One of these had been the giant Tenneco Corporation whose prior involvement in the Polar Gas project had finally precluded its participation in a second Arctic pipeline. Westcoast's largest customer, Northwest, was a logical candidate for partnership. Northwest was sufficiently encouraged by the results of its meeting with Westcoast officials that it commissioned Gulf Interstate—one of its parents—to conduct a crash feasibility study on the Fairbanks route. That route, Northwest hoped, would constitute a compromise acceptable to Alaska and might represent a useful lever in its negotiations over the state's royalty gas. But it would have to move quickly. The FPC hearings were expected to conclude by the end of May, and Northwest's gamble would certainly fail if it was made after the hearings were over. On April 6, therefore, Northwest made its formal bid for the royalty gas. In a letter to the state's Commissioner of Natural Resources, McMillian stated: "If a satisfactory commitment to Northwest is made, Northwest will sponsor and make all necessary applications in support of a Fairbanks-Alcan Highway pipeline alternative." To help to promote its bid, Northwest retained three lobbyists in Juneau, the state's capital. On April 14, the feasibility study was completed and, armed with its results, McMillian met Blair and Phillips in Calgary nine days later.

THE THIRD MAN IN

Ever since mid-March, Blair had come under mounting pressure from his partner Westcoast to support the Alaska Highway pipeline. Westcoast pointed out that one of Blair's key conditions in his testimony before the two Senate committees on March 24 had been fulfilled now that an American sponsor existed for the project. Furthermore, the reasons in the spring of 1976 for Foothills to propose a pipeline to carry Prudhoe Bay gas were even more compelling than they had been the previous fall when Westcoast had resuscitated Mountain Pacific: the reserve situation in the Mackenzie Delta had still not improved and Foothills' position was becoming increasingly untenable as a result. CAG, meanwhile, was reaping the profits of its extensive lobbying in the United States as a bill was introduced in the Senate in February to legislate American approval of a Mackenzie pipeline. If it hoped to defeat its rival, Foothills had to undercut CAG's mounting congressional support. An Alaska Highway pipeline would do just that. By forcing a delay in the American pipeline decision, it would buy time for Foothills. Time was important, because it would allow more exploratory drilling to take place both in Alberta and in the Mackenzie Delta.

Blair, however, still felt a strong commitment to the Maple Leaf proposal. He was reluctant to become drawn into a project that was so exclusively oriented to the American interest. He was concerned about the effect the promotion of a pipeline to carry American gas only would have on Foothills' credibility. He felt that if a congressional committee or members of the administration preferred an Alaska Highway pipeline, they should say so and Foothills would then consider making an application to build the line. Blair himself would not take the initiative of promoting Canada as a land-bridge between Alaska and the rest of the United States.

The man who helped to change Blair's mind was Tussing. Both men had talked extensively about the Fairbanks route before. When Tussing met Blair again, however, he no longer spoke only on his own behalf. After Blair's testimony before the two Senate committees, Tussing had informally canvassed officials in several government departments and agencies and had found a great deal of latent interest and even support for an Alaska Highway pipeline. Tussing was able to report to Blair that the construction of a Mackenzie pipeline was by no means assured and that an overland alternative following existing rights-of-way would be seen with a great deal of favour in some government circles, particularly in light of the disastrous cost overruns suffered by the Alyeska pipeline. This was exactly what Blair had wanted to hear. By mid-April, he was talked out of his opposition to an Alaska Highway pipeline.

Blair's reticence was typical. Contrary to the myths which have been built around him, Blair is a cautious man who avoids unnecessary risks. As he himself admits readily, "In many ways I follow more than lead. That's not some kind of artificial modesty. That's being clinical about the situation."[8]

The ability to listen to, and act upon advice is, of course, the mark of a successful businessman.

There were other factors too which contributed to Blair's change of heart. His attendance at several of Berger's community hearings had sensitized him to the deep opposition of the native people to a Mackenzie pipeline and the formidable obstacle that the unresolved land claims would represent to any pipeline project. Blair was also concerned that Ottawa might reject Maple Leaf because several government officials feared American retaliation if Canada did not give the United States overland access to Alaskan gas.

Ultimately, even if Blair prides himself on his nationalism, he is above all a pragmatist. And therein lies the key to his success. He may genuinely have felt in March that for a project with such obvious national implications as the trans-shipment of American gas across Canadian territory, the government should let Foothills know "that it was their choice that we endeavour to work out such an alternative" before proceeding any further. When it became clear, however, that AGTL's future growth might be circumscribed if it did not oppose Arctic Gas more effectively, Blair decided to define the national interest himself. Similarly, although he would have preferred not to "inherit complete responsibility" for the movement of all future gas production from the North Slope, AGTL would assume that responsibility if this was the only way it could protect its interests. For Blair, nationalism has a definite bottom line.

On April 23 in Calgary, AGTL, Westcoast and Northwest agreed to sponsor a new Arctic pipeline proposal. A letter of intent, outlining the obligations of the three companies, was drafted and signed on May 5. This letter established the broad principles under which the project would be pursued. In it, AGTL and Westcoast agreed to file applications to build the Canadian section of the line if certain conditions were met. Chief among these was that the Federal Power Commission hear the Northwest application conjointly with those of its competitors.

On May 7, the Northwest board of directors authorized the expenditure of up to $6 million to pursue the application. The very next day, however, Northwest received its first setback. On May 8, the governor of Alaska, Jay Hammond, announced that he was delaying the sale of the state's royalty gas (gas in lieu of royalties) indefinitely. The purchase of that gas, of course, had been the reason Northwest had decided to stretch its resources to their limit by sponsoring a multi-billion dollar pipeline. With characteristic determination, McMillian decided to persevere anyway on the belief that if Northwest could prevail on the route, it would stand a good chance of obtaining the royalty gas later. By the end of May, any momentary hesitation McMillian might have harboured was gone. Before the FPC, he declared brashly:

> There is a lot of self-serving interest here. We would expand our facilities. I mean I think we would have a better opportunity, in our opinion,

> to obtain Prudhoe Bay gas. There are a lot of advantages to us. We are not up here singing "Onward Christian Soldiers". It is a lot of self-service, self-interest we have here. We would double the size of our company.[9]

As a relatively small company filing an eleventh-hour application to build the largest privately-financed project in the world, Northwest was an interloper among some of the most powerful companies in the American natural gas industry. Arctic Gas had already spent six years and over $100 million studying the Mackenzie Valley pipeline, El Paso three years and almost $20 million studying the LNG alternative. Northwest only had one feasibility study that had taken one month to prepare. The FPC hearings were now scheduled to end in two months. The odds against Northwest were overpowering, and it would have to hurry if it wanted its project to be considered as a serious alternative to either Arctic Gas or El Paso.

The first step was to become recognized by the FPC as an official applicant alongside its more established competitors. Threatening to litigate "with every resource that we could possibly muster" if the FPC did not consolidate the Alaska Highway application in its current hearings, Northwest saw its request granted on July 23, two weeks after it had filed its application. This was the signal AGTL and Westcoast had been awaiting. Accelerating their own preparatory work on the Canadian sections of the pipeline, they submitted companion applications to the National Energy Board at the end of August. The NEB had no choice but to agree to incorporate these latest filings in its current hearings on the Mackenzie pipeline. This it did officially on September 10.

The original Alaska Highway proposal—it was modified several times later—called for the construction of a 42-inch pipeline from Prudhoe Bay, along the Alyeska oil pipeline right-of-way to Fairbanks where the line would then follow the Alaska Highway. The 731 miles of pipeline to be built in Alaska would be owned by a Northwest affiliate, the Alcan Pipeline Co.—since renamed the Alaskan Northwest Natural Gas Transportation Co. as a result of a formal complaint lodged by the Aluminum Company of Canada over the use of the name Alcan. The pipeline was to continue to parallel the Alaska Highway until Fort Nelson, in British Columbia, where it would interconnect with Westcoast. A new pipeline would be built between Fort Nelson and Zama Lake in northwest Alberta to link the project with AGTL. Both AGTL and Westcoast would be looped to accommodate the flow of Alaskan gas. The segment of the pipeline built in the Yukon would be owned by Foothills (Yukon) whose ownership in turn was divided equally between Westcoast and AGTL; all new facilities south of the 60th parallel would be owned by Westcoast and AGTL (Canada) except for any new line to be installed in Saskatchewan which would also be owned by Foothills (Yukon). The size of the pipe, the division of management responsibilities and the use

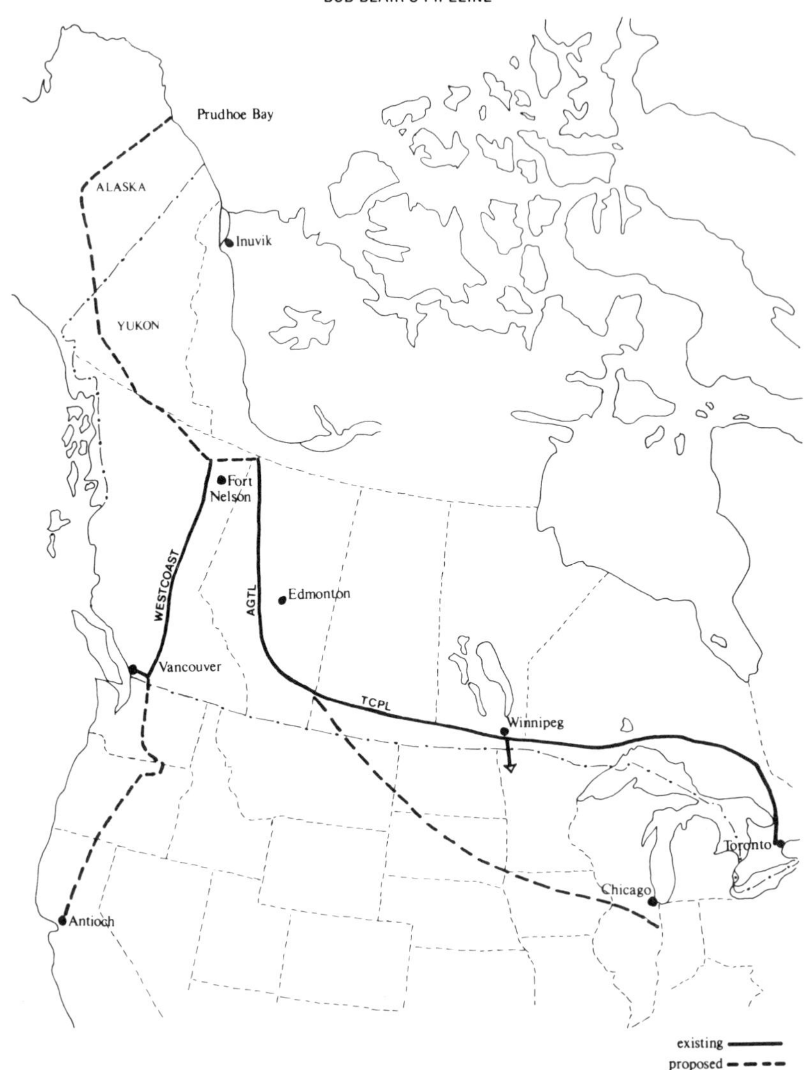

ALASKA HIGHWAY PIPELINE—ORIGINAL PROPOSAL

of existing systems all conformed to the conservative principles AGTL had followed since 1970. The total cost of the project was first estimated at $6.42 billion and the start of operations was set for 1980, one year earlier than Arctic Gas.

THE GOVERNMENT'S RESPONSE

The emergence of Alcan changed everything. Until Bob Blair was persuaded that Foothills should sponsor the Alaska Highway pipeline, it had seemed only a matter of time before a Mackenzie pipeline would be built. This assumption had underlain the government's planning for the last seven years and reflected closely the conventional wisdom of the time. Now that a third project had entered the fray, however, the pipeline issue could no longer be reduced simply to a choice between approving Arctic Gas and postponing development indefinitely. The victim of its own limited vision, the government was poorly equipped to make the decisions which were suddenly being demanded of it. It knew very little about the merits of an Alaska Highway pipeline, its environmental repercussions, its implications for native land claim negotiations in the Yukon, its impact on drilling activity in the Mackenzie Delta or its suitability for the development of Canada's own gas reserves. The Foothills (Yukon) application had multiplied the number of policy decisions the government now had to face.

In 1976, the uneven results of northern exploration were complicating the pipeline equation further by raising yet another possible alternative to a Mackenzie line: the Polar Gas proposal from the High Arctic islands. In contrast with the increasingly gloomy outlook in the Delta, the Arctic islands remained a bright spot for exploration. Panarctic, the 45% government-owned drilling consortium, had already accumulated twice as much gas as had been found in the Delta. Furthermore, the prospects for new discoveries were very good. Polar Gas, it is true, still had major technological hurdles to overcome before it could build its pipeline; more gas would also have to be found before the project could be economically viable. Nevertheless, if the domestic natural gas situation improved, thereby postponing the need for immediate frontier development, Polar Gas might yet become a serious alternative to a Mackenzie pipeline.

The government's task in choosing a northern pipeline was becoming more difficult at the same time as pressure for an early decision was mounting. That pressure was coming mostly from the United States where Congress was debating legislation to set a deadline of mid-1977 for the American pipeline decision. Although the Canadian government was obviously not bound to any American timetable, it could not ignore one either. A lengthy delay in the Canadian decision would be tantamount to rejecting an overland pipeline and would leave the US with no recourse but to approve El Paso. Arctic Gas, of course, had in the past exploited Canada's fears in this respect with considerable success. So when the American ambassador to Canada, Thomas Omstrom Enders, warned in June 1976, "It will be difficult for Washington to consider Canadian alternatives if the Canadian government does not take the initiative"[10] of conveying its pipeline decision quickly to the US government, his message did not go unheeded. Enders' warning prompted Dennis Timbrell, Ontario's Minister of Energy, to call publicly for an early decision on the northern pipeline, a call soon echoed in several newspaper editorials, notably the *Globe and Mail*. Being already predisposed to the construction of a pipeline, Cabinet was particularly vulnerable to such appeals.

As the date for a pipeline decision in the United States approached, the Canadian government therefore began to prepare itself to receive the recommendations of the NEB and the Berger Commission. Several government officials felt that the pipeline issue was just too important to leave in the hands of the NEB and that the government had to develop its own expertise to evaluate the various pipeline options. They also pointed out that, in the event that Berger and the NEB made conflicting recommendations, the government would have to be able to arbitrate between the two. In a variation of the same scenario, these officials raised the possibility that the NEB might not even make a recommendation, or issue one with so many qualifications, that it would force Cabinet to assume the entire responsibility for the pipeline decision. By questioning the board's competence to adjudicate the pipeline issue, these officials provided a powerful impetus for the formation of an interdepartmental task force to analyze the pipeline applications. There were other reasons too, for creating such a task force. The implications of an affirmative pipeline decision on government services and expenditures had to be weighed in light of the government's priorities. Furthermore, since the American decision-making process was more advanced than Canada's, the government had to be ready to react to any overtures from Washington and perhaps make a quick pipeline decision. Much of the technical analysis needed to meet these different requirements was already in progress by the time Foothills (Yukon) filed its Alaska Highway application. This work was carried out by the Northern Pipeline Study Group.

The nucleus of the study group had been formed in January 1976 when Treasury Board, the Department of Finance and the Department of Energy, Mines and Resources had decided to share the results of the work each department had been carrying out independently since the previous fall. A couple of months later, the study group was expanded with the inclusion of Indian and Northern Affairs, Industry, Trade and Commerce, Fisheries and Environment, and External Affairs. Typically, the initiative for the creation of the task force had come from within the civil service rather than from elected officials. It was middle-ranked bureaucrats principally who first identified the need for the study group and defined its terms of reference. Nominally, the study group reported to the influential Interdepartmental Committee on Oil, or the DM Oil Committee, as it is colloquially named in Ottawa because of its membership of deputy ministers. In fact, the study group was largely autonomous in the early months of its existence.

Throughout 1976, the study group prepared a series of background papers on world oil supply, environmental considerations, native concerns, economic implications, etc. These papers contained no recommendations as the study group's purpose was not to make policy decisions but merely analyze the options open to Canada: Arctic Gas, Arctic Gas with no Delta hookup, Maple Leaf, a Delta line to Prudhoe Bay, Polar Gas, no pipeline and, of course, Foothills (Yukon). Although the latter was recognized as an important alternative, the study group's emphasis remained on the Mackenzie Valley. Treasury Board, for example, did a cost/benefit analysis of both Arctic Gas and Maple Leaf but not of the Alaska Highway pipeline.

This work was conducted in secrecy. Circumstances had changed since 1968 when the government had proudly trumpeted the creation of the Task Force on Northern Oil Development. If the study group's existence became widely known, the government feared it would be charged with superseding the public inquiries it had set up to evaluate the pipeline applications. Although there were few parallels between the great pipeline debate of 1956, which had contributed to the fall of the St. Laurent government, and the situation twenty years later, Liberal strategists were still concerned that the government's handling of the pipeline issue could be exploited politically. There was therefore good reason not to provoke an already skeptical public by now lifting the veil of secrecy which surrounded pipeline policy-making.

Besides, the pace of events was now obviously accelerating, and the last thing the government wanted was for the pipeline to become a political issue. A public debate would not only expose some of the questionable premises under which the government had been proceeding since the early 1970s but would raise the risk of no pipeline at all being built if it entailed any delay in the Canadian decision. By October 1, barely a month after Foothills (Yukon)'s application, the US Congress had passed the Alaska Natural Gas Transportation Act (ANGTA) establishing a deadline of September 1, 1977 for the American pipeline decision. This was no longer the time to engage in soul-searching. If it hoped to meet the American deadline, the government would have to keep as tight a rein over the pace of events as possible.

THE ALASKA NATURAL GAS TRANSPORTATION ACT

The act was a major milestone in the Canadian and American selection of the northern pipeline. It governed the events of the following year in both countries and arguably influenced the outcome of the pipeline decision. In the United States, it transferred the ultimate decision-making authority over the northern pipeline from the FPC to the President and Congress. In Canada, it led to repeated accelerations in the pace of the NEB hearings with predictable and prejudicial results on the quality and completeness of the evidence the board received. In both countries, it was the Alcan consortium that benefited the most from the act's implementation.

The act established a four-step timetable to designate a route for the transportation of Prudhoe Bay gas:

1. the FPC would make a recommendation to the President no later than May 1, 1977;
2. Federal agencies, state governors and "any other interested person" would have the opportunity to comment by July 1, 1977;

3. the President would announce his decision by September 1, with an option of a ninety day delay;
4. Congress would vote on the President's decision within sixty days of having received it.

ANGTA had its genesis in congressional efforts to bypass the traditionally slow FPC and legislate approval for one of the pipeline routes. The reasons behind Congress'—and the Ford Administration's—desire to establish a timetable for the northern pipeline's construction were easily understood: gas production in the United States had peaked in 1973 and interstate pipelines had been forced to curtail deliveries to their customers ever since. In the face of mounting shortages, the Ford Administration and Congress were united in their determination to avoid a repetition of the delays that had plagued the Trans-Alaska oil pipeline.

By June 1976, four bills had been introduced in the Senate and five in the House of Representatives to expedite a decision on the pipeline: two supported El Paso, four Arctic Gas and three were procedural in nature, setting deadlines for various regulatory and executive decisions without endorsing a particular proposal. Arctic Gas had lobbied extensively for congressional support and its efforts had yielded impressive dividends. The Senate Bill S-2950, sponsored by Walter Mondale (who was to be elected Vice-President in November), had the support of thirty senators, including the Democratic and Republican leaders of the Senate, Mike Mansfield and Hugh Scott, former Vice-President Hubert Humphrey and other prominent senators such as Edmund Muskie and George McGovern. The bill would have directed the FPC to issue a certificate of public convenience and necessity to Arctic Gas within sixty days of its enactment; its companion bill in the House of Representatives, HR 11273, had seventy-six co-signatories.

Not surprisingly, Arctic Gas at first opposed the adoption of a procedural bill such as the one favoured by the Ford Administration. However, the intervention of the State Department and the American ambassador to Canada, Tom Enders, was successful in convincing Mondale that the passage of his bill might backfire since it would be seen in Canada as a heavy-handed attempt to force a favourable decision for Arctic Gas. Besides, it was in the interest of the American government to keep its options open until the Alaska Highway pipeline had been assessed more thoroughly. In early June, therefore, Mondale threw his support behind a new procedural bill, S-3521, similar to the one supported by the administration. The Senate passed this bill on July 1 and the House of Representatives on September 30, although not before an amendment delaying the deadlines for decision by three months had been included. Once again, the State Department and the ubiquitous Enders had intervened, this time to request the extension of the deadlines so as to mute the appearance of pressuring Canada into making a hasty decision based on an American timetable.

During this same period, however, Enders was also reassuring Arctic Gas that ANGTA would help to accelerate the Canadian decision. On September 29, Enders met with B.J. Clarke and Sy Orlofsky, two senior executives of Columbia Gas, an Arctic Gas member, who were concerned about the lack of momentum attached to the pipeline issue in Canada. The purpose of their visit was to ask whether there was anything that the US embassy or the White House could do to speed up a Canadian decision. Enders concurred with them that the Berger and NEB hearings were "indeed moving very slowly" but pointed out that any attempt by the Canadian government to bypass the normal regulatory process was fraught with dangers. "The only way we can speed up Canadian timing of a decision", Enders cabled back to the the State Department after his meeting, "is to have our own timetable which we now have in S-3521.... Only the pressure of our timetable which includes an independent US project option [El Paso] will maintain needed pressure on the Canadian government".[11]

This is probably not what Clarke and Orlofsky had come to Ottawa to hear but it shows that the American government was quite aware of the implications for Canada of setting a pipeline deadline. By the time Ford signed ANGTA into law in late October, the FPC hearings were almost over. By comparison, the NEB was not yet halfway through its own hearings, an indication of the time pressures the American timetable would soon impose on Canada if it wanted to keep in step with the United States.

The passage of the Alaska Natural Gas Transportation Act thus constituted an explicit signal to Canada that if it wanted to avert threatening domestic gas shortages, it would have to co-operate with the United States in reaching the pipeline decision. For Northwest, ANGTA represented a double victory: it muted congressional support for Arctic Gas at a time when CAG had garnered widespread backing; more importantly, it removed the final pipeline decision from an FPC which would soon show itself highly critical of the Alaska Highway pipeline proposal.

THE FPC HEARINGS

Since July, when Northwest had belatedly filed its application, Judge Nahum Litt had devoted the bulk of the Federal Power Commission hearings to an examination of the Alaska Highway proposal. Northwest did not fare well in those four months to the end of the hearings, the hasty nature of its application and its evident lack of preparation being exposed repeatedly. Much of the criticism the Alcan project endured before the FPC was focused on AGTL and Westcoast's proposal to combine the transportation of Prudhoe Bay and Mackenzie Delta gas in their systems.

Although the Maple Leaf and Alaska Highway projects were presented as separate entities, serving different needs, either or both of which could be built without jeopardizing the other, it was never clear how specific facilities for the transportation of Prudhoe Bay and Mackenzie Delta gas south of the

60th parallel would be segregated and their costs allocated to Canadian and American consumers.

If both Maple Leaf and Alcan were approved, AGTL would end up commingling three gas flows (from the Delta, Alaska and Alberta). The rate of expansion of AGTL facilities would depend on the construction schedule for both projects, the build-up of frontier deliveries, the number of gas discoveries in Alberta and the growth in both Canadian and American gas demand, all factors with varying degrees of uncertainty attached to them. Each eventuality would dictate a different system configuration and hence affect the costs of transporting frontier gas. In other words, the exact price American consumers would pay for Alaskan gas could not be predicted in advance. Intimately related to this issue was the question of "expansibility", or the rate at which capacity could be increased once the pipeline was in operation. This was a particularly nettlesome question for Alcan whose pipeline was rated at a lower capacity than either Arctic Gas or El Paso. If a case could be made for expanding existing low-pressure pipeline systems to accommodate the flow of either Mackenzie Delta or Prudhoe Bay gas, it did not follow that an equally persuasive case could be made to deliver a combined stream of frontier gas, particularly when AGTL was already operating at capacity.

Alcan posed an even more vexing problem for the US in that the timing of its construction was itself uncertain. Although the Alaska Highway line was scheduled for completion before Maple Leaf, Foothills insisted that the satisfaction of Canadian requirements remained its first priority. As both projects could not be built simultaneously because of their size, it was possible therefore that American regulatory approval of Alcan would effectively be frustrated by a Canadian decision to develop the Mackenzie Delta first. In the US, the NEB's 1975 report on Canadian gas requirements made this appear a plausible eventuality if enough gas was found in the Delta to support a Maple Leaf pipeline. Foothills' competing allegiance to its two projects thus placed the FPC in an impossible situation. The result was not difficult to foresee.

On December 7, 1976, less than a month after the conclusion of the hearings, the FPC staff released the first comprehensive assessment of the Northwest proposal by a public body in Canada or the United States. It was a devastating attack. The FPC staff accused Northwest of presenting a completion schedule that was unrealistic, cost estimates that were indefensible, a transportation tariff that was inequitable. It charged that there was no basis "for determining what the Alcan project would look like in *detail* [emphasis in the text], the detail required by the rules and regulations, if the Maple Leaf project were assumed to be delayed or never built".[12] The Alcan pipeline, the FPC staff continued, would be an uneconomic system. The Arctic Gas route, on the other hand, was overwhelming in its appeal, unassailable in its logic and vastly superior to its alternatives, according to the FPC staff.

To Northwest, the intensity of these criticisms came as a shock. After all, it had been the FPC staff itself which, by recommending the Fairbanks route on environmental grounds, had helped to induce Northwest to sponsor the Alaska Highway application. What Northwest was proposing, however, differed in two important respects from the FPC staff's favoured option: it was a smaller pipeline—42-inch instead of 48-inch—which would therefore be less efficient and would have to be looped earlier; this meant higher economic and environmental costs. Secondly, it assumed the construction of a Maple Leaf pipeline instead of the "Richards Island lateral" along the Dempster Highway for the delivery of Delta gas that the FPC staff had included in its environmental impact statement. For these reasons, the FPC staff found Arctic Gas to be environmentally superior to Alcan, although not to its own 48-inch Fairbanks pipeline with Dempster connection, a qualification which was not to be lost on Northwest.

With the FPC staff so emphatically opposed to its Alcan proposal, Northwest had to fear that both Judge Litt and the commission itself would also reject its application. Fortunately for Northwest, ANGTA, by having made the selection of the northern pipeline a political decision, gave it a second chance to be heard. This allowed Northwest to respond to its critics, modify its project accordingly and eventually overcome the disadvantage in which it had been placed following the FPC staff report.

In December 1976, however, it seemed to most observers that Northwest's gamble, taken several months before at a cost that had already mounted to $8 million, had failed.

In Canada, Foothills, too, was in trouble. It had lost much credibility. To many government officials the Alcan proposal was "pie in the sky". Foothills' only ally was Premier Bennett of British Columbia, who had organized earlier in the year a secret meeting in Seattle with the governors of the states of Alaska, Washington, Idaho and Oregon to win support for the Alaska Highway pipeline. But it was not a provincial premier with parochial development interests who would influence the course of events. The framework for a pipeline decision having been set, Foothills' and Northwest's fate rested squarely on the Berger and NEB reports in Canada and the FPC and the newly-elected Carter Administration in the United States.

CHAPTER SIX

THE YEAR OF DECISION

1977 started off well for Arctic Gas. On January 28, after two years of negotiations, Canada and the United States signed the Transit Pipeline Treaty forbidding the discriminatory taxation of each other's oil and gas crossing their own territory. The treaty, to which Trudeau had given his blessing in his energy message following the oil crisis (see Chapter Three), effectively precluded Canada from collecting the "economic rent", or windfall profit, which the United States would stand to receive by using the cheaper overland route. Because El Paso landed Prudhoe Bay gas in the US at a cost substantially higher than either Arctic Gas or Alcan, this rent amounted to several billions of dollars over the pipeline's economic life.

For Canada, the treaty meant that the US would not tax the Canadian pipelines already crossing American territory (there were three at the time). As some of these pipelines had been operating for over twenty years, it was clear that the driving force behind the treaty negotiations was not the desire to formalize a situation which had been acceptable for this long but rather to specify the gound rules under which future American pipelines would cross Canada. This conclusion is inescapable and, indeed, it is in this light that the US saw the negotiations. Baldly put, the United States did not want Canada to earn the rents its position as a land-bridge between Alaska and the "lower 48" created, and Canada surrendered that right in the negotiations.

The Pipeline Treaty removed a major stumbling block to the eventual construction of an overland pipeline. The risk that Canada might some day impose punitive taxes on a pipeline carrying Prudhoe Bay gas had, of course, been the argument on which El Paso had rested much of its case and had used to attack Arctic Gas. The signing of the Pipeline Treaty, therefore, paved the way for the eventual approval of a trans-Canadian pipeline. Four days later, the first step in that approval was taken with the release of the Litt report.

THE LITT REPORT

The Litt report[1] was not just another in the scores of documents that had already been published about the three pipeline proposals. It was to be the first exhaustive review of the issues raised by the transportation of Alaskan gas. From May 5, 1975 until November 12, 1976, Litt had presided over 253 days of hearings during which one thousand exhibits had been filed and 45,000 pages of transcript recorded. Litt's conclusions, therefore, would govern the Federal Power Commission's own recommendation to President Carter. The FPC's recommendation, in turn, would constitute one of the most important elements in the United States' choice of which pipeline to approve. Although the Alaska Natural Gas Transportation Act stipulated four more steps before this choice became final, Litt was in a position to sway the pipeline's fate decisively.

The *Initial Decision on Proposed Alaska Natural Gas Transportation Systems* was 430 pages long. Its conclusions were summarized on the second last page: "The Arctic Gas application is superior in almost every significant aspect when compared to El Paso"; "No finding from this record supports even the possibility that a grant of authority to Alcan can be made". A blunt man, who expresses himself in colourful language, Litt had a lot more to say about the virtues and defects he found in each of the pipeline applications: the looping of an Arctic Gas pipeline "would be a work of joy"; Alcan had an "overt Canadian bias"; "the El Paso Canadian Reply Brief [on the implications of shipping Alaskan gas through Canada] is as well crafted a chamber of horrors as this writer has ever seen and would do justice to the standards set by the Marquis de Sade if he had been interested in economics and politics".

The Litt report was extravagant in its praise of a Mackenzie pipeline. CAG's top executives were jubilant. Far from being embarrassing, they found the report's immoderate tone "objective and unbiased". They were convinced that Alcan was dead and that nothing could now stop their project. The enormous advantage the Litt report conferred upon Arctic Gas was further enhanced by the circumstances prevailing at the time of the report's release. At the beginning of February, the United States was in the midst of the worst gas shortage the country had ever known. As the result of an abnormally cold winter, particularly in the east, gas demand had surged and quickly overcome the ability of utilities to meet it. Schools and factories had closed; almost two million workers had been laid off; some people even died.

The crisis atmosphere that this economic emergency engendered provided fertile ground for Arctic Gas to sow its promise to deliver more gas more cheaply than either of its competitors. Alarmed by the dimensions of the gas shortage, some public figures seized on the Litt report to call for the speedy approval of the Arctic Gas pipeline. At the end of February, thirteen senators wrote President Carter a letter affirming their support for Litt's recommendation and urging an early pipeline decision. So did the governors of the thirteen states making up the Appalachian Regional Commission, the National Association of Regulatory Utility Commissioners, the United Auto Workers of America...[2]

This message was being widely echoed in the press. Not surprisingly, Alcan's fortunes plummeted in direct proportion to the rising chorus in favour of Arctic Gas. Stewart Udall, former Secretary of the Interior in the Johnson Administration, member of a prestigious law firm and future Foothills lobbyist (he would receive $110,875 for his services in 1977), conceded privately at the time that "Alcan is getting clobbered in the Washington press".

The Litt report, although its impact was ultimately to prove ephemeral, was nevertheless to leave at least one important legacy: at a crucial time in the Canadian and American evaluation of the northern gas pipeline, it reinforced CAG's already profound conviction that it was proposing the best project. Litt had upheld its choice of route, construction methods, financing plan and even its assessment of environmental and social impacts. Only a few months before, after Foothills and Northwest had decided to sponsor the Alaska Highway pipeline, Arctic Gas had re-examined quietly its old study on the Fairbanks route. It decided at the time to stay with its original Mackenzie Valley route. Horte would explain subsequently that "that really wasn't our objective—build any pipeline. Our objective was to build the best pipeline".[3] Today, Horte's explanation reads as much as an expression of unshakeable faith in the Arctic Gas project as a statement of corporate policy. In early 1977, of course, that faith seemed amply justified.

As a result, in the months ahead CAG refused to concede that several of the assumptions underlying the project were no longer tenable: the issue of Canadian need, CAG's ability to stay on schedule and within costs and adequate measures to offset frost heave would all prove suspect upon closer examination. By the beginning of 1977, however, Arctic Gas had become in a very real sense the captive of its own claims. It had spent five years and close to $150 million promoting its pipeline, answering its critics and attacking its rivals before regulatory inquiries in both Canada and the United States, members of Parliament and congressmen, the public and the media. It could not change its application substantially without at the same time losing its credibility. But even if it had been inclined to acknowledge the emerging flaws in its proposal, it had no incentive to do so. On the contrary, it was to its advantage—as it was to its rivals'—to continue making the same exaggerated claims it had made before. It knew that after it had obtained regulatory approval, Canada and the United States would have no choice but to accept any changes it made in its project because, by then, it would remain the only project in the race.

If the Litt report served to make Arctic Gas even more inflexible, it had the opposite effect on Alcan. McMillian would complain bitterly about Litt's "incredible bias and antagonism towards the Alcan project".[4] He would also accuse Arctic Gas of "trying to make Canada a Panama canal energy corridor",[5] fighting words that did not explain in what way Alcan was any different. McMillian, however, had not reached the top of his company by bemoaning adversity and subjecting himself to the vagaries of fortune. The Litt report galvanized the Foothills-Northwest partnership into a feverish reappraisal of its proposal. Samuel Johnson, the great English lexicographer, once wrote: "When a man knows he is to be hanged in a fortnight, it concentrates his mind wonderfully". Litt's savage criticism had a similar stimulating effect on Alcan's management. Foothills, particularly, appreciated only too well how desperate its position had now become. The Maple Leaf project was definitely dead in the wake of a downward revision of the estimates of the Mackenzie Delta reserves. All hopes of defeating CAG would therefore have to rest with Alcan, a project which had already been vilified publicly twice—first by the FPC staff and then by Litt. Having spent $22 million, Foothills could not afford to turn back.

THE 48-INCH ALTERNATIVE

Fortunately for both Foothills and Northwest, the Alaska Natural Gas Transportation Act had superseded the regulatory procedures that would have normally applied in the US. The act instructed the FPC to

> review all applications for the issuance of a certificate of public convenience and necessity relating to the transportation of Alaska natural gas pending on the date of enactment of this Act, *and any amendments thereto which are timely made*, and after consideration of any alternative transportation system which the Commission determines to be reasonable, submit to the President no later than May 1, 1977, a recommendation concerning the selection of such a transportation system. [emphasis added]

It was this provision which gave Alcan its second lease on life. Having argued so forcefully before the NEB and the FPC about the benefits of relying on operating pipelines and the wisdom of building a small, 42-inch pipeline, Alcan now sacrificed these principles in favour of a 48-inch express line with no interconnection to either AGTL or Westcoast. This new proposal, which Foothills coyly referred to as "the 48-inch alternative", was made public on February 16, barely two weeks after the release of the Litt report. Ironically, it had only been two months earlier that McMillian had argued against a 48-inch pipeline on the grounds that gas production at Prudhoe Bay would likely be too small to justify such a diameter. In the heat of battle, previous positions are sometimes best forgotten.

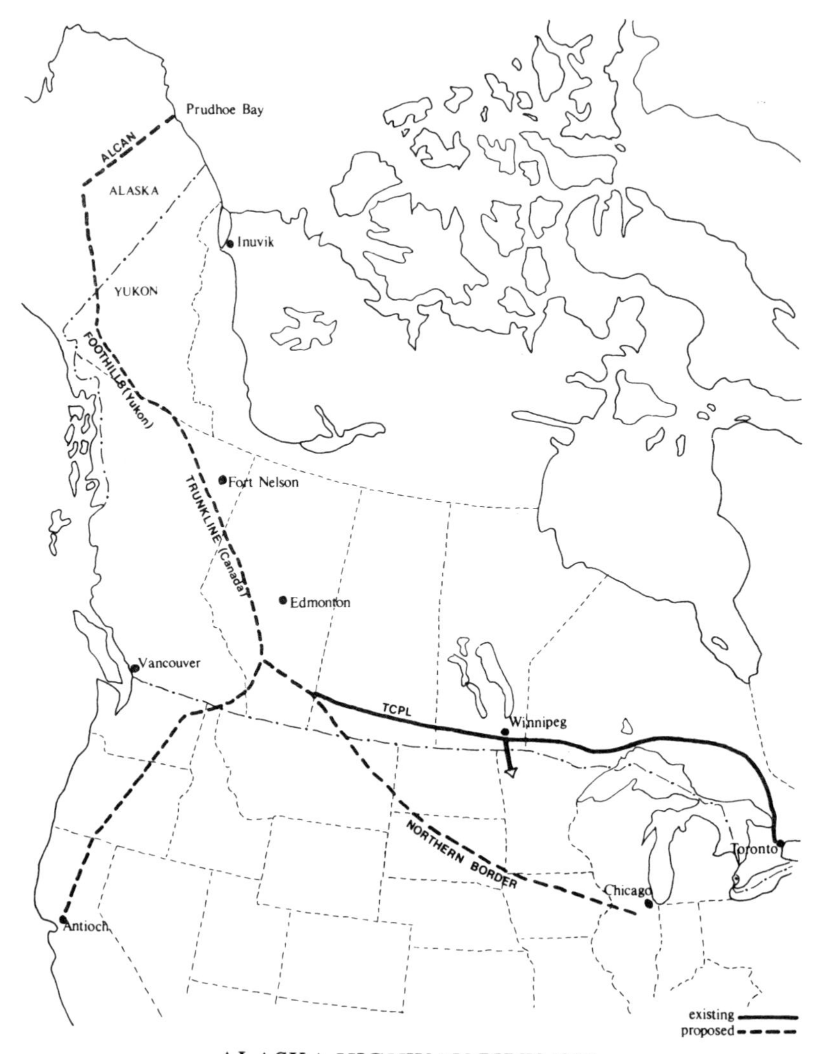

ALASKA HIGHWAY PIPELINE

But indeed, not only did Alcan announce its willingness to build a 48-inch pipeline, if asked to do so, it also stated its readiness to adopt a higher-pressure design for its pipeline even though it had attacked CAG's own proposed high operating pressure for being both untried and untested. Furthermore, Alcan was prepared to modify its southern delivery route, if so requested.

Foothills and Northwest clearly did not care what they built as long as they were allowed to earn a satisfactory rate of return on it. Alcan's "willingness to do anything anyone wants" as Litt had noted disparagingly was cynical but it reflected well the political realities of the time. As the date for a pipeline decision in both Canada and the United States approached, and consequently the stakes in both countries grew bigger, flexibility became all important. Alcan provided both governments with the flexibility they were seeking. Arctic Gas did not. In the end, this was to be a telling difference.

If, in March 1976, it had been Westcoast which had persuaded AGTL to sponsor the Alaska Highway pipeline in spite of Blair's reservations, in February 1977 it was AGTL which pushed for the adoption of the express pipeline over Westcoast's misgivings. Blair the nationalist, who in the past had expressed his concern over the implications of a "gun-barrel" pipeline carrying American gas across Canadian territory, was now proposing one himself, exposing thereby the full extent of his opportunism. This was the fifth pipeline proposal AGTL had sponsored in six years.

The vituperative intensity with which CAG greeted the "48-inch alternative" revealed the true nature of its concern over this latest application. Calling it "an irresponsible desperation bid which ignores Canada's needs for new energy supplies", Bill Wilder lashed out at Alcan's "flagrant abuse of the national decision-making processes in both Canada and the United States".[6] Arctic Gas indeed had reason to worry. Under the Alaska Natural Gas Transportation Act, the FPC had the authority to "provide for the presentation of data, views and arguments before the Commission". On March 11, three days after Alcan had filed the details of its new proposal, the FPC amended its general policy and interpretations to allow for the presentation of new evidence. This was the turning point for which Northwest had been hoping.

The "48-inch alternative" met most of Litt's objections to the original Alcan proposal: the problems of allocating cost between Canadian and American consumers of frontier gas no longer existed; a 48-inch pipeline provided ready expansibility; it was more efficient and therefore had lower transportation costs. The new Alcan project was now virtually identical to the FPC staff's own "Fairbanks alternative". Its major difference was that it did not include a Richards Island lateral. On April 4, Foothills repaired that omission.

A few months earlier, recognizing privately what it continued to deny in public, Foothills had begun studying alternatives to the Maple Leaf project. Included among these alternatives were studies of a Dempster pipeline. The Dempster pipeline would parallel the Dempster Highway between Inuvik and Dawson City in the Yukon where it would follow the Klondike Highway to Whitehorse. At Whitehorse it would connect to the Alaska Highway pipeline. When Blair revealed the existence of these studies in testimony before the NEB on November 26, 1976, he downplayed their importance because "as a policy and as a corporate objective", the route "that we believe is most appropriate for the flow of gas from the Mackenzie Delta is down the Mackenzie Valley".[7] By January 7, 1977, however, when another senior Foothills witness appeared before the NEB, the consideration of a possible

Dempster pipeline had become "high on our priority list of work which has been going on for the past month".[8] Three months later, the first three of the Foothills studies were released and the system which CAG had rejected in 1973 and the FPC staff had rediscovered in 1975 was born a third time.

Although the Dempster studies were so preliminary that they hardly qualified as such, they nevertheless offered the first real alternative for the delivery of Mackenzie Delta gas. A Dempster pipeline held two important advantages over a Mackenzie line: because it was shorter and had a smaller diameter, it required theoretically a much lower reserve threshold to be viable; secondly, it bypassed the politically explosive Mackenzie Valley where the unsettled land claims hung like a sword over the pipeline proposals. For these reasons this latest Foothills initiative was immediately the object of intense interest within both government and the NEB.

For the first time since the discovery of gas at Prudhoe Bay and the Mackenzie Delta, an alternative existed to a Mackenzie pipeline which did not require the simultaneous exploitation of frontier reserves in Canada and the United States. This was a far-reaching development with radical implications for Canadian pipeline policy: no longer would the rejection of Arctic Gas need to foreclose the timely development of the Mackenzie Delta. The government now had a choice, a fall-back position, in case Arctic Gas proved politically unacceptable.

THE RISKS OF ACCELERATION

At the same time, the modifications Foothills had made to its Alaska Highway pipeline proposal presented the Canadian government with a dilemma: if it was to adhere to the American deadline for decision, it would have to forego the rigorous review of the 48-inch alternative and particularly of the Dempster pipeline whose economic viability and environmental impact were unknown. If, on the other hand, it wanted to subject the Foothills project to the same scrutiny it had applied to Arctic Gas, it would not be able to meet the American timetable. Each alternative implied substantial risks but quite different political costs.

The government was under considerable pressure to adopt the American timetable. It was still haunted by its inept handling of the Mackenzie Valley oil pipeline when its hesitation and delays had helped to persuade the United States to opt for the trans-Alaska pipeline. The stakes in the development of frontier gas were infinitely greater, and the reasons for not allowing the US to make a pipeline decision for both countries for a second time were accordingly more compelling. Furthermore, the psychological effects of the American gas crisis, fuelled by alarmist media coverage, had spilled over the border: the unheated homes, the idle factories, the emergency rationing, all seemed to offer a prelude of what could happen in Canada too if frontier gas was not developed quickly. Arctic Gas and its sponsors had not lost an opportunity to exploit the situation and had intensified their lobbying after the release of the Litt report. The shortage psychology nurtured by Arctic Gas and its allies constituted an overpowering force in favour of an early decision.

There was little corresponding public pressure to examine the new Foothills proposals in depth and delay the Canadian pipeline decision. For their own opposite reasons, neither Arctic Gas nor Foothills wanted the Alaska Highway application reviewed in detail, Arctic Gas because of the delays it would cause, Foothills because of the incomplete nature of its proposal. The Council of Yukon Indians, who had the most to lose from Foothills' plans, was not as militant or as well-organized as the Northwest Territories' Indian Brotherhood, the Dene. Only a few public interest groups complained about the time pressures Canada's adherence to the US deadline would create. They did not have a broad political base and the government was satisfied that the long Berger and NEB hearings provided the illusion of thoroughness of review although, of course, not its substance given the eleventh-hour nature of the Foothills changes.

When the political costs were weighed, the balance was clearly in favour of an early pipeline decision. Within government itself, there was also emerging a consensus that the issue had to be forced. The pipeline had been around for eight years. It had been the subject of countless studies. The pipeline decision would be as thoroughly considered as any the government had ever taken. To the more impatient members of the Northern Pipeline Study Group and the Interdepartmental Committee on Oil, the Berger and NEB hearings seemed interminable. They saw the due process of presenting evidence, leading witnesses and engaging in procedural arguments as becoming increasingly unproductive. Without having to state their agreement explicitly, both Cabinet ministers and senior civil servants were coming to the same conclusion in early 1977: the Canadian pipeline decision should proceed in accordance with the American deadline.

Ottawa had publicly expressed its willingness to abide by the American timetable as early as February 1976, when Alastair Gillespie, the Minister of Energy, Mines and Resources, had declared that Canada "should be able to live with"[9] the series of deadlines President Ford had just proposed for the selection of the northern pipeline. A year later, a new president, Jimmy Carter, was in the White House. The pipeline decision would be one of the most important he would take during his first year of office and would be facilitated greatly by Canada's co-operation. Canadian-American relations had deteriorated under the Nixon and Ford administrations, and the government saw in the pipeline issue an opportunity to revive the special relationship that had previously existed between the two countries.

The occasion for Canada to show its readiness to co-operate with the United States came early in the new year. Acting on his election promise to pursue a good neighbour policy, Carter invited Trudeau in February 1977 to go to Washington on an official visit. The trip was a great success. After the visit, a senior adviser to Carter said he had never seen the President "relate so well or so quickly as he did to Prime Minister Trudeau."[10] The two leaders discussed a wide range of bilateral issues, including the pipeline timetable. During their talks, Trudeau assured Carter that Canada would meet the American deadline. Asked about the pipeline at the press conference he gave on the last day of his visit, Trudeau answered:

> Canadians generally—and certainly our government—want to be as helpful to the Americans as we can in this particular aspect. This is what our visit is all about. That is what friendship is all about.
>
> After all, it is American gas, to American consumers, and we don't want to be dogs in the manger about this.
>
> . . . We realize that we have to give you a final answer—whatever it be—before the end of the year. . . . Giving you *no* answer is *an* answer, in a sense and, if there is no pipeline from Canada, I suppose there is the El Paso route which is the one that the Americans would go for.
>
> It is a more costly one for you, and it has certain disadvantages for Canada too, and therefore we are very aware of the time strictures, and we will have to give you an answer at whatever deadline the President feels he has—likely one in September.[11]

Trudeau's answer, on the surface, appears remarkably disingenuous. In officially adopting the American timetable, Trudeau was announcing a policy decision of major importance, one which had the potential of influencing the very outcome of the consideration Canada was giving to the pipeline issue. Partly as a result of the disqualification of Marshall Crowe and the ensuing delay in the NEB hearings, Canada's assessment of the various pipeline proposals was lagging far behind the United States'. In order for Canada to reach a timely decision under the American timetable, a significant compression of the Canadian decision-making process would therefore be required. For Canada to subscribe to the American timetable represented accordingly a significant concession to United States interests.

It is also remarkable that Trudeau should have adopted the American timetable in the same breath as he acknowledged that El Paso was an inferior project for the United States and that Canada, by implication, could have bargained for a delay in the pipeline decision. It stood to reason that, if El Paso was as costly and impractical as all evidence was suggesting, the US would hesitate before approving it if all Canada required was a few more months to reach its pipeline decision. For the Canadian government, this was an important lever to ensure that it had the time to make the right decision. Yet there is no evidence that Trudeau used this argument during his stay in Washington. On the contrary, his readiness "to be as helpful to the Americans" as possible, by effectively circumscribing the Canadian decision-making process, showed his willingness to incur the risks of approving a northern pipeline even before its full environmental, social and economic implications were known.

The government's decision to expedite the consideration of the many issues raised by the northern pipeline came at a time when many of the assumptions under which it had been proceeding were being undermined by a rapid improvement in the outlook for conventional gas supplies and changes in the Arctic Gas as well as the Foothills applications. In other words, the acceleration in the Canadian schedule became more pronounced precisely as the decision of whether to approve a pipeline was growing increasingly complex. The risks of making the wrong decision were therefore increased substantially.

THE EMERGING GAS SURPLUS

Over the worst of the winter months, when shortages had been the most severe, the United States had been able to find some relief by importing additional quantities of gas from Canada. The NEB approved in quick succession several emergency exports which earned Carter's "deep appreciation" at Canada's "quick and generous response"[12] to the American request for assistance. The significance of these exports cannot be over-emphasized. It had been only a year and a half before that the NEB had warned that Canada was facing imminent shortages itself. Now, there was a surplus. Nothing could have illustrated more dramatically the rapid improvement in the Canadian natural gas situation—and the NEB's gross forecasting error in 1975—than a rise in exports at a time of peak domestic requirements.

The surplus arose from the combination of stagnant market demand and increased drilling in Alberta, both the result of sharply higher gas prices. By January 1977, internal studies by Energy, Mines and Resources already showed that Canada would not need frontier gas until the mid to late 1980s and that the construction of a northern pipeline therefore no longer constituted the priority it had been thought to be only two years earlier. For the first time since 1975, the option of not building any pipeline at all had to be considered seriously.

To the Arctic Gas sponsors who had argued for many years that the deteriorating supply outlook in both the United States and Canada dictated the expeditious construction of a frontier pipeline, this incipient surplus constituted a grave threat. They had to fear that, if Canada no longer needed a Mackenzie pipeline, the government might find it politically impossible to approve one, let alone guarantee its financing as they were asking. If, furthermore, Berger was to report that such a pipeline would entail large environmental and social costs, the chances for success became almost non-existent. It was imperative for CAG, therefore, to discount the recent exploratory successes in Alberta and continue to cultivate the impression that shortages were at hand. All the Arctic Gas sponsors had a vested interest in doing so.

There is no evidence that these companies did anything so sinister as manipulate reserve figures to establish the need for Arctic gas although there can be little doubt that they chose to interpret these figures pessimistically. Having been chastised in the past for their unwarranted optimism about Canada's oil and gas potential, the oil companies belonging to Arctic Gas found it easy in early 1977 to minimize the size of the "gas bubble" as TransCanada Pipelines deprecatingly dubbed the surplus. But if these companies did not set out to deceive the public, there is every indication that several of the Arctic Gas sponsors, most notably Imperial and TransCanada, misjudged completely the fundamental transformation in the Canadian gas outlook. Imperial, in particular, has had to pay a hefty price for its error.

At the end of 1969, the year it launched a major exploratory programme in the Mackenzie Delta, Imperial's overall reserves stood at 1.7 billion barrels of oil and 3.3 trillion cubic feet of gas. Eight years later, these reserves had declined to 1 billion barrels of oil and 2.2 trillion cubic feet of gas, not including the discoveries in the Delta. During that period, Imperial spent close to $350 million in northern exploration and reduced substantially its presence in Alberta. As a result, Imperial has been conspicuously absent from western Canada's most exciting "plays", the West Pembina oil discovery, the largest in Canada since 1965, and the giant Elmworth gas field in the Alberta foothills. Having staked the company's future on the North in the early 1970s, Imperial's management was forced in 1978 to pay inflated land prices in Alberta to regain a foothold in the province—after the best exploration prospects had been acquired by other companies. It is not surprising therefore that by the end of 1977, Imperial stock had declined by more than 60% from a 1972 high of over $50. Imperial's poor performance drew sharp criticism from the financial community as it sparked rumours of Exxon's displeasure with its subsidiary's management.[13]

TransCanada provides another example of a company which refused to accept the full nature of the changes in natural gas supply and demand which were taking place in 1976 and 1977. More fortunate than Imperial, however, TransCanada did not have to pay as dearly for its error. Although TCPL's chairman, Jimmy Kerr, admitted in January 1977 that "for the first time in several years, TransCanada now forecasts it will pay for gas during 1977 and defer its production to a future date", in his report to shareholders, Kerr nevertheless chose to emphasize "the importance of the attachment of frontier reserves to fulfill long-term Canadian requirements".[14] Barely a year later TransCanada was forced to delay production of 200 billion cubic feet of gas, a third of Ontario's annual consumption, and under its contractual obligations pay for a substantial proportion of that gas anyway and leave it in the ground.

The fact that large corporations with the human and financial resources that Imperial and TransCanada can command should have erred so spectacularly in a vital aspect of their daily business is not one likely to be underlined by apologists for the role played by these companies in the formation of Canadian energy policy. The multinational companies which dominate the Canadian oil industry will sometimes be accused of duplicity, engaging in uncompetitive practices and even of gouging the public, but almost never of incompetence. Being the biggest, the wealthiest and the most sophisticated, it is held as an elementary tenet of our economic system that their decisions will not only be guided by the profit motive but, in the long run, will invariably achieve maximum profits. Thus, when Imperial, Gulf and Shell began allocating an increasing percentage of their expenditures to Arctic exploration in the early 1970s, it was widely understood that Alberta's gas reserves were rapidly approaching exhaustion.

This, as well as the alarmist pronouncements on the inevitability of domestic shortages if a Mackenzie pipeline were not built as soon as possible, implanted a shortage mentality in the minds of the Canadian public which became a powerful stimulus in favour of the Arctic Gas proposal. Once implanted, the belief that shortages were imminent proved hard to change. Even though as much gas, for example, was added to reserves in Alberta in 1976 as had been found in six years of exploration in the Mackenzie Delta, the discoveries were dismissed as counterfactual because they defied conventional wisdom. The persistence of the myth that Canada had to build a northern pipeline would not only help a government favourably inclined towards one to approve it but would indeed almost force it to do so. In politics appearance is everything, and it would have to be an extraordinarily compelling argument that would lead to the rejection of all pipeline applications.

The repeated warnings of the Arctic Gas sponsors helped to establish the context in which the government made its pipeline decision. Along with the NEB's 1975 gas report and the American gas crisis, they predisposed public opinion towards the approval of a pipeline. Furthermore, they had a great impact on the National Energy Board. Of the eight interveners who presented evidence on natural gas supply to the NEB hearings, four were Arctic Gas sponsors, one was affiliated to CAG through a member of the consortium and one was Arctic Gas itself. Their evidence, of course, indicated that domestic need dictated the construction of a Mackenzie pipeline.

Only two interveners contested CAG's pessimistic supply projections. One was Dr. John Helliwell of the University of British Columbia, whose extensive computer modelling of natural gas supply and demand indicated that there would be no need for frontier gas until the early 1990s. Although

Helliwell's work was taken very seriously by officials at both the Privy Council and Energy, Mines and Resources, the NEB did not seem prepared to accept the implications of Helliwell's conclusions. The board's evident prejudgement of the issue led an otherwise even-tempered Helliwell to write in frustration:

> It was increasingly clear that the evidence from the model was not acceptable to the NEB, and that great efforts would be made by the NEB to discredit the evidence from the model and to permit the NEB to continue to conclude that gas from the frontier regions would be needed in the early 1980s.[15]

The second intervener to present evidence showing an improvement in the domestic gas outlook was AGTL. Blair testified in early May that the natural gas situation in Alberta was "a new ball game" and that Mackenzie Delta gas would not be needed domestically until 1986 or 1987 at the earliest. The board's reaction was one of ill-concealed skepticism. Once again, the implications of this testimony were too great. They would have dictated a more thorough assessment of natural gas supply and demand than the board had time for. Although Helliwell's calculations as well as Energy Probe's testimony on the potential for conservation were therefore received politely, they were not believed. In the headlong rush to reach a timely decision, everything, including the questioning of whether a pipeline was still needed, would have to be subordinated to the exigencies of the Alaska Natural Gas Transportation Act.

Cabinet could not be unaware that the virtual unanimity of views the NEB received on gas supply carried far-reaching implications for the board's recommendation. Nor could it ignore the limitations an NEB recommendation in favour of a pipeline on the basis of an alleged domestic need would impose on its own latitude in making its decision. It is significant, therefore, that the government chose not to make public the advice its own civil servants were providing it on the improvement in the natural gas situation. On the contrary, the government actively contributed to the impression that frontier gas would have to be developed soon. In May 1977, for example, Gillespie would declare in a TV interview that it was "very important that we bring down that northern natural gas."[16]

Although in early 1977 the government did look at the possibility of turning down all the pipeline applications, it is fair to say that its lack of bias was more relative than absolute. Cabinet backing for a pipeline was strong. Gillespie himself admitted to being predisposed towards a pipeline and the disgruntled Jack Horner, who had been lured from the ranks of the Conservatives in April with the promise of a Cabinet portfolio, did not disguise his support for Arctic Gas.

The emergence of a domestic natural gas surplus in early 1977 had fundamental implications for Canadian energy policy on at least two levels. First, it meant that for the first time since 1971 the government had to consider whether to increase gas exports. The pressure for new exports was already building up in Alberta, coming mostly from small independent producers. Leading the drive for greater exports was Pan Alberta Gas, an AGTL subsidiary, which began making the case for exports as early as January.

Second, the domestic surplus held implications for pipeline policy. It could buy Canada more time to decide whether to develop the Mackenzie Delta or the Arctic Islands; it could increase the probability of settling the native land claims before pipeline construction began. The government, however, had already committed itself to reaching a pipeline decision by September 1, largely in the interests of closer relations with the United States. The extent of the gas surplus, therefore, was not fully determined before the pipeline decision was taken. This, of course, was one of the risks that the government had accepted in agreeing to meet the American deadline.

THE RISKS OF ACCELERATION II

But there were also other risks. The pipeline applicants were making substantial changes to their projects. Foothills had adopted a bigger pipeline and proposed a Dempster spur as an alternative to Maple Leaf. Arctic Gas too made important modifications to its application at that time, amounting to a revision of half of its pipeline route through the Mackenzie Valley. The government's already difficult task of assessing the various pipeline options was now becoming so complex that it demonstrably exceeded its ability to carry it out thoroughly.

CAG had been forced to redesign its line extensively when tests conducted by the National Research Council had shown that the measures it had advocated for almost three years to control frost heave were ineffective. This, as well as a year's slippage in the proposed start of operations, had increased the pipeline's estimated costs by half a billion dollars.

The frost heave redesign demonstrated perhaps better than any other factor the enormous risks that the large-scale application of new technology pose in a poorly known environment. The heaving of frost-susceptible soils could, if unchecked, rupture the pipeline; both Foothills and Arctic Gas, therefore, had spent significant sums of money to devise appropriate measures to control it. Arctic Gas had developed a technique to mitigate the effects of heaving in zones of discontinuous permafrost that had withstood cross-examination before Berger, the NEB and the FPC. It was one which had cost CAG over one million dollars to develop and in which it expressed total confidence. Unbeknownst to all until late 1976, however, the laboratory equipment on which Arctic Gas had relied to conduct its experiments had malfunctioned. This malfunction was only discovered when the National Research Council had attempted to duplicate CAG's experiments and failed.

This incident showed that Arctic Gas was proposing a pipeline whose implications it still did not understand fully after seven years of study and the investment of $150 million. More importantly, it showed that there existed serious gaps in scientific knowledge to assess the impacts of the pipeline projects. It also exposed the dangers of relying on industry assurances about the effects of their proposals. These were sobering thoughts at a time when government was rushing its consideration of the three pipeline applicants in order to meet an American deadline.[17]

The frost heave redesign injected a measure of uncertainty in the Arctic Gas application that had not existed before. But, as the NEB hearings progressed, it was not to prove the only element which put the feasibility of a pipeline into question. In late 1976, it had become apparent that none of the major producers in the Mackenzie Delta—Imperial, Gulf and Shell—had yet completed economic studies on the development of their reserves. These studies, in the case of Gulf and Shell, were not expected until mid-1977, or *after* the conclusion of the NEB hearings. What these companies were therefore asking in effect was that the NEB approve a pipeline after which they would decide whether and when they would start producing gas. In other words, the decision as to whether the pipeline was built, if it was found in the national interest, would ultimately be made not by the Canadian government but by three foreign-owned oil companies. This was an intolerable condition which tested even the NEB's patience. The oil companies' repeated refusal to commit themselves firmly to a pipeline, even though they advocated its construction and indeed were members of Arctic Gas, finally broke down the usual reserve of the board members hearing the evidence and led one of them, Geoff Edge, to ask sarcastically:

> Well, I guess the problem we are wrestling with is, we are really talking about a design which is to a certain extent, hypothetical, because we do not have any contracts to look at. We are talking about contracts which do not exist, which someone is expecting in some way to come into existence. We are talking about financing which is hypothetical because there are no contracts to support financing. It seems to me that we are getting close to talking about a hypothetical public interest with a hypothetical certificate with hypothetical conditions in it, but where is the substance that the board is looking at in relation to this project?[18]

Although it had been delivered with a smile, this was a strong rebuke indeed for an agency which has not distinguished itself in the past for its aggressive regulation of the gas industry.

The uncertainty surrounding the economics of Mackenzie Delta production made it impossible to establish conclusively the financial viability of an Arctic Gas or a Dempster pipeline. As it was, the "financeability" of CAG was already conjectural because it depended on government guarantees. The request for guarantees was meeting with strong resistance, particularly in the United States, but also in Canada which would already have to bear the bulk of the pipeline's environmental and social costs. Government guarantees were even more distasteful in light of the ten-fold increase in the costs of the Alyeska pipeline and, of course, the composition of the Arctic Gas consortium itself.

The emerging gas bubble, the frost heave redesign, the uncertainty surrounding the economics of Delta production and the request for guarantees all constituted so many questions which begged for answers before a pipeline decision could be made. Some of these questions also applied to Foothills: was it reasonable to expect that an Alaska Highway pipeline, too, would not some day require some form of financial assistance, even though in 1977 Blair expressed his confidence in being able to raise the money needed privately? The natural forum in which to address all these matters, including of course the 48-inch alternative and the Dempster lateral, was the National Energy Board. Being constituted as an independent agency and being composed of a large professional staff, the board not only had the legal mandate to hear pipeline applications but the resources to adjudicate them. Furthermore, the board had developed procedures to test evidence and allow the public to present its views. The NEB, however, is also a creature of government and, as such, subject to political pressure. The board did not feel it could ignore the accelerating march of events. To have done so would have embarrassed the government and invited an explicit abrogation of its jealously guarded autonomy. This was an eventuality to be avoided at all costs and the board therefore chose to quicken the pace of its hearings itself.

The NEB had already lengthened its hearing day—at CAG's invitation—on May 3, 1976, only three weeks after the start of the hearings, and then again in August, the second extension coinciding, perhaps only fortuitously, with an Arctic Gas complaint about the slow pace of the proceedings. Although the board had stated in May that afternoon sittings—the board was then sitting only in the morning—were not feasible because of the large amount of work that NEB staff and all interveners had to do on a day-by-day basis to prepare for cross-examination, in August this impediment to the rapid progress of the hearings had inexplicably vanished. The board announced that it would start sitting full days for a trial three-week period. Arctic Gas was alone in rejoicing at the board's ruling. Mike Goldie, the chief CAG lawyer, captured the impact of the Board's announcement in his quip that "nothing expedites cross-examination like exhaustion".[19]

The trial run was a failure, and the board was forced after three weeks to revert back to morning sittings, albeit much longer ones. Still, the hearings were evidently proceeding with insufficient dispatch for, on February 4, 1977, the NEB extended the hearing day for a third time. In April, the board began sitting evenings as well. By then, the hearings were beginning at 8:00

in the morning and often did not conclude until 7:30 in the evening, a pace which the board lawyer subsequently admitted had been "killing". The final acceleration in the schedule came just before the start of the most important phase of the hearings, that on natural gas supply and demand, which would determine whether any pipeline was needed. By this time, however, the NEB's concern with the substance of evidence being presented seemed little more than perfunctory. Expedience had become an end in itself and the hearings an endurance test for all the participants, including board staff whose own resources had been overwhelmed long ago by the furious pace of the proceedings.

As a result of the NEB's haste, several matters were left unresolved when the hearings concluded on May 12. They included the question of the effectiveness of measures to mitigate frost heave and thaw settlement in zones of discontinuous permafrost, sale and transportation contracts for both Prudhoe Bay and Mackenzie Delta gas, a detailed assessment of the environmental and socio-economic effects of the Alaska Highway and Dempster pipelines and the economic viability of gas production in the Mackenzie Delta, all matters to which the board admitted in its report. The government's single-minded determination to bend to the American timetable forced it to make its pipeline decision without that information and without a rigorous appraisal of conventional supply and demand. The NEB's expedition of its hearings, partly the result of Arctic Gas pressure, in effect lowered the standard of proof to be met by the pipeline sponsors, two of whom, of course, were advancing projects whose *raison d'etre* was primarily, if not exclusively, the delivery of American gas to American markets.

Once the government had committed itself formally to meeting the US deadline, it had accepted these risks. There would simply be no time to weigh new factors such as the emergence of the domestic natural gas surplus, or even a new alternative such as the Dempster lateral. In a period of rapid change, such as prevailed in early 1977, this represented an appreciable narrowing of options. But there was no going back once the commitment to the United States had been made: the domestic and international repercussions would have been too great.

THE NEED FOR COORDINATION

Trudeau's promise to abide by the American timetable accentuated the need to co-ordinate the Canadian and American assessments of the pipeline proposals. On each side, the stakes were too high to allow any ambiguity to remain or any area of uncertainty to be left unexplored before the decision was reached. Each country had therefore to be apprised of the factors the other would consider in making its decision. Furthermore, it was necessary to start setting the stage for negotiations in the event both Canada and the United States approved an overland route.

On March 3, therefore, only nine days after Trudeau had met with Carter, Gillespie went to Washington where, the following day, he held separate discussions with Carter's chief energy adviser, James Schlesinger, Vice-President Walter Mondale and Secretary of the Interior Cecil Andrus. The American ambassador to Canada, Tom Enders, attended each of these sessions.

In his meeting with Schlesinger, Gillespie reiterated[20] first Canada's "commitment to doing everything we could to arrive at a decision, at least in principle, by September 1" and proceeded to outline Canada's own timetable and the organization the government would establish to make the pipeline decision. Gillespie then listed five points which needed to be considered by both countries:

1) the question of government financial assistance to the successful pipeline applicant;
2) the problem posed by native land claims. A number of native leaders and representatives of Canadian public interest groups would be testifying before a congressional subcommittee during the middle of March and Gillespie was concerned that "these submissions might well cause worries in US quarters as to Canadian attitudes". In order to dispel any misgivings this testimony might create in Washington, Gillespie therefore briefed Schlesinger and Andrus about "the native problem—the numbers involved, and the difference of view between the Metis and the Indian Brotherhood in the Mackenzie";
3) the price. Gillespie explained that frontier gas would be priced in the Canadian market at full value, that is, that it would not be "rolled-in", or averaged with existing low-cost supplies as the United States planned to do. Since Mackenzie Delta gas was expected to cost at least twice as much as gas then being sold in Toronto, Gillespie feared a good deal of resistance to its development. This, he felt, "would be an argument for the Alcan route";
4) the barriers to the export of Canadian petrochemicals created by the high American tariffs;
5) the creation of a Northern Pipeline Authority to oversee the construction of a pipeline.

Gillespie's list of what ought to be considered in a pipeline decision is interesting both for its inclusions and its omissions. The reference to petrochemicals constituted a bow to Alberta's aspirations to promote the growth of this industry but could not properly be deemed as a factor affecting the determination of which pipeline to build, if any. On the other hand, other factors which logically belonged to such a list, such as the environmental impact of a northern pipeline and its implications for Canadian gas export policy, to name only two, were absent. The most striking feature of Gillespie's list, however, was its implicit premise that a pipeline would be approved. The high cost of Mackenzie Delta gas, for example, did not militate against a pipeline altogether, only in favour of a different one.

But by early March 1977, of course, there was a growing body of evidence in Canada to indicate that no pipeline should be approved. In spite of the natural gas shortages that winter, the United States, too, had reason to proceed cautiously in light of the uncertainty affecting the pipeline proposals. Prudhoe Bay gas would contribute only 4% of American supply, a volume which Schlesinger acknowledged in his meeting with Gillespie would be "helpful, but not really significant in terms of... overall consumption."

The import of that fact seemed to be lost at the time on the Canadian government. If Alaskan gas was not really significant, the concessions Canada was making by subjecting itself to the American pipeline timetable were unlikely to return the large dividends in improved bilateral relations Ottawa was expecting. From the very beginning, Canada's hope of winning its neighbour's gratitude by accommodating its need seemed to be premised on a faulty appraisal of the importance the United States was attaching to the pipeline. It was therefore bound to be frustrated in the long term.

With the date of the pipeline decision approaching rapidly, it was clear that more than ministerial meetings with the Americans was needed if Canada was to be ready in time. The government faced essentially two new tasks: it had to assess the Alcan option formally to respond to the growing public demands for a Berger-style inquiry in the Yukon and it also had to establish an internal mechanism to coordinate the different inputs it would be receiving from the NEB, Berger, the Northern Pipeline Study Group and the Alaska Highway pipeline assessments. The creation of a centralized agency would, as an added advantage, simplify liaison with the US.

THE GOVERNMENT ACTS

The creation of a special commission to evaluate the regional impact of the Foothills (Yukon) proposal seemed logical given the precedent of the Berger Inquiry. Indeed, this was why there was such widespread public support for such a commission. It was precisely the Berger precedent, however, which caused the government to hesitate for six months before Warren Allmand, the Minister of Indian and Northern Affairs, announced on March 9 that a socio-economic inquiry would be appointed in the Yukon. Berger, on the other hand had been named the very day Arctic Gas had filed its application.

There were many in government who wanted to prevent a repetition of the Berger hearings. They felt that he had exceeded his terms of reference and contributed to the growing political activism among the native people in the North. Most importantly, Berger had turned the Mackenzie pipeline into a political issue by maintaining a high public profile throughout his inquiry. As a result, he had reduced the government's latitude in reaching the pipeline decision by forcing it to give what was considered a disproportionate weight to environmental and social concerns. In the minds of these officials, therefore, the inquiry constituted a mistake to avoid rather than an example to emulate. The government's delay in establishing a socio-economic inquiry could be ascribed in part to the continuing perception of the Alcan project by Gillespie and some of his colleagues as no more than "a serious option so far as contingency planning was concerned"[21] rather than an equal contender to the Mackenzie pipeline.

Nevertheless, in spite of the apprehension in some quarters about a repetition of the Berger hearings, it was impossible to resist the political pressures in favour of an inquiry in the Yukon. To have done so would have given the appearance of having prejudged the issue and succumbed to American demands for an early decision. The government found the solution to its dilemma in offering the form of public hearings without granting their full substance. The manner by which the government succeeded in retaining tight control over the environmental and socio-economic assessments of the Alaska Highway pipeline is instructive. It reveals not only the true nature of its commitment to the public inquiry process but also the ranking of its priorities: in this instance, the end of reaching a timely pipeline decision justified the means of establishing what would amount to only token public consultation.

The government first separated the environmental and socio-economic considerations and convened two sets of hearings. While it made for greater speed, such a separation did not contribute to a thorough understanding of the issues—the social implications of certain environmental impacts, for example, would be obscured—nor did it necessarily assist Yukon residents in preparing submissions to the hearings. If the assessment process was fragmented, it was also incomplete because the environmental and socio-economic inquiries were restricted to examining only the Yukon portions of the Alaska Highway pipeline.

On March 21, Cabinet referred the pipeline proposal to the Environmental Assessment and Review Office of the Department of Fisheries and the Environment. The office had been established in April 1974 to prepare environmental evaluations of projects initiated by federal departments or involving the use of federal funds or property. Although the Environmental Assessment and Review Process (EARP) includes public hearings, interveners are usually not allowed to cross-examine each other. In this case, therefore, opponents of the pipeline would not be able to challenge directly the evidence of Foothills. But this was not the only control the government would exert on the environmental hearings. The EARP panel is recruited from within the civil service and is therefore less likely to oppose government policy than would a panel of outsiders. Of the six panel members reviewing the Foothills application, three, including the chairman, Dr. H.M. Hill, were from the Department of Fisheries and the Environment, one was from the Department of Indian and Northern Affairs, one from Energy, Mines and Resources and one worked as an environmental consultant to the

Yukon government. Furthermore, the Alaska Highway Pipeline Panel was given only until August 1 to submit an interim report. This ensured, of course, that the government would meet its deadline but also that the panel would not be able to give more than superficial consideration to the environmental implications of the pipeline routes through the Yukon. By the spring of 1977, there were no fewer than three separate routes being considered through the southern Yukon: the original one along the Alaska Highway, one further north along the Tintina Trench and one further north still along the Klondike Highway which had the advantage of being 200 miles closer to the Mackenzie Delta. Lastly, the very terms of reference the EARP panel was given—to propose measures to mitigate the environmental impacts of a pipeline rather than to decide whether a pipeline was environmentally acceptable—helped to bias its conclusions in a very definite direction.

In meeting the political need for a public inquiry or royal commission, a government will usually retain enough control over its conduct to minimize the possible adverse effects of its creation. This, it can do by appointing the members of the inquiry, restricting its budget or the duration of its mandate and dictating its terms of reference. In this way, the appearance of independent review can be provided with few of the risks it would entail. In naming the Mackenzie Valley Pipeline Inquiry, the government had neglected to stipulate a date by which Berger had to submit his report; it had also given him, by including in his purview the 1972 pipeline guidelines, very broad terms of reference. This time, the government was making sure that EARP would not escape its control in the same fashion as had Berger.

The government established a second inquiry to examine the socio-economic impact of a pipeline in the Yukon which became known as the Lysyk Inquiry, after the name of its chairman. Appointed on April 19, Lysyk was given little more than one hundred days to prepare an initial socio-economic assessment of the construction and operation of an Alaska Highway pipeline. By comparison Berger, who had admittedly conducted an inquiry of greater scope and over a wider territory, had taken three years to complete his report.

Lysyk was well-suited to his task. Dean of Law at the University of British Columbia, he had also done some research for and advised both the government and native organizations on land claim issues. His two co-panelists were Willard Phelps, a Whitehorse lawyer nominated by the Yukon government, and Edith Bohmer, Executive Director of the Yukon Association of Non-Status Indians, nominated by the Council of Yukon Indians (Ms. Bohmer would later work for Foothills). The presence of a Yukon government appointee and a native representative on the socio-economic panel was designed to secure the cooperation of each and demonstrate the government's fairness. The panel's composition accomplished these two goals.

There was also another reason why the government chose to name a panel rather than an individual to head the socio-economic inquiry. An individual proceeds unfettered by the pressures of compromise. An important reason for CAG's alarm at the Mackenzie Valley Pipeline Inquiry was that Berger alone would decide what he would write in his report. A tripartite commission, on the other hand, is forced to make numerous accommodations to each of its members before it can reach a mutually satisfactory common ground. Although each of the Alaska Highway Pipeline Panel members would be allowed to write a minority opinion—none did—the momentum towards consensus would prove overwhelming over the life of the inquiry.

Here again, the appointment of a panel rather than an individual, the tight time-frame, the terms of reference (Lysyk, for example, was not allowed to hold hearings outside the Yukon as Berger had done, with resulting widespread media coverage) were designed to ensure that the Lysyk Inquiry did not acquire the dimensions of the Berger hearings. Having set what appeared to be an elaborate public process to gather information and formulate recommendations, the government in fact offered only the illusion of full consultation with the people who would be most affected by an Alaska Highway pipeline.

In addition to the creation of a formal assessment process for the Alcan line, the government faced in early 1977 the much more daunting task of preparing itself to make the pipeline decision. At the beginning of April, the Northern Pipeline Study Group submitted the results of its work, a two-inch-thick report entitled *Northern Gas Pipeline Issues*. The report had been written to provide the government with the background analysis it would need to evaluate the Berger and NEB reports and decide which pipeline to build if any. Although the number of policy options Canada faced was still growing as Foothills continued to introduce new alternatives to its applications, there were essentially three courses of action from which to choose: Arctic Gas, Alcan and no pipeline. With its work completed, the Northern Pipeline Study Group was formally dissolved although its members would continue to work individually on pipeline matters until the end of the summer. Now that the date for a decision approached, it was up to senior civil servants and politicians to start weighing the alternatives.

On April 26, an updated summary of the study group's work, setting out the various policy options facing Canada, was submitted to the ad hoc Cabinet Committee on the Northern Pipeline. The creation of a special committee to oversee the pipeline decision testified both to its importance and its political sensitivity. The committee was chaired by Allan MacEachen, the Deputy Prime Minister and President of the Privy Council. MacEachen had been chosen over other Ministers because Trudeau wanted a neutral chairman who was not associated with any of the departments directly implicated in the pipeline decision. It is a moot point, however, whether there would have been a need for an outside chairman had Trudeau trusted Gillespie more. As former Finance Minister John Turner would reveal in one of his expensive newsletters after returning to private life—a few large corporations pay $15,000 each for the insights Turner's years in power can give them—Gillespie "is generally perceived to lack the confidence" of the Prime Minister. MacEachen's appointment was a rebuff for Gillespie who is reported to have considered resigning over the issue. The other members of the ad hoc committee were Warren Allmand, the Minister of Indian and Northern Affairs; Romeo Leblanc, the Minister of Fisheries and Environment; Donald Macdonald, the Minister of Finance; Jean Chretien, the Minister of Industry, Trade and Commerce; Don Jamieson, the Secretary of State for External Affairs and Jack Horner who had just joined the Liberals on April 21 as Minister without portfolio.

Two days after the ad hoc committee's first meeting, the government announced the formation of a Northern Pipeline Commission to be headed by Basil Robinson, the Under-Secretary of State for External Affairs. The need to find a "Mr. Pipeline" to bring together the many strands of the pipeline decision had been recognized at the beginning of the year and had been discussed in the meeting Gillespie had held with Schlesinger. The Pipeline Commission was established late, however, reflecting the limited amount of forward planning the government is usually capable of undertaking. As it was, the creation of a special agency to deal with a specific issue was an innovation which few issues in the past had warranted.

But then there never had been an issue that had reached into so many different areas as the northern pipeline. That fact alone made it unique and the natural focus of interdepartmental rivalries. Which department should be the lead agency in the pipeline decision, Energy, Mines and Resources or the Department of Indian and Northern Affairs? Senior EMR officials did not impress their counterparts in other departments, particularly at Finance and Treasury Board, with their insistence that Canada had to move on all energy fronts at once because of the long lead times in developing new resources. Given the enormous costs of frontier projects, this was hardly a realistic position and it lost EMR much support for its arguments. For its part, DINA had been sensitized by the Berger experience and was unhappy at the bias towards Arctic Gas it perceived in EMR. The solution was to find a neutral forum which no department would dominate. The practical result was to lessen EMR's influence over the pipeline decision.

Although he came from External Affairs and had made his career as a diplomat, Robinson, the new Pipeline Commissioner, knew the pipeline issue well. For the five years between 1970 and 1974, he had served as deputy minister of Indian and Northern Affairs. He had thus been a member of the Task Force on Northern Oil Development. This past was undoubtedly considered an asset at a time when the pipeline decision would have to be reached quickly.

As befitted its task, the Pipeline Commission was centrally located, opposite Parliament Hill and only one block from the Privy Council Office. It had a small staff of five, a number which underlined its role as co-ordinator: it was not to supersede the work already being carried out in existing departments. As commissioner, Robinson acted as chairman of the ad hoc committee of deputy ministers on the northern pipeline, the bureaucratic counterpart to the Cabinet committee. Its membership was large because the pipeline decision affected virtually every department. Nevertheless, a core group composed of the deputies of Energy, Mines and Resources, Indian and Northern Affairs, Treasury Board, Finance, Justice, External Affairs, Environment and senior representatives from the National Energy Board and the Privy Council Office emerged as the team who would guide the decision through Cabinet. During the hectic months that followed, this group met regularly, usually on Thursday mornings for breakfast.

The Northern Pipeline Commission's task was clear. The priorities for the work to be done were obvious and the time pressures considerable. There was little time to do anything more than make use of the information already available and try to build on that information by taking into account new developments as they arose. One of Robinson's responsibilities included consultations with the United States, a job for which he was admirably suited. In External Affairs he had come to know well the staffs of the Canadian embassy in Washington and of the American embassy in Ottawa. Robinson was able to take advantage of these contacts in his tenure as pipeline commissioner to stay on top of events in the United States. As the months went by and the Canadian and American schedules came to fit perfectly, this aspect of his work would involve less time than had been originally anticipated.

The month of April 1977 was a critical one in the Canadian consideration of the northern pipeline. It had begun with Foothills announcing yet another pipeline project, this one along the Dempster Highway. Both the environmental and socio-economic assessments of the Alaska Highway pipeline had been launched. April was also a month of transition. The initiative which, until then, had rested firmly with the bureaucracy began shifting to Cabinet as the pipeline decision approached. Outwardly, this period was characterized above all by the lull before the final acceleration of events. In the space of the next three months, six government reports on the pipeline would be released in Canada and the United States. In early May, the Federal Power Commission and Berger would submit their recommendations, to be followed two months later by the reports of the White House Task Force on the pipeline and the National Energy Board; finally, in late July, the Environmental Assessment Panel and Lysyk would both issue their findings.

The process by which a pipeline would be chosen or rejected was now in place. All that remained was to weigh the results of over three years of formal evaluation of the options. The denouement was about to begin.

CHAPTER SEVEN

THE TIDE TURNS

Two major events marked the first few days of May 1977: on May 2, the Federal Power Commission recommended that the United States government approve an overland pipeline through Canada—either Alcan or Arctic Gas; on May 9, Judge Berger stated categorically that no pipeline should be built in the Mackenzie Valley for ten years. In the space of that one week, the tide had turned. To many in government both recommendations came as a shock. The emergence of the Alaska Highway proposal with its associated Dempster lateral was in many ways still too recent to have reversed completely the inertia of almost nine years of thinking. The work of the Task Force on Northern Oil Development, the 1970 and 1972 Pipeline Guidelines and the NEB 1975 gas report all constituted a legacy which pointed in one direction and one direction only: the Mackenzie Valley. Besides, Arctic Gas had been in existence for almost five years; it had done the most work on its project; it had won the most support, not only from within the ranks of industry but also among politicians in both Canada and the United States. Moreover, it was the only proposal to have received preliminary regulatory approval. On May 1, 1977, it seemed logical to expect that Arctic Gas would ultimately build the northern pipeline.

THE FPC REPORT

On May 2, however, all this changed. Unable to agree among themselves on the choice of a best route for delivering Prudhoe Bay gas, the Federal Power Commissioners issued a split recommendation, two favouring Arctic Gas and two preferring Alcan. For Arctic Gas, whose project had been endorsed so forcefully by Judge Litt only three months earlier, the FPC report represented a stunning setback. For Foothills and Northwest, the report marked an extraordinary recovery. The daring gamble of devising a "48-inch alternative" after they had seemingly been eliminated from contention, had paid off. That they had been able to take that gamble at all, of course, had only been made possible by the provisions of the Alaska Natural Gas Transportation Act. But the act had been of even greater benefit to Alcan by affecting the very form of the Federal Power Commission recommendation. Without ANGTA, the FPC would have been forced under the 1938 Natural Gas Act to approve one project or dismiss them all; in such circumstances, it is very likely that the FPC Commissioners would have confirmed Litt's opinion—if only because so much more was known about Arctic Gas than either of its competitors. ANGTA, however, had instructed the FPC to weigh the advantages and disadvantages of each alternative without necessarily endorsing a particular one. This provision had been designed to give the President maximum flexibility in making his choice and in negotiating with Canada. Fortunately for Alcan, it also allowed the FPC to avoid having to make a difficult and controversial decision which would almost certainly have gone against the Alaska Highway project.

In its report, the FPC indicated that all three applications—Arctic Gas, El Paso and Alcan—were economically viable although it found an overland route through Canada to be clearly superior to the combination of pipeline and sea transport advocated by El Paso. By refusing to choose between Arctic Gas and Alcan, the FPC therefore shifted the decision of which pipeline to build to the Canadian government but with the understanding that, if Canada imposed unreasonable conditions, the United States would opt for El Paso.President Carter was thus given a strong bargaining position with which to approach Canada.

If the FPC recommendation already constituted a grievous blow for Arctic Gas, the Berger report released only a week later sounded its death knell. It was not only the recommendations it contained—that no pipeline be built across the northern Yukon *ever* and none in the Mackenzie Valley for ten years—that proved so damaging to Arctic Gas but more so the extraordinary publicity which surrounded them. Until then, public awareness of the pipeline issue had been limited. After the Berger report, public opinion became a factor in the pipeline decision. It was one which would contribute to CAG's eventual demise.

THE BERGER HEARINGS

The publicity which accompanied the release of the Berger report was entirely owing to the unique nature of the Mackenzie Valley Pipeline Inquiry itself. Nothing like it had ever happened before; it is unlikely anything like it will happen again. Judge Berger was fond of repeating that he was "embarked on a consideration of the future of a great river valley and its people".[1] But the Mackenzie Valley Pipeline Inquiry, of course, had been more, much more than that: from an inquiry into a gas pipeline, it became an inquiry into the future of the North and, finally, an inquiry into the future itself.[2] This made the inquiry's existence itself and its hearing process as important as its eventual outcome. Reflecting upon his mandate in mid-1977, Berger would say that his inquiry would have been a success even if he had never written his report because it had promoted a greater awareness of the issues facing the North. To Berger, the journey had all along seemed more important than the destination. In order to understand the impact of his report, it is necessary therefore to understand something also about the inquiry itself, how it operated, how it outflanked the NEB and how it captured the public's imagination.

From the very beginning, the inquiry had become the focus for the discussion of social, ethical and political issues, as well as environmental and engineering problems. This was because it represented in a microcosm the clash between two cultures, two sets of values, two definitions of progress. On one side, stood Arctic Gas and, to a lesser extent, Foothills who believed, in the words of Bill Wilder that:

> nowhere in the Yukon and the Northwest Territories is the need for development as great as in the Mackenzie Delta and Mackenzie Valley. That is where the major social and economic problems exist. If the pipeline goes away, these problems won't.[3]

The Dene, as the Indians of the Mackenzie Valley call themselves, held a radically different view of what the pipeline would mean to them. In August 1975, Frank T'Seleie of Fort Good Hope, an Indian community on the Mackenzie River, denounced the pipeline companies in ringing tones that captured headlines across the country. Addressing himself to Bob Blair—with a single exception, senior CAG executives did not attend Berger's community hearings—T'Seleie declared:

> You are like the Pentagon, Mr. Blair, planning the slaughter of innocent Vietnamese. Don't tell me you are not responsible. You are the twentieth century General Custer. You are coming with your troops to slaughter us and steal land that is rightfully ours. You are coming to destroy a people that have a history of thirty thousand years. Why? For twenty years of gas? Are you really that insane?[4]

Wilder and T'Seleie epitomized the two diametrically-opposed views about the future of the North. This dichotomy ran as a theme throughout the entire Berger hearings and was reflected in the title Berger chose for his report: *Northern Frontier, Northern Homeland.*

In order to give the inhabitants of the Mackenzie Valley an opportunity to be heard, Berger went about to create an inquiry "without walls". This he accomplished by visiting every community that might be affected by a pipeline, thirty-five in all; there, he received the testimony of a thousand witnesses who spoke in seven languages. At the very first community hearing in

Aklavik in the Mackenzie Delta, Berger established the informal tone which would prevail for the rest of the hearings:

> I am here so that you can tell me what you think, and so that you can say what you want to say. I want you, the people who live here, who make the North your home, I want you to tell me what you would say to the Government of Canada if you could tell them what was in your minds.[5]

To break down the walls of the inquiry even further, Berger arranged for extensive coverage of the proceedings by the CBC Northern Service. A summary of the day's events was broadcast in English and the native languages every day that the inquiry was sitting. The consequences were profound. One of Berger's senior staff members noted that "everyone in the region was thus able to keep informed and knew, before the inquiry arrived in their community, which issues had been debated by the experts and what their neighbours in other communities had said".[6] As a result of its unique procedures, its conscientious efforts at stimulating broad participation and the pervasive importance of the issues the pipeline brought into focus, the inquiry became a giant consciousness-raising exercise and a milestone in the political development of the Dene and the North itself.

The inquiry and the native people very quickly developed a symbiotic relationship. Each needed the other as much as it was needed itself. To the Dene and the Inuit, Berger represented perhaps the last chance to gain some measure of control over their future. The inquiry's findings would play a crucial role in their land claim negotiations. In order to succeed and leave a lasting impact, the inquiry, on the other hand, had to develop a constituency, a strong base of public support. This it could achieve only by being rigorously fair and thorough and encouraging as many people as possible to participate in the hearings. Berger went to the people because he believed there is as much wisdom in Old Crow as there is in Ottawa. But there was also another reason.

At various times throughout its existence, the Pipeline Inquiry faced the thinly-disguised hostility of the government that had created it. In November 1974, Donald Macdonald, the Minister of Energy, Mines and Resources, had suggested that Cabinet might have to change Berger's terms of reference if he insisted on forcing the disclosure of certain government documents on the pipeline. In March 1975, on the very day the inquiry began, Mitchell Sharp, who was acting Prime Minister at the time, refused to commit the government to wait until it had received Berger's report before making a decision on the pipeline. Only three days later, Jeanne Sauve, the Minister of the Environment, would pledge her department's support to the inquiry while noting pointedly that no development would ever take place if all environmental questions had to be answered first. On March 12, Judd Buchanan, the Minister of Indian and Northern Affairs, announced that he would not refer the construction of gas processing plants in the Mackenzie Delta to the Berger Inquiry, even though they formed an integral part of a Mackenzie pipeline, but would have his department examine them internally instead. In other words, the example of the Berger Inquiry was not to be repeated. Buchanan also hesitated several months until July 1975 before asking Berger to include the new Maple Leaf application in his terms of reference. The public declarations of Cabinet ministers as well as the reduction in funding to various interveners appearing before Berger directly challenged the inquiry's legitimacy. The government's behaviour could only undermine the confidence of the public in the inquiry's ability to conduct full and fair hearings.

It is not surprising therefore that Berger should have sought to circumvent the effects of this hostility by establishing a power base of his own. His staff lawyers were instructed to brief the editorial boards of major newspapers and maintain a good rapport with reporters. The inquiry's high profile was raised further when it took its much-publicized swing through southern Canada in the late spring of 1976. Berger had declared his intention to hold southern hearings almost two years before when he had released his preliminary rulings on the conduct of the inquiry. These hearings could not, however, have been scheduled at a better time. Stopping in ten cities from Vancouver to Charlottetown, Berger received 400 briefs from groups and individuals in an exercise which he himself described as a "travelling teach-in". Berger would say later: "Suddenly all the issues we had been dealing with—industrial growth and whether or not it should dominate social concerns, patterns of energy consumption, native rights, protection of the northern environment—all this came together".[7] Along with it came sustained media coverage which not only familiarized Canadians with the pipeline but made Berger a household name. The results of a public opinion poll conducted between January and March 1976, long before the southern hearings began, must have given the government cause for reflection: more respondents ranked the protection of the environment as the most important issue raised by the construction of the pipeline than security of energy supply and the production of energy as cheaply as possible. The government, it was clear, would be able to ignore Berger's recommendations only at its own peril.

It was Berger's resolve "to do things right" that was responsible for the strong public support behind his inquiry. Doing things right included resisting government and industry pressures to accelerate his hearings. He would ask in Inuvik in February 1976: "If Canada can't take the time to make an informed decision on what's going to happen in our northland, then what's Canada got time for?"[8] Berger also knew that he had much to lose by submitting a report prematurely. The pipeline equation was changing so rapidly that the danger of his report becoming obsolete as a result of developments before the NEB and the FPC—such as the filing of an Alaska Highway application—could not be discounted.

In mid-1976, however, Berger himself decided that his hearings would have to move faster. By then, they had been in progress for over a year, and Berger was starting to feel that he had heard all the evidence he needed to write his report. Besides, time was growing short. Congress was considering legislation to set a deadline for the American pipeline decision. Furthermore, the NEB hearings were still expected to conclude by the end of the year. If he was to have any impact, Berger believed he had to come first. Starting during the summer, the rhythm of the hearings was quickened, the hours lengthened, cross-examination shortened. On October 15, 1976, after 283 days of testimony, 1,700 witnesses and over 40,000 pages of transcript, the Berger hearings concluded in Yellowknife. There still remained a week of final argument that Berger had scheduled in mid-November to give each participant the opportunity to present draft terms and conditions to be imposed on a pipeline's construction and operation if one was approved. At that time, interveners would also be able to comment on the report Berger had asked his staff to prepare.

The staff report was an innovation in the Canadian context. Berger had borrowed the practice from the United States because he wanted the participants at the inquiry to be given the chance to criticize the advice he himself would receive from his staff. Released on October 29, the five-inch thick staff report was unequivocal in its two main conclusions. Berger's staff felt that

> in order to protect the unique environment of the northern Yukon and the Mackenzie Delta, as well as the way of life of the native people in this region, the Prudhoe Bay pipeline should not cross the northern Yukon along either the coastal or the interior route, but rather should follow a more southerly route or corridor.[9]

Furthermore, the staff concluded that not only land claims should be settled before a pipeline was built but that "a substantial period of time, in our estimate ten to fifteen years, must be allowed before major development, to permit the implementation of the settlement."

If adopted, these recommendations would have spelled the end of Arctic Gas although they would not have precluded the overland delivery of Prudhoe Bay gas. Berger's staff noted that the Fairbanks corridor offered "environmental advantages over the routes of the Northern Yukon" which made it preferable to a Mackenzie pipeline for the transportation of American gas. As far as Canadian gas was concerned, the staff recommended that "the Dempster Highway route should be assessed and reviewed, on a priority basis, as an alternative to the Mackenzie Valley route for transport of gas... southward from the Mackenzie Delta".

The Berger staff conclusions confirmed CAG's worst fear. Did they reflect the views Berger wanted to hear? Arctic Gas suspected that they did. CAG's top executives were convinced that "Berger had been dedicated to killing the project from day one". As the hearings progressed, they had become increasingly dismayed at the turn the Pipeline Inquiry had taken. CAG had been particularly disturbed by the native peoples' growing unrest which it believed the inquiry was helping to foster. This unrest, native leaders had warned several times during the hearings, might eventually erupt into violence. However remote a possibility this was, it was one which could not be ignored because its mere mention was enough to inhibit potential investors and the government from backing the pipeline.

The lack of progress in land claim negotiations was at the root of the native peoples' militancy and Arctic Gas therefore urged the government repeatedly to settle the Dene and Inuit claims. The rapid succession of ministers of Indian Affairs and Northern Development—three between 1974 and 1976—as well as the split and deepening rancour between the Metis Association and the Indian Brotherhood of the Northwest Territories, however, prevented any breakthrough in negotiations between the government and the native peoples. In September 1976, in a desperate bid to break the deadlock, CAG even presented a legal memorandum to the government which it hoped might serve as the basis for a settlement. But by then it was too late. The Berger report would be released in a few months and the government understandably wanted to study its recommendations before launching any new initiative. Thus, when two senior executives of Columbia Gas System, an American member of Arctic Gas, met Tom Enders in Ottawa on September 29 to discuss ways in which the pipeline decision might be expedited, the three men were forced to agree that although the CAG submission had been "a necessary and helpful gesture it would not by itself resolve the difficult claims issue."[10]

CAG's secret intervention—which Arctic Gas officials hotly denied when it became known in the spring of 1977—revealed the true extent of the consortium's alarm at the lack of progress in land claim negotiations. From the very beginning of its existence, CAG had strived doggedly to dissociate its project from the claims. It had argued that the claims were not only a matter for the government and the native people to settle—which they obviously were—but that the pipeline's prior construction would not prejudice a settlement—a much more tenuous argument.

As time went by, Arctic Gas found it increasingly difficult to maintain its role of passive observer. It knew that in the fall of 1971, the major Prudhoe Bay producers had been instrumental in persuading a dilatory Congress to pass the Alaska Native Claim Settlement Act after almost three years of debate. CAG's legal memorandum was premised on this precedent and the danger that unresolved native claims in the Mackenzie might scuttle the pipeline.

Had Arctic Gas succeeded, it would have been the third time in the history of the Northwest Territories that the government would have signed an agreement with the native people as the direct result of economic imperatives.[11] It is a telling testimony of the government's neglect of the native people that it has repeatedly waited for the pressure of resource development to become irresistible before trying to settle claims.

Arctic Gas spent the better part of two days during the week of final argument before the Berger Inquiry rebutting the Berger staff conclusions. At the time, Arctic Gas could only hope that both Foothills' and its own strong opposition to the staff recommendations would moderate Berger's report. In mid-November 1976, of course, Arctic Gas was still the overwhelming favourite to receive final government approval. The FPC hearings had just concluded and Arctic Gas knew that it was ahead of its rivals in the United States; in spite of difficulties before the NEB, CAG was confident that the NEB would also choose its project over either Maple Leaf or the Alaska Highway line. The Berger staff report, although worrisome in its implications, did not appear to detract significantly from CAG's overall advantage over its competitors.

THE BERGER REPORT

By the time he heard final arguments, Berger had already started preparing his own report. Indeed, on the last day of the hearings on November 20, he had presented to his senior staff a draft of what he intended to say. Berger wanted his report to come in two volumes, the first to contain his principal conclusions and recommendations and the second the terms and conditions for a Mackenzie pipeline. The first volume had to be simple and direct so that it would be read widely. Having been a Member of Parliament once, Berger knew only too well that he would not reach MPs with long dissertations on frost heave or caribou migration patterns.

Berger was also acutely aware of the latitude he enjoyed in writing his report. The emergence of a pipeline proposal which did not cross the northern Yukon or the Mackenzie Valley gave him more freedom to criticize a Mackenzie pipeline. Berger had also followed closely the most recent developments in the Canadian natural gas situation. He held numerous discussions with Marshall Crowe during this period and knew that the pressure to exploit the Mackenzie Delta reserves as quickly as possible was receding. This, too, removed the need for compromise in the report.

But in order to have the impact he wanted, Berger had to submit his recommendation before the NEB's. He therefore pressed his staff relentlessly. He and they remained in Ottawa from November 1976 to May 1977 working around the clock at the inquiry's offices on Nicholas Street. Throughout, they kept an anxious eye on the progress of the NEB hearings held across town on Albert Street. In spite of the innumerable drafts—the first and the final one for each chapter were always Berger's—and the NEB's repeated acceleration of its proceedings, they knew by early 1977 that their report would come first.

The Berger report[12] was finally released on May 9, 1977, at three o'clock in the afternoon, when Warren Allmand, the Minister of Indian and Northern Affairs, tabled it in the House of Commons. Ever concerned with keeping a high profile, Berger had asked that his report be made public on a Monday when he would not have to compete with the hockey playoffs then in progress. It was immediately apparent that the report's presentation in two volumes, published on separate dates, had achieved its desired end. It focused public attention on whether to build a pipeline rather than on how to build one. This, of course, made it much more difficult for the government to ignore the central issues the pipeline raised. But for Berger, there was another advantage as well: by dividing the report into two sections, he not only set the mood against which the NEB decision would be judged, he also reserved the right of rebuttal in Volume II.

The Berger report had an enormous impact. The day of its release, it was the subject of a special two-hour programme on CBC radio while CBC TV devoted an hour to its analysis that same evening. The report was also accorded front page coverage in the press. More important than all the news stories was the fact that it became a best-seller and had to be reprinted only a few days after its publication. In keeping with the precedent-setting nature of the inquiry, the presentation of the report itself was unique: no effort had been spared to maximize its impact. It was lavishly illustrated, photographs of witnesses giving greater immediacy to quotations, pictures of the land emphasizing its vulnerability to environmental damage.

Berger's evocative and limpid prose and his uncompromising moral tone spoke with a compelling force that attracted widespread public support:

> What happens in the North... will be of great importance to the future of our country; it will tell us what kind of country Canada is; it will tell us what kind of people we are.
>
> ... There is a myth that terms and conditions that will protect the environment can be imposed, no matter how large a project is proposed. There is a feeling that, with enough studies and reports, and once enough evidence is accumulated, somehow all will be well. It is an assumption that implies the choice we intend to make. It is an assumption that does not hold in the North.
>
> ... The evidence is clear: the more the industrial frontier displaces the homeland in the North, the greater the incidence of social pathology will be. Superimposed on problems that already exist in the Mackenzie

> Valley and the western Arctic, the social consequences of the pipeline will not only be serious—they will be devastating.

Berger's recommendations that, for environmental reasons, no pipeline *ever* be built across the northern Yukon, and none in the Mackenzie Valley for ten years to allow the settlement and implementation of the native claims represented a disastrous reverse for Arctic Gas; this reverse was all the more damaging from following so closely upon the FPC report. It was the finality of Berger's recommendations that was particularly harmful. For the first time since it had been considered, the Mackenzie pipeline now no longer appeared a certainty. But if Arctic Gas had suffered a defeat of major proportions, it had by no means yet lost the war. The NEB report was still to come. Arctic Gas also had many friends in the media, industry and, most importantly, Cabinet.

ARCTIC GAS COUNTER-ATTACKS

Immediately upon the release of the Berger report, Arctic Gas and its supporters launched an all-out campaign to neutralize its effects. That campaign was first evident in the media. On May 9, the *Globe and Mail*, acknowledged as the most influential newspaper in Ottawa, had published a long feature article by Bill Wilder opposite its editorial page. If the publication of this article the same day that the Berger report was released was no more than a coincidence, it was a particularly happy one for Arctic Gas. In the past, the *Globe* had written editorials favourable to CAG; predictably, its own reaction to the Berger report was lukewarm. Arctic Gas also had the support of the *Financial Post*, Canada's largest business newspaper, which criticized the Berger report in terms CAG itself had used. Aimed towards a broader public were the full-page ads placed by Imperial Oil in several Canadian magazines, such as *Maclean's* and *Saturday Night*, proclaiming: "As a Canadian, you'll get more than you might expect from a Canadian Arctic gas pipeline".

It was natural that Imperial, the richest oil company in Canada and the discoverer of Taglu, the largest gas field in the Mackenzie Delta, would assume a leading role in promoting a Mackenzie pipeline in the critical early months of 1977. The most active of Canada's oil companies in pressuring the government, Imperial has also over the years been the most effective. One reason, advanced by Bill Hopper, Petrocan's president, is that "you could put the people in Energy, Mines and Resources who know anything about oil and gas in one corner of Imperial's corporate economic department".[13] One of Imperial's greatest successes came in 1975 when it engineered the dramatic showdown with the federal and Alberta governments over the $2 billion Syncrude tar sand plant. When the project had been put in jeopardy after the withdrawal of one of its original sponsors, Imperial had threatened to abandon it unless the two governments rescued it. They did. This victory flushed Imperial with confidence. When it had raised the stakes high enough, Ottawa had capitulated. Imperial believed that the same tactics would also work for a Mackenzie pipeline and their initial success helped to convince it to stay in the Arctic Gas consortium even after Exxon, its corporate parent, withdrew in February 1975.

Impatient at what it perceived as CAG's ineffectual lobbying, Imperial decided in January 1977 to seize the initiative itself. Once again, it chose to raise the stakes: a speech was prepared to announce that Imperial would halt further drilling in the Mackenzie Delta until Arctic Gas was approved. With the government intent upon doubling oil and gas exploration in the North, this threat revealed clearly the leverage Imperial enjoyed. At the very last minute, however, Imperial changed its mind. In a newspaper interview following the release of the Litt report, Gillespie had declared that he would not be blackmailed into supporting a Mackenzie pipeline. Gillespie had not known about Imperial's intentions but the company realized immediately that this was not the time to pressure the government publicly into supporting Arctic Gas. The speech was therefore quietly shelved.

If Gillespie's warning was instrumental in persuading Imperial not to make its threat public, the other oil companies with interests in the Delta were not similarly deterred. On April 28, only a few days before the release of the Berger report, Bill Daniel, Shell's president, took advantage of the company's annual meeting to declare that Shell was suspending all future drilling plans in the Delta until a Mackenzie pipeline was approved. Daniel was grandstanding. Shell had already explored all the attractive prospects it controlled in the Delta and, indeed, had begun shifting its exploration effort back to Alberta a year and a half earlier. Daniel's threat was thus a hollow one aimed strictly for public consumption. On May 9, Jack Gallagher, the chairman of Dome Petroleum, the company which had pioneered offshore drilling in the Beaufort Sea, warned that the construction of a pipeline was essential if exploration was to continue in the area. Less than a month later, on June 3, Gulf and Mobil announced that they, too, were suspending further drilling in the Delta until Arctic Gas was approved and royalty regulations in the north clarified.

Arctic Gas, however, was not another Syncrude. This time, there was an alternative and the oil companies' tactics did not achieve their desired effect. Nevertheless, the decision by Shell, Gulf and Mobil to suspend exploration, Imperial's consideration of the same and Dome's warning that it might follow suit, illustrated for all to see the length to which these companies were prepared to go to shape government policy. By being members of Arctic Gas and having dedicated their reserves to other CAG companies, Imperial, Gulf and Shell had allied themselves to a specific pipeline proposal and were therefore already in a position to influence the selection of the company that would build the northern pipeline. By controlling the pace of exploration, the majors enjoyed potentially a far more powerful weapon, one they had not hesitated to use in the past.

During this period, Arctic Gas, of course, was stepping up its pressure also. The day after the release of the Berger report, Horte and Bill Brackett, the president of CAG's sister organization in the US, went to see Enders. The visit was important enough that Enders cut off a previously scheduled appointment in order to see them. As American ambassador to Canada, it was to be expected that Enders would play a pivotal role in the pipeline decision. He was not doing so as an impartial arbiter, however, a fact underlined by Horte and Brackett's surprise visit. Indeed, Enders had already revealed where his sympathies lay several times at diplomatic dinner parties. The purpose of Horte and Brackett's call was thus not to inform Enders of what Berger had said. It was to discuss CAG's fate.

Reduced to its simplest terms, the strategy Arctic Gas adopted in the spring of 1977 to minimize Berger's impact was designed to stress Canada's "growing dependency on uncertain supplies of imported oil".[14] CAG knew that to attempt to discredit the Berger report directly would almost certainly backfire. Indeed, a Gallup poll conducted in early June would show that more Canadians supported the Berger report than opposed it. CAG therefore toned down its attacks on Berger's conclusions and emphasized instead the advisory nature of his inquiry: here was but one piece of the puzzle, the argument went, and not even the most important one at that; the key element in the pipeline decision would be the NEB's recommendation, not Berger's. "It would be wrong to regard Berger's as the sole report on this matter", Horte said at a press conference on May 9. "We are disappointed in the Berger report but certainly we still feel confident.... a way will be found in that the interest of the natives and other Canadians will be served."[15]

At the same time, Arctic Gas continued to insist that the construction of a Mackenzie pipeline was essential to the fulfilment of Canada's goal of energy self-reliance. To a Cabinet that had not forgotten the trauma of the 1973 oil embargo, CAG's argument in favour of increasing the security of Canada's energy supply was endowed with considerable appeal. The already discovered reserves in the Mackenzie Delta, according to Arctic Gas, would displace $17 billion worth of oil imports over twenty years, reducing Canada's balance of payments deficit as it enhanced its security in energy supply.

This argument was to be the last twist in CAG's evolution from an essentially export-oriented project to one of allegedly compelling necessity to one, finally, designed to lessen Canada's dependence on oil imports. This latest justification for a Mackenzie pipeline underlined how events were passing Arctic Gas by and how the company was becoming the prisoner of its former claims in the process. It was not at all clear that expensive Mackenzie Delta gas would succeed in displacing oil imports without some form of subsidy. The obvious alternative to this dubious proposition, however, the export of Delta gas, was one which the Berger report had foreclosed. Only if a case for urgent domestic need could be made, would the government be able to override Berger's recommendations and approve a Mackenzie pipeline. The ever-expanding "gas bubble" meant that this case was increasingly difficult to make.

The "gas bubble" indeed was making new enemies for Arctic Gas. If a Mackenzie pipeline was built before the domestic market could absorb its flow, Alberta production would in all probability have to be curtailed because Mackenzie Delta gas could not be shut in once put into production: the enormous pipeline investment precluded that option. It would be the Alberta producers therefore who would pay the price of bringing frontier gas on stream before it was needed. Those who stood to suffer the most from the surge in northern supply and the accompanying reduction in southern production were the small independents whose vigorous exploration effort was responsible for the bulk of the newly-made discoveries in Alberta.

Starting in the spring of 1977, therefore, some of the independents began to lobby the government, claiming they could deliver gas to market in greater quantities and more cheaply than Arctic Gas could. Theirs was a persuasive argument: their discoveries in 1976 alone had cut the expected domestic shortfall in the 1980s by half; the prospect for greater finds still was excellent and, besides, the gas could be transported to eastern Canada at a fraction of the cost of frontier supplies.

Although the small producers' "*prise de conscience*" was slow in coming—none of them had intervened before the National Energy Board to protect its interests, for example—the representations they made to the Canadian government in the critical middle months of 1977 eroded much of the appeal Arctic Gas once had.

THE GOVERNMENT REACTION

Arctic Gas was not the only one to be jolted by the Berger report. For its part, the government felt placed in an awkward position. Only three months before it was to make its pipeline decision, it was suddenly confronted with the possibility that it might have to approve a pipeline about which it realized it knew very little. After both the Berger and the FPC reports, the Alaska Highway pipeline could obviously no longer be treated merely as "a serious option so far as contingency planning was concerned". The government was forced to reassess its strategy.

The release of the Berger report brought into focus the split in the Cabinet over the northern pipeline. When the Berger Inquiry had been set up, the Mackenzie Valley pipeline had been received religion in Ottawa. The pipeline hearings had helped to change these attitudes. In fact, the media had an impact not only on the public but on ministers and senior civil servants too. They had read about the hearings in the *Globe and Mail*, they had heard reports on the CBC about the pipeline's apprehended impacts, they had seen statements made on television by the native people in their villages and they had been affected by all these things. By the time the Berger report was handed down, many ministers and their deputies had moved a significant distance away from the consensus that had existed in 1974 in favour of the pipeline.

But many had not. Some Cabinet ministers felt that Berger had exceeded his terms of reference, that he had made a decision that was not his to make. "Mr. Berger was not invited to recommend against a pipeline", Gillespie said curtly the day the report was released. Along with many of his colleagues, he felt that Berger's uncompromising recommendations had reduced the number of options available to the government at a time when the need for flexibility was at a premium. The government could not afford to lose control of the pipeline issue when it was facing the delicate task of co-ordinating its decision-making process with the United States. Yet, this was precisely what Berger had caused by recommending that no Mackenzie pipeline be built for ten years.

In spite of this recommendation, there still remained much latent support for Arctic Gas in Cabinet. Jean Chretien, for example, did not hide his disappointment with Berger's conclusions. It was left to Jack Horner, however, to deliver the bluntest attack against the Berger report:

> ... I look at it like this. If Berger had been around a hundred years ago, we would still have the buffalo herds in the West and the CPR wouldn't be built because that would disturb the migration pattern of the buffaloes and Jack Horner would have been born in Quebec and I by this time would've been bilingual and Ottawa wouldn't have the problem of the Prairies because the Prairies would be looking after itself. Berger came a hundred years too late.[16]

Horner's logic was obscure and convoluted but both his comments and Gillespie's showed that Cabinet would have a difficult time in establishing a consensus on the pipeline issue. It was already divided over land claims, with some ministers, led by Allmand, pressing for an agreement in principle with the native people before a pipeline decision while others, Gillespie and Horner among them, argued for the quick development of frontier gas. Unable to agree on the substance of the Berger recommendations, Cabinet decided to maintain a neutral public posture which paid tribute to the excellent work Berger had done while it remained silent on the issues he was raising.

The Cabinet's ostrich-like reaction was tested very quickly when the New Democratic Party introduced a motion in Parliament urging "the government to accept the principal recommendation of the Berger report that no pipeline be built in the Mackenzie Valley for at least ten years". The motion was only indirectly aimed at the government. Its true target was the Progressive Conservatives. As long time opponents of Arctic Gas, the NDP hoped that if they could rally the vacillating Tories to their cause, they would help to dissuade the government from endorsing a Mackenzie pipeline.

This stratagem seemed to offer a good chance for success, for the day the Berger report was released Joe Clark had declared on television: "It would be very hard to contest Mr. Berger's evidence indicating that we should not proceed directly with the Mackenzie Valley pipeline". Clark however, had been partly goaded by reporters and his surprising statement did not have the support of a large number of Conservative MPs. The dissension within his party—the Conservatives were much more divided over the issue than the Liberals—forced Clark to make a humiliating *volte-face* on the day the NDP motion was debated and espouse a position little different from that of the government. Since they could not pronounce themselves on the pipeline, the Conservatives limited themselves to calling for a parliamentary debate on the pipeline and a delay in the final decision until all relevant information became available.

Thus, even though the government was highly vulnerable to criticism for its longstanding support of a Mackenzie pipeline and its adherence to an American timetable for decision, it escaped the debate unscathed. Indeed, MacEachen, the minister responsible for the pipeline, took advantage of the opportunity to argue piously that the government would not be rushed into any pipeline decision. Coming from the same government that had been prepared to build a Mackenzie oil pipeline in 1972 with no knowledge of its environmental effects, that had given Lysyk and EARP three months to review the impact of an Alaska Highway pipeline in the Yukon and had pledged to do everything possible to give the United States a decision by September 1, MacEachen's homily was obvious cant.

In light of the Conservatives' dismal performance, it was not long before the government agreed to a longstanding opposition request for a full-scale parliamentary debate on the pipeline. Liberal strategists who had worried that the opposition might seek to exploit the pipeline issue to its own advantage came to realize after the release of the Berger report that there would be no repetition of the 1956 pipeline debate.

The government nevertheless remained very concerned about the degree of public opposition to a Mackenzie pipeline. This opposition, it believed, had been catalyzed in great measure by the Berger southern hearings which had given pipeline critics unprecedented media coverage. The broad basis of this opposition, comprising church and labour groups as well as environmentalists and native people, gave it a political clout that the few public interest groups intervening before the NEB had never possessed. In order to retain its control over events, the government began to feel that it would have to take special counter-measures. Anticipating a national letter-writing campaign against Arctic Gas as the date for decision approached, Energy, Mines and Resources programmed a computer to handle the anticipated flow of mail. The government also started to prepare legislation on a contingency basis to pre-empt a legal challenge by opponents of a pipeline. The pipeline decision was clearly becoming politicized and was calling for greater sensitivity to public attitudes. The government's response was characteristic: it retained the services of Goldfarb Consultants Ltd., a firm which regularly conducts public opinion polls for the Liberal Party.

In order to gauge the response of Canadians to Berger, Goldfarb was asked to carry out two highly confidential polls, one immediately before the release of the judge's report and one a few weeks after. The results of the first poll, received in early June, were reassuring. The majority of respondents trusted the government to give Canadians accurate information on the pipeline issue. Goldfarb wrote in his report:

> The federal government comes off in this analysis as a very credible adjudicator and force both in the dissemination of information about and the formulation of the decision regarding the pipeline. That is, Canadians are really looking to the government for objective leadership in the northern pipeline issue.[17]

Goldfarb also found broad support for the government's decision to settle the pipeline issue quickly in accordance with the American timetable, rather than wait two or three years until more information became available. This support seemed to stem from a widespread belief that a gas shortage would occur in Canada before the mid-1980s. "The implications", Goldfarb remarked, "is that Canada should participate with the United States and build a pipeline." The public's acceptance of impending shortages was in part of the government's own making. Through the National Energy Board 1975 gas report and its silence over its internal assessment of supply and demand, the government had helped to propagate the industry's alarmist warnings. Even though the domestic outlook had improved considerably over the previous two years, the government now had to contend with the expectations of a majority of Canadians that a pipeline had to be built.

The Goldfarb poll contained some warnings, too. Environmental issues ranked highest among those the public wanted resolved before a pipeline decision. The settlement of native claims was also listed as a major concern. Goldfarb concluded that "at least on an emotional level, people will tend to support the findings of Berger."

Public attitudes, it was clear, were not going to stand in the way of government approval of a pipeline. Indeed, they favoured it. They did suggest, however, that a decision in favour of the Alaska Highway pipeline was likely to meet with much less opposition than one which endorsed Arctic Gas.

The government's decision to conduct its own private poll was revealing in the preoccupation it showed over Berger's impact. The government obviously feared that the pipeline issue would be extremely sensitive politically in spite of the Conservatives' ineffectual opposition and had to be handled therefore with the utmost concern towards public opinion. The questionnaire Goldfarb used in his survey was interesting in itself: although it ran to 27 pages—the average interview lasted an hour and a half—only once did it refer to the Alaska Highway pipeline. The government's apprehension about the political ramifications of its pipeline decision obviously did not extend to the Alcan line.

The Berger report cooled considerably the government's ardour for a Mackenzie pipeline. Cabinet ministers, even personal friends of CAG's top executives, began to dissociate themselves immediately from the consortium. It took Gillespie, for example, only eight days following the publication of the Berger report to make a well-publicized tour of the Yukon, ostensibly to survey the Alaska Highway route. The true purpose of Gillespie's trip, however, was not so much to ascertain first-hand what terrain an Alcan pipeline would cross as to protect his political reputation. Even though he had once privately told Imperial Oil that he would not stake his career on defending Arctic Gas, Gillespie was perceived to lean towards a Mackenzie pipeline. It was known that Wilder was a friend of his and an occasional tennis partner. Both men owned adjoining farms just outside Toronto. Gillespie, therefore, felt that he had to dispel the image that he was CAG's man in Cabinet. This message, of course, was not lost on Arctic Gas.

Gillespie's trip at the time raised eyebrows for the unexpected endorsement it seemed to give to an Alaska Highway pipeline. Interviewed on CBC as he was flying above the highway, Gillespie declared that he saw no environmental impediment to pipeline construction. This was a daring remark for a man who had admitted in the previous sentence that he was not qualified to judge the feasibility of building a pipeline because he was not an engineer. Gillespie's extemporaneous assessment showed his eagerness to appear neutral on the pipeline decision: not necessarily neutral on the question of whether to build a pipeline but neutral on where it should be built.

THE NEB DECISION

With Cabinet support waning, CAG realized that only an unequivocal endorsement from the NEB would overcome the impact of the Berger report. Such unqualified support, however, was no longer very likely. The NEB hearings had ended in a final burst of speed on May 12 with many issues concerning each of the pipeline applications still unresolved. Under normal circumstances, there is little doubt that the NEB would have felt compelled to adjourn until more evidence had become available. But because the board was determined to submit a report by early July, the numerous gaps in both the Foothills and CAG applications did not slow down the furious pace of the hearings to any appreciable extent. Indeed, in order to save time, NEB staff began writing the report long before the hearings themselves had concluded.

By early April, the board lawyers were openly reading drafts of the report in the hearing room itself while cross-examination was going on.

On March 25, the NEB staff had been sent a confidential timetable setting deadlines by which certain portions of the report had to be written. The covering letter accompanying the timetable described how the report was to be written:

> There are actually three distinct sections to each write-up. First is the summary of the submissions and evidence presented. Much of this can be written prior to the sub-phase concerned occurring, with modifications then made on evidence brought forward through the cross-examination process. The second section deals with the "Views of the Board" and should contain the board's analysis, but *not* any recommendations.
>
> The third section is not for direct publication in the report but rather is a "Conclusions and Recommendations" memorandum that will be forwarded to the Hearing Panel and used by them in their drafting of the actual decision, including an overall "Conclusions and Recommendations" section.[18]

The last deadline specified in the letter was June 10. The hearings adjourned on May 12; June 6 was set as the date for submission of final argument; rebuttal argument was allowed until June 20 at which time the record was officially closed. The NEB report was released July 4.

The board's haste was such that major sections of the report were written not only when the hearings were still underway but indeed before interveners had even finished stating their case. The NEB had obviously felt it more important to meet its deadline than to take the time necessary to synthesize all the information it had received.

For the board, of course, the pipeline decision would be the most crucial in its eighteen-year history. Alone among the commissions of inquiry and assessment groups that were investigating the various aspects of the pipeline issue, the NEB exerted a peremptory power over the ultimate decision. It had the authority to choose which pipeline should be built, if indeed any. Only through legislation could the government overturn its decision, an awkward remedy fraught with political liabilities. The NEB must have believed that this power imposed upon it a particularly onerous responsibility that could be used only with the greatest circumspection.

This helps to explain why the board felt forced to consider, in drafting its report, several factors extraneous to the evidence which had been presented during the pipeline hearings. It did not think it could ignore, for example, the forcefulness of the recommendations of the Berger Commission and the wide degree of public support they had encountered, both of which imposed an obvious constraint on the government's future latitude in making a decision. Nor could it be oblivious to the recommendation of the US Federal Power Commission which signalled a shift away from the unequivocal endorsement Arctic Gas had received earlier in the year from Judge Litt. A decision in CAG's favour would not only constitute a potential political embarrassment for the government which would have to reconcile publicly diametrically opposed advice, but it also created the risk of isolating the NEB as the only major agency supporting a Mackenzie pipeline. In writing its report, the board could not be unmindful either of the proposals which had recently been discussed in Cabinet to limit the authority of regulatory agencies. A decision which created too much difficulty for the government invited that these proposals be translated into policy and the NEB's independence be promptly circumscribed. A sensitivity to the government's position, including its evident predisposition towards accommodating the American interest, was therefore imperative.

As a last concern, the NEB also had to consider the distasteful possibility of litigation—a more likely prospect in case of an affirmative decision towards Arctic Gas than one favouring Foothills. To a greater extent than the other pipeline proposals, CAG had acted as a lightning rod for native groups, environmentalists and nationalists. Foothills had aroused considerably less opposition because it had remained the underdog until the very end and its negative impacts appeared less severe. This, however, was a deceptive situation: if the Alaska Highway line looked relatively more benign than a Mackenzie pipeline, the less rigorous examination which the project had received was at least as responsible as its nature.

All these factors militated in favour of an NEB decision with a strong political character. This is exactly what the board delivered on July 4.

The date's irony—it was Independence Day in the United States—was unintentional, a coincidence due to the fact that this was the earliest the report would be ready. The board had announced a few days before that it was inviting all interveners to attend a lock-up starting at five o'clock on Monday July 4, at which time it would release its decision. This was a highly unusual procedure as NEB decisions are traditionally released with little fanfare. This time, all the actors who had participated in the drama for the previous two years would be present to receive the board's verdict in person.

The secrecy surrounding the report had been absolute. Only the most senior board staff knew in advance what the recommendation would be. Even some of the the board's branch directors had not been informed, an indication of how few people had participated in the decision. The day the report was released, one of them informally tipped off a friend that Arctic Gas had won.

As five o'clock approached, clusters of men representing the elite of the Canadian and American oil and gas industry made their way from nearby downtown hotels to the Trebla Building where the NEB is located. In anticipation of a large crowd, the ninth floor hearing room had been cleared of desks and additional rows of chairs had been installed. The room filled rapidly. Arctic Gas had flown in its top executives from Toronto and Washington; its fifteen sponsor companies were well-represented too. They were confident, in spite of a newspaper story that morning that had claimed that the NEB would approve Alcan. Arctic Gas had prepared a large publicity campaign that it would launch immediately upon the release of a favourable NEB recommendation. Imperial had gone further. It had asked Wood Gundy, Canada's largest and most prestigious brokerage firm, to write a prospectus for a $50 million Eurobond borrowing to finance its gas gathering facilities in the Mackenzie Delta. The prospectus had been ready for several days and only the advice of its public relations department had persuaded Imperial to await the release of the NEB report before making its financing plan public.

Officials of the Foothills group of companies had also turned out in force. They too were hopeful, although they felt they had ended the hearings on the wrong note. Having withdrawn their Maple Leaf application, they were staking everything on the "48-inch alternative" filed only four months earlier. All in all, there were some three hundred representatives of the biggest law firms in the country, the most powerful petroleum interests in North America and a smattering of public interest groups gathered in the hearing room as Jack Stabback, the NEB's vice-chairman, started reading the board's Reasons for Decision.[19] Alternating with the two other members of the panel, he was to read for over an hour. Tension built up quickly as the board outlined one by one the reasons which had led it to its conclusion without, however, revealing until the very end what that conclusion was.

Stabback first gave the board's assessment of the natural gas situation: "... a case has been established for the connection of Delta gas as early as 1982 providing it can benefit from being transported in association with the larger volumes of Alaska gas". Arctic Gas executives thought they had won. More reasons for optimism came from the board's discussion of the various proposals' design and engineering. Here again, despite reservations about both major applications, the board seemed on balance to favour the Arctic Gas plan. The section on financing dealt CAG its first blow: the board categorically rejected the concept of government backstopping; it also spent an inordinate amount of time describing the possible corporate re-structuring of Foothills (Yukon), the first indication of the board's choice. The panel then went on to transportation charges, the risk of cost overruns, Canadian content and economic impact which, taken together, seemed to favour Foothills. The section on socio-economic impact was critical of both applicants. Only when the panel broached environmental matters did its decision become unmistakably clear: Arctic Gas, the most powerful consortium of oil and gas companies ever assembled in Canada, which had spent $150 million in pursuit of its application and had once enjoyed the overt support of the government, had lost its bid to build the Mackenzie pipeline to a partnership of western transmission utilities that was barely a year old.

The NEB decision came as a shock to the members of the Arctic Gas consortium. For Imperial in particular, this was the biggest defeat in the company's history. It had been associated with Arctic Gas to a greater extent than any other member of the consortium. "There's no point staying around this goddam place," Imperial's executive vice-president Don McIvor snapped as he stormed out of the hearing room. The champagne that had been brought especially for the occasion aboard the company's executive jet remained uncorked on the flight back to Toronto.

At eight o'clock that evening, Arctic Gas held a press conference at the Four Seasons Hotel. Vulture-like, a crowd of reporters gathered to hear Bill Wilder read a statement and answer questions. Everyone sensed that Arctic Gas had received the coup de grace and no protest to the contrary by the consortium's officials managed to dispel this impression. Visibly bitter, Wilder denounced the NEB decision as political, not based on facts. The press conference was short and afterwards the weary Arctic Gas group retired for dinner to a nearby French restaurant. The restaurant's name was La Guillotine.

THE NEB REPORT

The NEB report was one of the most, if not the most, important documents on which the government relied to reach its decision on the northern pipeline. By statute, of course, this would have been the case in any event: the report is invested with the legal authority of the National Energy Board Act. With the approach of negotiations with the United States, the report also became part of the government's bargaining posture and acquired an added significance as a result. On another level, it had an important symbolic value as well: coming after a year and a half of hearings, it commanded an implicit measure of public credibility based on the belief that the NEB's assessment of the competing pipelines had to have been thorough to have taken that long; confirming the recommendations of the Berger report, it automatically enjoyed wide public acceptance. The government could therefore, and did, use the NEB report to justify its final decision. This it was able to do in spite of a circularity of cause and effect which made it difficult to identify precisely the extent to which the NEB had influenced the government and vice-versa.

The NEB report owed much to the board's interpretation of its political milieu. It is apparent, for example, that the board did not so much embrace Alcan as it backed away from Arctic Gas. In doing so, it forced itself into the position of having to make substantial changes to the original Alaska Highway proposal: politically, it could not approve a project which would do nothing to increase domestic energy supplies when its pessimistic forecast of the Canadian natural gas situation dictated that the Mackenzie Delta reserves be connected to market; the only alternative which remained, however, a Dempster pipeline, was uneconomic because of the distance between the

Delta and the Alaska Highway. The solution therefore lay in rerouting the Foothills line further north to reduce that distance. This proposal became known as the Dawson diversion.

The board redrew the pipeline route with what can only be described as breathtaking abandon. In justifying its decision, the board wrote:

> Recognizing that the amount of engineering design work and environmental and socio-economic studies and planning needed to meet final design requirements on the Alaska Highway route would be substantial in any case, it is the board's opinion that the Dawson diversion would not significantly alter the existing proposal or the construction schedule.[20]

With these words, the board was applying a lower environmental and socio-economic standard to the Yukon than it had accepted for the Mackenzie Valley. But the acceptance of that standard in the Northwest Territories had been strictly opportunistic. That the board had truly rejected Arctic Gas "on the evidence before it... including particularly the environmental and socio-economic problems" was an absurd proposition. The board had spent only a week reviewing environmental evidence. Its expertise in socio-economic matters was strictly limited. In any case, the NEB's endorsement of the Alaska Highway pipeline, about which it admitted little environmental and socio-economic evidence existed at the time, and its approval in principle of the Dempster pipeline, about which even less was known, demonstrated more clearly the real depth of the board's concerns. In the aftermath of the Berger report, these same concerns constituted of course, unassailable reasons for justifying publicly the board's decision. The board could not have paid Berger a more explicit compliment than it did when it used strikingly similar language to phrase its rejection of a Mackenzie pipeline. It could not have acknowledged more plainly either how it had become upstaged by his inquiry.

What the decision to divert the Alcan pipeline to Dawson lacked in elegance, the board hoped it would make up as a potential bargaining lever in any future negotiations with the United States. Another NEB recommendation, that Foothills pay up to $200 million into a socio-economic compensation fund, seemed to be advanced even more explicitly in anticipation of these negotiations. Although there were grounds to believe that the imposition of such a payment was precluded under the terms of the Canadian-American Transit Pipeline Treaty, its value as a tool to extract concessions from the US was self-evident.

As a result of the NEB's political acumen, the government not only received a recommendation that it could easily accept but a ready-made bargaining position as well. At the same time, it was confronted only a few weeks before it was to make its decision with a major change in the route of the Alcan pipeline, one which increased the project's costs by some $500 million. Furthermore, it had to accept the risk of making the future fulfilment of domestic gas needs dependent upon the unstudied Dempster pipeline. Both recommendations carried enormous financial and economic implications. Locked into the American timetable, however, the government would have no time to analyze either in depth.

The national interest would undoubtedly have been better served had the NEB concerned itself less with politics and more with the substance of the applications it adjudicated. By concluding that Canada too needed the pipeline, the board did more than officially sanction the government's preferred policy: it fundamentally and irretrievably undermined Canada's real bargaining advantage vis-a-vis the United States. Once Canada had conceded that it wanted a pipeline, it forfeited any opportunity to impose unilateral conditions on its construction. More importantly, it abandoned any claims to the considerable advantages the US would reap from an overland pipeline. Estimated conservatively, these advantages were worth $6 billion to the United States.

The NEB report therefore influenced decisively the outcome of the pipeline negotiations between Canada and the US. It is important because of this to examine how the board justified its decision. If the NEB had found that there was no short or medium-term domestic need for frontier gas, the *raison d'etre* for a pipeline as far as Canada was concerned would have been questionable at the very least. The board acknowledged that "on balance, pipeline projects probably have a negative social impact"; it also noted that an "... analysis of the project shows that it has limited potential for net economic gain ..." The weight of social, economic and environmental evidence, on the board's own recognition, was thus at best equivocal and it was not on the basis of these criteria that a persuasive case could be made in favour of the pipeline. Hence, only if Canada needed access to northern gas in the early 1980s, and only if a Dempster pipeline represented the best alternative to deliver that gas, could the board properly justify its decision.

This, of course, is exactly how the NEB argued its conclusion. To support its recommendation that a pipeline be built, the board claimed that gas shortages could begin domestically as early as 1982. It was here that the NEB report's incongruous logic was most evident. Not only can a Dempster pipeline not mitigate shortages should they arise by 1982 since the earliest the pipeline could have begun operations was thought to be 1985 at the time (it is now later), but the relief it may bring must remain entirely speculative in the absence of firm estimates concerning both the transportation and the development costs of Delta gas. The NEB's proposed remedy did not correspond therefore to its public diagnosis of the gravity of the natural gas situation. Did this mean that the board was contemplating a potential domestic gas shortfall with equanimity or that it was prepared to reduce Canada's gas exports? Or did it imply that the board accepted that its assessment of the Canadian gas outlook was unduly pessimistic?

The board indeed recognized the existence of a gas bubble in its report although it down-played its importance. If, in the board's opinion, the domestic gas surplus was too small to justify a delay in the construction of a frontier pipeline, it could postpone slightly the need for northern gas if it was exported now to the United States in exchange for equivalent volumes of American gas later. Such a swap offered a second advantage: the pre-building of parts of the Alaska Highway pipeline. Under the board's proposal, the southern sections of the line would be built earlier and Canadian gas exported through them. This would bring forward the realization of part of the pipeline's economic benefits. When the rest of the pipeline was completed, the gas that had been exported would be replaced with Alaskan gas.

To the United States, the possibility of obtaining additional volumes of Canadian gas immediately, even if it had to be returned at some unspecified date in the future, made the Alaska Highway pipeline a great deal more attractive. It provided a bridge in time until Alaskan gas could start to flow and also offered cost savings for the whole pipeline since a considerable portion of its length would be built almost right away. The American decision to develop Prudhoe Bay gas was acquiring a new dimension, the securing of more Canadian supplies as well.

In recommending a gas swap, the board was treading a narrow line indeed. It was acknowledging the emergence of a surplus but only a small one. The board's failure to recognize the true dimension of the transformation in the domestic gas outlook was the result of several factors. As has already been mentioned, the NEB was influenced by the testimony it had received on supply and demand from the Arctic Gas sponsors. The continuing legacy of the 1975 gas report warning of shortages was another factor which should not be underestimated. To have declared in 1977 that a large surplus was developing would have been an implicit admission of failure, a confession of its inability to forecast accurately even over the short term. That, indeed, has been the case in the past. Shoddy analysis was largely responsible for the wild fluctuations in estimates of natural gas supply and demand made between 1970 and 1975[21], and shoddy analysis was also in part what led the NEB to conclude in 1977 that a northern pipeline would be needed soon. The board's pipeline report implied for example a yearly growth in natural gas demand of almost 10% between 1977 and 1980 even though actual consumption in the preceding three years had risen by less than 3% annually. On the supply side, however implausible it may seem, the board's estimate of production over time added up to less than what the board recognized physically existed in the ground and was available![22]

The board's repeated errors and its reliance on improbable assumptions when forecasting both supply and demand raise numerous questions concerning not only its competence but also its role in Canadian energy policy. Although it is quite likely that the government would have decided in favour of the construction of an overland pipeline even if the NEB had not indicated an upcoming domestic shortage, there can be little doubt that the NEB report made the government's task much easier. And here lies the ultimate irony in the board's recommendation: in seeking to anticipate the government's wishes in its report in order to retain its independence, the board only demonstrated the illusion of its autonomy.

Having already compromised its integrity by accelerating the pace of its hearings to the point where the quality of the evidence it was receiving had been gravely eroded, the board produced a report whose chief distinguishing feature was its political expedience. As one ministerial aide observed after the report's release, "the board managed to show it wasn't a dead horse".

CHAPTER EIGHT

THE PIPELINE AGREEMENT

Tuesday, July 5, was "Black Tuesday". On the Toronto stock exchange, the value of the shares of the companies most adversely affected by the National Energy Board decision—Imperial, Gulf, Shell and Dome—fell $230 million before edging up at the close of trading. Imperial stock alone had dropped $80 million by the end of the day.

During the morning, Imperial's board of directors had met to assess the options they faced. These were essentially two. They could mount a massive lobbying effort against Alcan to have Cabinet reverse the NEB decision. This was a risky proposition because it entailed the possibility that no pipeline at all would be built. Imperial's $350 million investment in the Mackenzie Delta in this case would be lost—perhaps forever. The alternative was not to do anything and accept the Alcan/Dempster combination, however distasteful it was. Imperial chose not to fight. Later in the day, nevertheless, the company made one last desperate attempt to salvage its position. McIvor, Imperial's executive vice-president, went to see Gillespie to explore the possibility of a forced merger between Foothills and Arctic Gas.

Such a union was no longer in the cards. There was now too much animosity between the two groups to contemplate any repetition of the 1972 shot-gun marriage between the Northwest Project and Gas Arctic. Having won, Foothills was in a position to dictate its terms. It did so just as Imperial's board was meeting: it was ready to welcome new partners but not the major oil companies. "Exxon tried to exercise too much muscle" in pushing Arctic Gas, Blair explained, referring to Imperial by its corporate parent's name.

Imperial's decision not to challenge the NEB decision was the first confirmation that CAG's days were numbered. Although Wilder had bravely declared at his press conference the night before that "we haven't given up by any means", there was very little that Arctic Gas could do. Even if it had been inclined to fight, CAG's management was captive to the companies in the consortium. These, as Imperial had demonstrated, were not so committed to a Mackenzie pipeline that they were willing to incur the risk of losing the only alternative they had and see El Paso triumph. An appeal was therefore considered and rejected. Though the Lysyk report and the parliamentary pipeline debate, both scheduled for the beginning of August, offered only the slimmest hopes of a reprieve, Arctic Gas decided at its last executive board meeting on July 20 to await the final government decision before disbanding formally. Even this symbolic gesture proved too onerous for some of its member companies. Nine days later, all of CAG 's American sponsors announced that they would henceforth support Alcan, the same company they had previously described through CAG as incompetent, unrealistic and underfinanced. Arctic Gas was dead. Why had it died?

Arctic Gas had been a dinosaur. It had been unable to adapt to changing conditions. After the NEB decision, Wilder would say bitterly, "We could have changed the proposal and altered the routes. But we didn't.... I guess that's what you get for being honest". Of course, it was not honesty but inflexibility that lost Arctic Gas the northern pipeline. From the very beginning, all CAG sponsors had held as an article of faith that they were proposing the best pipeline. For them, the best pipeline was the shortest and the most economically efficient.

Thus, when Arlon Tussing met Bill Brackett on a flight from Toronto to Washington in late 1975 and suggested Arctic Gas include an Alaska Highway alternative in its application in case a Mackenzie line was found unsuitable, CAG refused. Tussing then went to Blair. Although CAG's refusal was understandable at the time, its insensitivity to the changes occurring around it would prove fatal. Nothing, not the disappointing reserves in the Mackenzie Delta, the unresolved land claims, the risk of cost overruns, the environmental impact on the North Slope, succeeded in shaking CAG's blind adherence to its dogma.

There were other factors too, of course, which accounted for CAG's demise: the emergence of the "gas bubble" reduced the need for frontier gas; the demand for government financial guarantees constituted a major handicap; the delay in the NEB hearings as a result of Marshall Crowe's disqualification gave Foothills time to prepare its Alaska Highway application; the uncompromising tone of the Berger report politicized the pipeline issue at the worst possible time for Arctic Gas.

Foothills, on the other hand, had all the advantages of a latecomer. It could learn from CAG's mistakes and tailor its project more precisely to the circumstances prevailing at the time. Being small, it could react quickly. It did not face the same incompatible deadlines Arctic Gas had to confront as a result of the Alaska Natural Gas Transportation Act and the unresolved land claims in the Mackenzie Valley. But more importantly, Foothills mastered the regulatory game. It did not propose a finished solution and ask the government to approve or reject it. Instead, it stated explicitly that it was willing to subordinate all private imperatives to political considerations. Having no stake in gas production or distribution as the Arctic Gas members did and being assured of a return on its investment if it won, Foothills was free from the constraints which hampered CAG. It was this independence and a large dose of opportunism which gave Foothills its victory.

THE PIPELINE LOBBY

If in Canada the NEB decision spelled the end for Arctic Gas, in the United States, not surprisingly, it also injected new life into El Paso. By recommending that the Alaska Highway pipeline be rerouted and that it cover its indirect socio-economic costs, the NEB had substantially increased the costs of the project. El Paso did not fail to exploit these changes. The $200 million levy was described as "discriminatory taxation", a violation of the Transit Pipeline Treaty between Canada and the United States before it had even been ratified by the US Senate. El Paso also noted, with considerable justification, that the Alcan pipeline was now "literally a combination of assertions by the applicants and as yet unstudied Canadian modifications".[1] By contrast, El Paso could claim that it was still sponsoring the same project that had withstood exhaustive cross-examination before the Federal Power Commission.

The cause of the all-American pipeline thus gained greater momentum as the pipeline decision drew near. Congressmen wrote Carter urging him to endorse El Paso to avoid "placing a major resource of the future within the jurisdiction of a foreign dominion".[2] One of these letters, signed by sixteen congressmen, even sought to capitalize on an issue on which the Carter Administration had taken a strong stand: human rights. The letter asserted craftily that the construction of an Alaska Highway pipeline would violate the rights of the Yukon Indians by denying them a fair land claim settlement.

The El Paso lobby, in Blair's words, was fearsome and ferocious. It enlisted the support of several large organizations, such as the biggest labour unions (the AFL-CIO and the Teamsters) and powerful business interests, such as Tenneco and Southern Gas, the third largest utility in the United States. Another important ally was the State of Alaska which not only committed its royalty gas to Tenneco, Southern and El Paso if a trans-Alaskan pipeline was approved but also pledged up to $900 million in bonds to help to finance the project.

Northwest, however, was equally adept at the lobbying game. As the battle shifted from the regulatory to the political arena, it too stepped up its efforts. Lobbying Congress is not cheap and during 1977 Northwest spent more than $2 million in legal fees and services alone. Like El Paso, it solicited letters of endorsement from senators and congressmen. One of its prominent supporters was Senator W. Proxmire, chairman of the Senate Banking Committee. Proxmire wanted an overland pipeline because it offered

> a golden opportunity for the federal government to make amends for its serious error in judgement in approving a trans-Alaska oil pipeline four years ago.
>
> As everyone knows, that decision was a disaster for American energy policy. We are now shipping oil vitally needed east of the Rocky Mountains through a multi-billion dollar pipeline to nowhere.
>
> The West Coast is already awash in oil. It would be unconscionable to set her afloat with gas.[3]

This was Canada's trump card. The Alyeska pipeline had begun operating in June and immediately created a large oil surplus on the US West Coast. Because there was no pipeline to ship Alaskan crude inland to Midwest markets, the excess oil had to be sent at considerable expense to American ports on the Gulf of Mexico and the East Coast through the Panama Canal and even around South America. American approval of El Paso, as Proxmire pointed out, would have compounded the problem by giving rise to a similar gas glut in California.

In spite of the considerable political heat the El Paso lobby was generating, it was clear that the Carter Administration would not be able to use the renewed vigour of the "all-American" alternative to strengthen its bargaining position with Canada. This was a key point as the negotiations between the two countries approached: no matter what the El Paso supporters argued, Alcan was clearly the superior alternative for the United States. Canada, therefore, would have the superior hand when the pipeline negotiations began.

THE WHITE HOUSE TASK FORCE REPORTS

To help in the pipeline decision, the Carter Administration had commissioned as provided for under the Alaska Natural Gas Transportation Act ten inter-agency task forces to analyze the relative merits of the three pipeline applications. The task forces' reports were ready on July 1. The White House had carefully co-ordinated the preparation of these reports to ensure that they did not foreclose any options in future negotiations. They had therefore avoided ranking the pipeline projects although it was clear that on balance they favoured an Alaska Highway pipeline. Alcan's advantage over El Paso, however, had been reduced considerably from the evaluation the Federal Power Commission had made in May. At that time, the FPC had found that the difference in transportation costs between the two projects—the most important criterion in choosing between them—amounted to thirty cents per thousand cubic feet; the White House Task Force reduced the difference to only seventeen cents by attributing a greater risk of cost overruns to Alcan. The revised calculations, of course, did not make any allowance for the increase in Foothills' costs as a result of the NEB decision. The implications for Canada's bargaining position were obvious.

The tone of the US agency reports stood in striking contrast to the orthodoxy which was still stifling the Canadian government. The White House task force was unencumbered by prior assumptions and did not hesitate to question even the desirability of developing the Prudhoe Bay reserves. By contrast, the NEB had uncritically accepted that "the need to connect Alaska gas to US markets would appear self-evident" although it had also been forced into the embarrassing admission that the absence of contracts for the sale of Prudhoe Bay gas made it difficult to identify specific markets for its use.

The difference between the American and Canadian approaches yielded revealing results. The Working Group on Supply, Demand and Energy Policy Impacts of Alaska Gas, for example, calculated that the implementation of Carter's National Energy Plan, unveiled two and a half months earlier, would eliminate gas shortages, albeit temporarily, by the mid-1980s and balance supply and demand at a price lower than that of Alaskan gas. By 1990, the working group estimated that shortages would reappear even with the delivery of Prudhoe Bay gas. The accelerated leasing of oil and gas prospects in the Gulf of Mexico constituted another option which would have "a supply impact that is comparable to gas deliveries from an Alaska gas project"[4] at a likely lower price. Imports from Mexico represented yet one more alternative to a northern pipeline. The working group's conclusions could not be described as a clarion call for the prompt exploitation of Alaskan gas and, not surprisingly, led American officials to study carefully the no pipeline option.

The news was greeted with apprehension in Canada. Cabinet was poorly briefed on the intricacies of American energy policy and the possibility that the United States might choose to defer the development of Prudhoe Bay gas was not one to which the government had given much attention. The American rejection of a pipeline was indeed unlikely, but it was obvious in light of the reports emanating from Washington in early July that it could not be dismissed altogether. With the pipeline decision only a few weeks away and the start of negotiations expected before the end of August, the need to grasp the United States position more clearly was becoming inescapable. Accordingly, Basil Robinson, the Canadian pipeline commissioner, went to Washington in the last week of July to hold an exploratory meeting with his American counterpart, Leslie Goldman, one of James Schlesinger's chief advisers. Domestically, the visit carried an element of risk since it could easily be used by the Opposition to accuse the government of prejudging the issue. Once again, the concern of government officials was unfounded. The pipeline issue was proving much easier politically for the government to deal with than it had feared only a few months earlier.

The purpose of the Washington meeting was to establish terms of reference for the upcoming negotiations. It was necessary for both sides to understand in advance the implications of their decisions for any future bargaining. It was not surprising, therefore, that the United States should have taken advantage of the meeting to attack strongly the conditions that the NEB had attached to its pipeline recommendation. The Americans stated flatly that they considered the $200 million socio-economic payment a violation of the Transit Pipeline Treaty and that the resolution of this issue and "any other significant costs or uncertainties associated with the terms and conditions proposed by the National Energy Board will necessarily bear upon the President's decision".[5]

The same message was repeated publicly two weeks later by Cecil Andrus, the US Secretary of the Interior. On August 9, he declared that El Paso

> is still a viable contender because if you add the $200 million for the social economic impact that has been discussed, and you add the construction cost of 300 to 500 million dollars for the Dempster loop, and you add the western leg into the Rocky Mountain areas of America, you're looking at an additional cost in excess of $1 billion. And I think that will probably have a voice in the determination that the President has to make.[6]

The Americans' statements were a classic negotiating gambit: they were designed to weaken Canada's bargaining strategy and elicit concessions prior to the start of negotiations. Even though their very nature hinted that they should not be taken at face value, they nevertheless caused much concern in government circles. The government had expected the United States to be unhappy with the NEB recommendations but not to reject them so categorically. This was a new factor that would have to be weighed very carefully in the pipeline decision.

THE FINAL ACCELERATION

Events were now moving very rapidly. On July 27, the government received an outline of the terms and conditions Berger would propose in his second volume for the construction of a Mackenzie pipeline. Although an Arctic Gas pipeline was now unthinkable in spite of Trudeau's public caution that he "wouldn't eliminate any route", Berger's recommendations would have obvious application to an Alaska Highway pipeline. On July 28, the Environmental Assessment and Review Panel under Dr. Hill submitted its preliminary environmental assessment of the Foothills project. The panel concluded that an Alaska Highway pipeline would be environmentally acceptable but that more study would be needed to mitigate its impact. The panel indicated on the other hand that there was not enough information to evaluate a Dempster pipeline.

The Lysyk report[7] followed on August 2. Upon its appointment in the spring, it had been expected that the Lysyk Commission would constitute a "mini-Berger Inquiry". The expectations that Lysyk would play a determinative role in the pipeline decision had been fuelled by the impact of the Berger report itself. The Lysyk report, however, was anticlimatic. The NEB decision had not only put enormous pressure on the Lysyk Commission to approve the Alcan project but had indeed made it marginal to the decision-making process: the NEB recommendation in favour of the Dawson diversion in particular had made the commission appear almost irrelevant.

Nevertheless, Lysyk and his two colleagues produced an important document. They indicated that the uncertainty remaining over the comparative advantages of the Dawson diversion and the original pipeline route meant that "to choose now a particular pipeline route through the southern Yukon would be to run the risk of selecting the wrong route". Lysyk echoed the NEB recommendation regarding a socio-economic payment and suggested Foothills contribute $200 million to a Yukon Heritage Fund. Because the three commissioners had "no doubt that the achievement of a just settlement and the implementation of the Indian land claim is much more important to the future of the Yukon than any pipeline", the Lysyk Commission recommended that the start of pipeline construction in the Yukon be delayed one year to August 1, 1981. The report made it clear that an even greater delay should be imposed on the Dempster pipeline because it could not "be considered a feasible alternative at this time".

Released so soon after the NEB decision, Hill and Lysyk's conclusions about the viability of a Dempster pipeline underlined tellingly the flimsy nature of the evidence on which Cabinet would have to base its pipeline decision. The conundrum Cabinet faced was obvious: if it approved Alcan, it could not be certain that a Dempster pipeline would ever be built; but if a Dempster pipeline was uncertain, how could Alcan be justified in the national interest?

This was the crux of the question before Parliament as it began the much-awaited pipeline debate on August 4, only two days after the publication of the Lysyk report. Called ostensibly to allow all parties in the House of Commons to have a say in one of the most important decisions Canada would make in the 1970s, the debate's true purpose was entirely different: it was to win support for the government's policy. All through the early spring, the government had resisted repeated Opposition demands for a debate. The simmering dissension within Conservative ranks, however—dissension which the release of the Berger report had exacerbated—helped to convince Liberal strategists that, far from constituting a threat, a debate might represent a unique opportunity to score political points. On May 13, therefore, MacEachen finally surrendered to Opposition pressure and announced that a debate would take place during the summer and that Parliament would be recalled of necessary.

Inevitably, the debate became an elaborate parody, full of grandiloquent statements and empty rhetoric. A Liberal backbencher made the improbable claim that "the building of the pipeline is just as necessary in keeping Canada together as is our handling of the Quebec problem". A statement by Joe Clark was only slightly less extraordinary:

> I want to remind the House that Canada has two basic interests in pipeline policy. Our primary interest, our primary goal, is to deliver Canadian resources to Canadian markets. Our secondary goal is to help our neighbour and ally, the United States, deliver their resources to their markets.

Never before had a Canadian political leader expressed as a goal of this country's pipeline policy, if only a secondary one, the delivery of American resources to their markets.

By the evening of August 4, all three opposition parties in the House of Commons, the Conservatives, the New Democrats and the Créditistes, had endorsed the Alaska Highway pipeline. The Liberals alone maintained the fiction of neutrality, this in spite of their years of vigorous promotion of a northern pipeline in the early 1970s. As the government had anticipated, the Conservatives were unable to reconcile completely their profound differences and could only agree to press for the adoption of the recommendations which the government had received. The Conservatives' position on the pipeline thus became an undigested mix of the conclusions reached by Berger, the NEB, Hill and Lysyk.

As for the NDP, its effectiveness as a critic had been irretrievably crippled back in February when Tommy Douglas had unexpectedly made a speech in support of a modified Alcan proposal. The NDP's qualified endorsement of a large resource project had been designed to refurbish the party's image by presenting it as a responsible advocate of alternatives to government policies. It was a fundamental political error. Not only did it fail in its intended purpose but it reduced the NDP to playing an inconsequential role during the pipeline debate. Ed Broadbent did point out quite correctly that what was at stake was "the entire question of the way in which we choose to treat our northland". Coming after he had set out his reasons "for making an unequivocal commitment in principle to the Alcan route", however, Broadbent's argument was wanting in conviction.

Lacking a coherent set of policies they could call their own, the two major opposition parties were unable to attack the government forcefully. Indeed, since the beginning of the year, they had limited themselves by and large to criticizing the process by which the government was making its decision rather than the substance of the issues themselves. This had allowed the government to disarm the Opposition through the simple expedient of establishing public inquiries in the Yukon and calling a parliamentary debate. These ritualistic concessions not only successfully muted Opposition attacks but also, ironically, served to legitimize the pipeline decision itself. The release of a series of highly visible reports within a short time-span gave the government an appearance of thoroughness and responsiveness all the while it was carefully orchestrating the decision-making process to meet the American timetable.

By the end of the pipeline debate on Friday August 5, Cabinet could justifiably look back with satisfaction on its handling of the pipeline issue. It had succeeded in projecting an image of impartiality in spite of its history of support for a northern pipeline; it had generated broad support for its acceleration of the pipeline decision in spite of the risks this entailed; it had skillfully outflanked the Opposition by yielding on symbolic issues while it maintained a tight rein over the pace and breadth of the decision-making process; it had kept the public trust, in part by enforcing strict secrecy over the work conducted by various government departments. The pipeline decision, which carried so many political risks, was turning out to be extraordinarily easy to make. As a result, the apprehension which had beset Cabinet in late winter was transformed into a mood resembling euphoria.

THE GOVERNMENT DECISION

Cabinet met during the week-end at the Prime Minister's summer residence in the Gatineau Hills just outside Ottawa. It is a paradox that a government had seldom commanded so much information on which to base a decision and yet at the same time was so ill-prepared to reach that decision. To a significant extent, of course, the wealth of information at Cabinet's disposal was illusory. The NEB report, for example, had been completed with a haste that had prejudiced its quality; similarly, the terms of reference given to the environmental and social assessment panels in the Yukon—particularly their deadlines—had made a normal evaluation of the Alaska Highway pipeline impossible. Some facts crucial to an informed decision were therefore missing. More important than the information gaps was the lack of a framework in which Cabinet could weigh the inputs it had received and make trade-offs among the competing interests affected by the pipeline decision. The absence of clearly-defined goals to evaluate the policy alternatives was partly the result of having fragmented the decision-making process into components that had examined different aspects of the same problem in isolation from each other; but it was also the result of not having a well-articulated industrial strategy or energy policy to determine which policy alternative best satisfied national goals. Without these two essential prerequisites to a sound resolution of the pipeline issue, it was inevitable that Cabinet's deliberations would be biased towards short-term economic and political considerations.

The path of least resistance was certainly to approve the NEB recommendation: it gave the United States the land-bridge it wanted to develop its Alaskan reserves; it did not foreclose the possibility of later connection of the Mackenzie Delta; it was less environmentally damaging than a Mackenzie pipeline; it faced less intractable native claims; it would create jobs; in the wake of CAG's demise, it enjoyed wide industry and political support. The alternative would have been to build no pipeline. This was much the tougher course to follow although the growing gas bubble in western Canada was making this into an increasingly viable option: the updated Energy, Mines and Resources forecast of supply and demand showed no Canadian need for frontier gas now until 1990. The uncertainty remaining over many key issues related to the Alcan/Dempster combination, particularly economic and financial ones, constituted another reason for rejecting the pipeline. What additional expenditures, for example, would the Alaska Highway pipeline imply for the government? Nobody knew the answer, and it is not surprising that the absence of this information as well as the lingering suspicion that government financial assistance would eventually be required led Treasury Board analysts to recommend against a pipeline.

Their conclusion, by necessity, was hedged. There were too many unknowns to establish beyond a doubt that a pipeline should not be built. The onus in the pipeline decision, of course, should have rested with those who favoured a pipeline, not those who questioned its desirability. The momentum of the original Cabinet consensus in favour of a northern pipeline, however, had reversed the burden of proof: it was assumed a pipeline would be built unless a compelling case could be made against it. Thus, when Bob Andras, the President of the Treasury Board, presented to Trudeau the result of his staff's work, qualifications and all, he was politely rebuffed.

The no-pipeline option was pre-ordained to lose although until the very end it had its advocates. The thrust of Canadian energy policy was not towards conservation or renewable energy, two logical alternatives to a $10 billion investment, but rather towards encouraging the development of frontier oil and gas. On this point, officials at Energy, Mines and Resources were concerned about the drop in exploration in the Mackenzie Delta and were looking for an incentive to bring the oil industry back. Short of further tax write-offs, this incentive would have to be a pipeline. Did it matter if the pipeline was five or ten years premature? Most Cabinet ministers preferred to build one too early than never. As one senior civil servant who attended the Cabinet deliberations recalls, "there was a thirst for a major project" and that thirst overrode the fine economics of optimal pipeline scheduling.

With no pressing domestic need for frontier gas, the overriding argument in favour of a pipeline became an economic one. The pipeline decision was made against a background of high unemployment, persisting inflation, a falling Canadian dollar, a rising balance of payments deficit and sluggish economic growth. The deputy minister of Finance, Tom Shoyama, insisted that the government had to give the business community a positive signal which would renew their confidence in the economy. The pipeline decision would be that signal. It would represent "the light at the end of the tunnel so far as the unemployment situation is concerned" as John Munro, the Minister of Labour, would later claim hyperbolically.

The Alaska Highway pipeline, in spite of its long-term policy and energy implications, was approved in large measure because it represented a short-term economic palliative. Berger and the NEB had made the tough political decisions. All Cabinet did was to ratify them. It did not want to antagonize the young Carter Administration by denying the land-bridge across Canada that was so obviously in the American interest. Besides, the second Goldfarb poll had shown that Canadians preferred an Alaska Highway to a Mackenzie pipeline and continued to trust the government to make the right decision. The Alaska Highway pipeline had taken everybody off the hook.

At noon on August 8, Trudeau called Carter to inform him of the Cabinet decision and make sure that the US was still interested in discussing the construction of an overland pipeline. Both agreed that the negotiations should begin as quickly as possible in order to reach an agreement in principle "within a very few number of weeks".

That afternoon, the Prime Minister's Office issued an anticlimatic press release[8] which made all the obligatory references to the careful "weighing of the many economic, social and environmental factors involved" and "the appropriate conditions and safeguards" which would be imposed on the Alcan project. Ironically, it had been only three and a half years earlier that Jean Chretien had stated the government's support for a Mackenzie pipeline in almost the same terms. In spite of this, or perhaps because of it, no one ever thought of asking Trudeau at his press conference why the government had endorsed the pipeline.

Although, at the prodding of reporters, Trudeau made a few perfunctory remarks about the toughness of the upcoming talks with the United States and the attendant risk that they might fail, the dominant tone of his press conference was one of unwavering trust in their outcome: "We are going into this with great optimism, we are confident that it will succeed and that it is in the interest of both countries". For good measure, Trudeau added that "we are not going into this in order to take the Americans for a ride". Indeed, when he was asked whether Canada would insist that the United States pay for the indirect socio-economic costs of a pipeline, he replied:

> Well, if I can tell you a secret, we'd like to have the Americans pay as much as possible. But we realize that at some point we have to be reasonable with them. We've got to keep in mind, and I think it's appropriate to remind the Canadian public through you at this press confer-

> ence, that we have pipelines to the United States.... Now, in the North there are special circumstances and we intend to plead them. But we intend being reasonable in this.

Trudeau's readiness to compromise stood, of course, in direct contrast to the unequivocal position the US had staked on the same issue during the preliminary meeting Canadian and American negotiators had held at the end of July. Trudeau's refusal to take a tough bargaining position publicly, as Cecil Andrus would do the next day at his press conference, revealed more than a difference in style between Canada and the United States. It testified to the prior judgements the government had made all along in the development of its northern pipeline policy. The pipeline was assumed to be a desirable end in itself and contrary evidence such as that dealing with adverse social impacts, for example, was not allowed to alter this first assessment.

The statements Trudeau made that day constituted an uncritical endorsement of the Alcan pipeline, and implicitly a Dempster pipeline, which was scarcely moderated by vague allusions to unspecified "conditions and safeguards" which might be later applied to the project. Trudeau's press conference marked the first public expression of official support for the pipeline. A justification of the government's decision in light of the apprehended impacts of the project, a statement about the extent to which the Cabinet accepted the NEB, EARP and Lysyk recommendations, an outline of the conditions that the government would impose on the pipeline, and an explanation of the degree of the government's commitment to the unstudied Dempster pipeline all appeared to be in order but were not offered. Indeed, the reasons which had led the government to its decision were themselves left studiously vague. The Prime Minister's Office press release only made an oblique reference to the government having been influenced by the NEB's conclusion that Canada could start experiencing gas shortages without stating, however, how much weight the Cabinet had attached to that conclusion.

By publicly announcing its support for the pipeline, the government shed its image of detached regulator to assume the role of active promoter. This transformation is of fundamental importance to an understanding of the outcome of the pipeline negotiations. By endorsing the Alcan pipeline before the United States had done so, Canada put itself in the position of seeking to convince the US that an overland pipeline was in the American interest rather than force the US to demonstrate why an Alaska Highway pipeline would be in Canada's interest. By shifting the burden of proof upon itself, Canada entered the pipeline negotiations from a weakened bargaining position. In January, the government had already signed the Transit Pipeline Treaty under which it was precluded from collecting any share of the benefits the US would reap from a cheaper overland pipeline; furthermore, it had no fallback position should the negotiations fail while the US had a proven economic alternative in El Paso; finally, it was supporting a pipeline for reasons that the US could easily exploit.

This underlying weakness was compounded by the fact that Canadian officials were forced during the negotiations to rely on Foothills for some technical information, such as estimates of capital costs. This gave Foothills, of course, an extraordinary opportunity to ensure that the negotiations would succeed. What was particularly alarming about this incestuous arrangement was that the Foothills numbers allowed in some cases for a wide margin of error because of the haste with which they had been calculated. Those concerning the Dempster pipeline in particular had an Alice in Wonderland air about them: the government believed them because it wanted to believe them. It was on the basis of this at-the-time tenuous information that Canada negotiated with the United States an agreement of enormous consequence to the country's future.

THE NEGOTIATING STRATEGIES

The Canadian and American delegations who met in Ottawa in mid-August to begin the pipeline negotiations offered an interesting study in contrast. The American team was young, its average age around thirty. Its leader, Les Goldman, was only 32. An ambitious Democrat who had started his career in Washington as an aide to Senator Adlai Stevenson Jr. before becoming assistant to Dr. Schlesinger, Goldman hoped to establish his reputation by driving a hard bargain with Canada. The average age of the Canadian delegation, by comparison, was about 45. As a group, its restraint accentuated the verve of the Americans. Basil Robinson, who headed the Canadian team, was 58. He was approaching the end of a long and successful career in External Affairs.

The age discrepancy helps to explain perhaps the difference in negotiating approaches between the two countries. The United States began the talks by announcing a minimal position from which it would not budge. Canada, on the other hand, was prepared to negotiate everything. The American delegation had come armed with elaborate computer models which allowed it to calculate almost instantly the result of any change in assumptions. The Canadian delegation did not rely on such electronic wizardry, believing that so many of the numbers on which the negotiations were based approached the mythical that such precision was unnecessary.

More important than the difference in style between Canadian and American officials were the diverging perspectives with which each entered the negotiations. The attitudes of the Canadian negotiators had been shaped to a large measure by almost ten years of government policy towards the northern pipeline. Several members of Canada's negotiating team, most prominently among them Basil Robinson who had served as deputy minister of Indian and Northern Affairs between 1970 and 1974, had indeed been personally responsible for the development and implementation of that policy. As such, they were not inclined to ask soul-searching questions about the desirability or impact of building a northern pipeline. On the contrary, they tended to espouse the view attributed to a Cabinet minister by the *Financial Post* that "we weren't going to take the Americans for every cent we could on this pipeline, for it would have been foolish to push them to the wall on this project and face retaliation later".[9] This pusillanimity led Canada to relinquish an immense bargaining advantage for nothing more than the future goodwill of the United States.

The objectives of the Canadian negotiators reflected this conciliatory approach. They were modest and largely of secondary importance: the supply of gas to the Yukon, the optimization of the pipeline's Canadian content, the recovery of the project's socio-economic costs. Even the achievement of these limited goals was incomplete. The optimization of the pipeline's Canadian content will depend on the interpretation of Article 7 of the Pipeline Agreement which states: "Each Government will endeavor to ensure that the supply of goods and services to the pipeline project will be on generally competitive terms". The recovery of the pipeline's social costs was at best an illusive goal in the absence of firm estimates of those costs. The choice of a pipeline route that would not inhibit the timely development of the Mackenzie Delta reserves represented a questionable insurance policy, given the uncertainty clouding the viability of a Dempster pipeline.

If the Canadian negotiators limited themselves to achieving tactical gains, the Americans on the other hand sought to realize strategic objectives. The chief American negotiator was James Schlesinger, Carter's energy advisor. Educated at Harvard, Schlesinger had been director of strategic studies for the Rand Corporation before serving in various capacities in the Nixon Administration, including Director of the Central Intelligence Agency and Secretary of Defense. Immediately before joining Carter's staff, he was a visiting scholar at Johns Hopkins University's School of Advanced International Studies.

Better than most, Schlesinger understood the geopolitical implications of building a 4,800-mile pipeline from one of the world's great oil and gas fields to consuming centers in the United States. To the US, the pipeline was more than a conduit for the 26 trillion cubic feet of gas at Prudhoe Bay. The pipeline guaranteed the security of existing Canadian exports by providing Canada access to its own reserves in the Mackenzie Delta; these exports were greater than the pipeline's planned daily throughput. More importantly, the pipeline implied new Canadian exports, through the National Energy Board's pre-building proposal. An Alaska Highway pipeline would also create a major new North American energy corridor which could one day accommodate an increased flow of Alaskan gas—the potential for discoveries in northern Alaska remains promising—and perhaps an oil pipeline as well. Foothills indeed had already begun studying the construction of an oil line parallel to the gas line and would make a formal application towards it in 1979 (see Chapter Ten).

In order to achieve these greater objectives, Schlesinger was quite willing to compromise on relatively minor issues such as pipeline alignment and property taxes.

THE PIPELINE NEGOTIATIONS

The pipeline negotiations began on Wednesday morning, August 17, in the Langevin Block, the building occupied by the Prime Minister's Office. The purpose of this first meeting was to clarify the specific points of disagreement between Canada and the United States before the real bargaining that was to get under way the following week. Here is what happened.

WEDNESDAY, AUGUST 17: Both sides present their positions. Canada wants the pipeline routed further north to provide possible future access to the gas reserves in the Mackenzie Delta; Canada is also asking that the US cover the indirect socio-economic costs of the project; they are estimated at $200 million. The American negotiators balk at both requests. They insist that the pipeline follow its original route along the Alaska Highway. They strongly urge that the pipeline company loan the Canadian government the $200 million as an alternative to a compensation fund paid for by the American gas consumer. The Americans remind their Canadian counterparts that if Canada imposes too many conditions on an Alaska Highway pipeline, the United States will approve instead the "all-American" El Paso proposal. The talks last nine hours.

At the end of the day, Robinson describes the meeting as having been "solid and very satisfactory". Goldman says the talks were "fruitful".

TUESDAY, AUGUST 23: The Canadian negotiating team lands at Andrews Air Force Base near Washington, where the second round of negotiations is to take place. The two sides make considerable progress. The US proposes to pay for part of the costs of a Dempster spur between Whitehorse and Dawson City—which would meet the Canadian objective of rerouting the pipeline closer to the Mackenzie Delta—in return for keeping the pipeline along the Alaska Highway. The possibility of having the pipeline company prepay part of its property taxes in the Yukon to cover its indirect socio-economic costs is discussed further.

Canada and the United States now seem close to resolving their differences. All the divisive issues have been defined and preliminary compromises identified. Unless the negotiations break down unexpectedly, an agreement should be reached by September 8 when Prime Minister Trudeau will be in Washington to witness the signing of the new Panama Canal Treaty. It is time for the political representatives of both countries to take over.

WEDNESDAY, AUGUST 24: White House Press Secretary Jody Powell announces that President Carter will delay issuing his decision on the pipeline until Congress reconvenes on September 7. Under the Alaska Natural Gas Transportation Act, Carter was to have made his decision by September 1 although he had the option of delaying it by ninety days.

THURSDAY, AUGUST 25: Alaska Senator Ted Stevens, a strong El Paso supporter, meets Carter for half an hour to share his misgivings over transshipping American gas across Canadian territory. After his meeting, Stevens claims that El Paso is "still very much a viable option". The United States is not yet conceding publicly that it much prefers the overland pipeline through Canada.

FRIDAY, AUGUST 26: Allan MacEachen, the President of the Privy Council and the Canadian minister responsible for the pipeline, meets in Washington with James Schlesinger, the future American Secretary of Energy. The session lasts five and a half hours but ends in deadlock. MacEachen and Schlesinger cannot agree to a cost-sharing formula for the Dempster spur, and MacEachen returns to Ottawa with new American proposals. The American negotiators had hoped that the talks would wind up the following week. They are clearly disappointed. One of them warns: "If progress at the political level is not made next week, we are in real trouble". Is Canada asking for too much?

MONDAY, AUGUST 29: Trudeau and Carter talk to each other over the phone. They are both unhappy at the slow pace of the negotiations. They agree, therefore, to instruct their respective teams to be less intransigent. The American negotiators are angered at this interference. They had felt that they were scoring important gains.

WEDNESDAY, AUGUST 31: Carter convenes a meeting of his top advisers, including Schlesinger, Vice-President Walter Mondale and Secretary of the Treasury Michael Blumenthal. Also in attendance are representatives of the Office of Management and Budget and the White House Domestic Council. They discuss the two pipeline proposals and the options the United States faces. They agree that the Alaska Highway pipeline represents the much superior alternative and that it is this project which must be built. Schlesinger is accordingly told not to return from Ottawa, where the next round of talks is taking place, without an agreement. However, in case another deadlock should occur, Carter drafts a letter to both the President of the Senate and the Speaker of the House of Representatives announcing that he would delay issuing his decision yet again to September 15.

The same day, the Canadian Cabinet meets for two hours to discuss negotiating strategy.

THURSDAY, SEPTEMBER 1: MacEachen and Schlesinger meet in the morning and have lunch together at External Affairs. The meeting drags on longer than expected and lasts five hours. Although both sides had stayed in contact by phone after Washington to prepare for this session, the talks bog down once again. Canada is no longer arguing that the pipeline should be rerouted north to Dawson and is asking the United States instead to pay for the Dempster spur. The US wants to make such a payment conditional upon Canada's ability to control cost overruns on the pipeline. The US is also looking for an assurance that Canada will not raise property taxes once the pipeline is approved.

Officials for both sides work late into the night to try to resolve the substantive problems that still divide the two countries. Schlesinger had hoped to return to Washington that night but just in case had brought an extra shirt with him.

FRIDAY, SEPTEMBER 2: MacEachen spends the morning closeted with the members of the Cabinet ad hoc committee on the pipeline. Schlesinger, an amateur ornithologist, goes bird-watching.

The two men meet again in the afternoon. They ratify the agreement their officials had reached the night before about property taxes. They also settle the last outstanding issue, the cost-sharing formula for the Dempster spur. Although the main principles of an agreement have now been resolved, the language that would determine its political acceptability to both sides provides a last stumbling block. Finally, after a gruelling seven hours, that too is set. After toasting their success with champagne, the tired MacEachen and Schlesinger emerge from the negotiating room at a quarter to nine and descend the wide staircase of the Langevin Block to announce to the waiting crowd of reporters that Canada and the United States have tentatively agreed to the construction of the Alaska Highway pipeline.

TUESDAY, SEPTEMBER 20: The Agreement between Canada and the United States of America on Principles Applicable to a Northern Natural Gas Pipeline is signed in Ottawa.

TUESDAY, NOVEMBER 8: President Carter signs Congressional Joint Resolution 621 on the Alaska Natural Gas Transportation System into law. This being an important occasion, there is an opportunity for a few speeches:

> CARTER. This joint resolution to approve the construction of the major natural gas pipeline from Alaska down through Canada to our country is a very important demonstration of our nation's commitment to provide adequate energy supplies in the future....
>
> ... I'm particularly glad that the ambassador for Canada is here. I

hope that he will relay directly to Prime Minister Trudeau my deep gratitude at the co-operative attitude that has been taken by the Canadians in working with us on this project....

SCHLESINGER. I think what the President has said underscores the close relationships that we should maintain with Canada in regard to what are common problems. This will help restore an era of good feelings between the two countries and, that this project, large as it is, is a splendid symbol of that cooperation....

SENATOR STEVENS. Mr. President, I think this is just the first of a series of transportation systems to bring Alaska's resources to what we call the South 48. We have a lot more oil and gas and we'll hopefully get on those other areas, too, soon. So, I congratulate you....

CARTER. Although we don't look on Canada as coming under the purview of the Foreign Relations Committee, Frank—because they are so much of a part of our country—would you like to say just a word?

SENATOR CHURCH. Thank you Mr. President. I think the route that's been chosen is the correct one.... I think this bill will serve the country well.

CARTER. Jim? [sic]

McMILLIAN. It's my pleasure. This is my project. I want to thank you for choosing it, the confidence you had in us. We're going to uphold that confidence of both yourself and the Congress and do what we said to bring this energy source to you as quickly and reasonably as we can.

CARTER. We worked very closely with Jim, in preparing this, and I want to thank you for it.

The transcript did not record the reaction of the Canadian ambassador, Peter Towe, to Carter's remark that Canada was so much of a part of the United States.

THE RESULTS

The Pipeline Agreement or "The Agreement between Canada and the United States of America on Principles Applicable to a Northern Natural Gas Pipeline", was released with much fanfare in Canada. The government felt it had scored significant gains during the negotiations. Indeed, the fact sheet accompanying a statement issued by MacEachen on September 9 promised a veritable cornucopia of benefits: the creation of 100,000 man-years of employment, the "injection of a substantial boost to the economy" as a result of expenditures reaching perhaps as high as $4 billion, property tax revenue in the Yukon of over $1 billion, an improvement in Canada's balance of payments, the delivery of gas to Yukon communities, a stimulus to petroleum exploration in the western Arctic and transportation savings on the future delivery of Mackenzie Delta gas of $1 billion. This was an impressive achievement for only seventeen days of negotiations!

A more dispassionate assessment of the Pipeline Agreement yields sharply divergent results. For Canada, the most important elements of the agreement are those dealing with the pipeline route, the provisions for the possible future delivery of Mackenzie Delta gas and the level of property taxes in the Yukon. What does the agreement stipulate in each of these areas?

Routing: The National Energy Board's recommendation that the Alcan pipeline be diverted north to Dawson would have added 119.9 miles to the pipeline route while increasing its costs by an estimated $542.7 million. Since it is cheaper to built a 34-inch pipeline (the proposed diameter of a Dempster line) than a 48-inch line, the United States argued during the negotiations that it would be more economic to extend the Dempster pipeline from Dawson to Whitehorse than reroute the main line itself. The difference in capital costs between these alternatives is almost $100 million. Thus, it was to the advantage of the US to agree to pay for a portion and, indeed the totality, of the costs of the Dempster spur to Dawson in order to keep the Alaska Highway route for the transportation of Prudhoe Bay gas. Indeed, as James Schlesinger noted, "It is in the long-run interest of US consumers to assist Canada in developing"[10] their Mackenzie Delta reserves. The security of gas supply the US purchased from Canada by agreeing to share the costs of the Dempster spur came cheaply.

The sliding scale formula which covers the cost-sharing clause of the Pipeline Agreement regarding the Dempster spur provides the US with another significant benefit. As the American share of the costs of the Dempster spur to Dawson is to decline in direct proportion to cost overruns on the main line in excess of 35%, this clause, in Schlesinger's words, "... creates a formidable incentive for Canada to build the main line as efficiently as possible, and decrease the overall cost of service to US consumers to the maximum extent". It is a moot point whether this formula will not also inhibit Canada in imposing conditions on the pipeline's construction (e.g., environmental standards) which would drive costs upwards. The United States may thus get a pipeline which is not only environmentally superior from their point of view to what its alternatives (Arctic Gas and El Paso) would have implied but one moreover whose ultimate cost may not cover fully the environmental damage it will cause in Canada.

Canada too stands to gain from the retention of the original pipeline route—if a Dempster pipeline is built and if cost overruns on the Alaska

Highway pipeline are kept to 35%. The United States, it is interesting to note, expected overruns to amount to 40% at the time the Pipeline Agreement was negotiated.

Canada and the United States may also jointly benefit from the decision to increase the capacity of the pipeline south of Whitehorse. Assuming, obviously, that this capacity will be utilized, the higher gas throughput will result in a more efficient pipeline and, hence, lower transportation costs. The practice by pipeline companies of recovering a disproportionate share of capital costs in the early years of operation (in financial jargon, the tariff is front-end loaded) implies that in this case American consumers will pay for the bulk of the costs associated with the additional capacity as the pipeline would deliver only Alaskan gas initially. This increased capacity, of course, is also available for any future exports of Canadian gas.

The sections of the agreement regarding the pipeline route, the cost-sharing arrangements and the line's increased capacity led the Canadian government to claim that, in the event that the US paid for the whole Dempster spur, "... the resulting savings would represent a reduction of approximately $1 billion in transportation costs for the existing reserves of 5.2 trillion cubic feet (tcf) already discovered in the Delta as compared to the Dawson routing proposed by the NEB".[11] This claim, like many others made by the Canadian government at the conclusion of the negotiations, is highly misleading. A more meaningful estimate of the present value of this benefit in 1977 would be $200 million, assuming the Dempster pipeline were built by 1990.[12]

As it is, this number probably overstates the value of this benefit as it assumes that the extra pipeline capacity installed south of Whitehorse will be efficiently utilized. The transportation savings postulated by Canada and the United States will be realized only as the pipeline approaches its optimal throughput of 3.6 billion cubic feet a day (bcfd). Prudhoe Bay, however, will deliver only 2.0 bcfd, at least during the first few years of pipeline operation; present proven reserves in the Mackenzie Delta can only supply .7 bcfd. Thus, unless gas production at Prudhoe Bay is increased significantly—which would imply increasing the Alcan pipeline's capacity north of Whitehorse—or large economic discoveries are made in the Delta (an additional 3.5 tcf would be needed to reach a production level of 1.2 bcfd), the pipeline will operate below its rated capacity south of Whitehorse and the claimed transportation savings will not be realized fully.

Neither of these conditions seems very likely: an increase in gas production at Prudhoe Bay could reduce the ultimate recovery of oil by lowering prematurely the pressure in the Prudhoe Bay reservoir; it is unlikely major discoveries will be made in the Delta soon because exploration there has virtually stopped. Although prospects in the Beaufort Sea are more encouraging, the high costs of exploration and development may not make the delivery of gas through a Dempster pipeline economic for several years to come.

It is also difficult to judge today whether a Dempster pipeline will constitute the most attractive energy option available to Canada in the late 1980s or early 1990s. A significant discovery in the Arctic archipelago could, for instance, postpone the development of the Mackenzie Delta and perhaps even preclude it together. Conversely a large strike in the Beaufort Sea could accelerate the development of this frontier region although not necessarily by a Dempster pipeline. If the reserves are large enough, a Mackenzie pipeline may be economically preferable to a Dempster pipeline. It is also conceivable that this gas would find its way to market by tanker. None of these alternatives is contemplated under the Pipeline Agreement. One must conclude therefore that the government did not consider any of them in its negotiations with the United States and has made a policy commitment to only one method of developing frontier gas. This commitment, like so many similar ones in the past, seems to have been made without adequately weighing other options.

The $1 billion saving proudly claimed by the government is at this juncture therefore largely speculative if not indeed illusory. If the assumptions that underlie it are examined, it loses much if not all of its value.

Taxation: Under the Yukon Property Tax, the territorial government will collect $30 million annually, adjusted for inflation, when the pipeline begins operations, and smaller payments during the pipeline's construction. Although not part of the Pipeline Agreement itself, the prepayment by Foothills of up to $200 million in taxes to cover the socio-economic costs of the project was described as an important advantage resulting from the negotiations. In its fact sheet, the government claims that "even after amortization of the company's advance payment, the proposed tax system would yield more than $1 billion over the twenty-five year economic life of the system if annual inflation averaged 5%". Once again, this number is highly misleading. The present value of the Yukon Property Tax in 1977 was closer to $250 million.[13]

Will it be adequate to cover the socio-economic costs of the project? The costs mentioned in the NEB and Lysyk reports include not only the incremental public expenditures generated by the project for roads, utilities, health services, law enforcement, environmental monitoring, administration, etc., but also some effects which may be very difficult to quantify such as labour shortages, a possible reduction in the tourist trade, the congestion of transportation facilities (e.g., the Alaska Highway), the deferment of certain industrial projects such as the opening of mines and inflation. The potential costs of some social impacts, such as a probable increase in alcohol and drug abuse or the disruption of hunting and trapping activities or a higher incidence of stress, however, cannot be calculated.

As it approached the pipeline negotiations, the government did not know what additional costs it would have to bear as a result of the construction of an Alaska Highway pipeline. To obtain an approximation of these costs, the

Department of Indian and Northern Affairs was forced to apply to the Yukon estimates it had previously made for the Mackenzie Valley. These rough calculations indicated that the federal and Yukon governments could expect to spend about $155 million for the period 1978 to 1981 as a direct result of the pipeline's construction. The addition of a Dempster pipeline was expected to push these costs up to $207 million.

Given its inability to estimate the full range of costs associated with a pipeline, it was important that in its negotiations with the United States the government not tie itself to an inflexible revenue-raising scheme which would prevent it, for example, from increasing taxes should the NEB or Lysyk proposals prove insufficient to cover the pipeline's socio-economic impact. This, however, it failed to do. At the Americans' insistence, Canada dropped the concept of a socio-economic compensation payment in return for a higher rate of property taxation on the Yukon section of the pipeline. This new rate, it must be pointed out, merely brings the Yukon Property Tax in line with the taxes the State of Alaska is already charging to the Alyeska oil pipeline and will collect from Alcan. More importantly, the Yukon Property Tax sets a comprehensive ceiling on the taxation that the government can levy on the pipeline.

The United States, therefore, achieved their twin objectives of eliminating the politically unpalatable compensation fund and limiting their future tax liability in Canada at a cost which, in the words of James Schlesinger, "... represents only a modest increase over the level of taxes included in the original cost of services estimates for Alcan."

Although it is true that the NEB's recommendation in favour of a compensation payment raised difficult problems of application (what projects should cover their social costs?) and definition (what costs should be included?), this particular section of the agreement raises an important question as well: should Canada pay for even a portion of the social costs of a pipeline designed fundamentally to service American natural gas demand?

When it dropped the concept of a compensation payment, the government, for political reasons, adopted the imaginative artifice of having Foothills prepay a portion of its property taxes, thereby creating the impression that the pipeline company was going to cover its socio-economic costs after all. This illusion was reinforced by fixing $200 million as an upper limit on this prepayment, the same figure which both the NEB and Lysyk Commission had referred to in their reports. This sum, of course, will have to be repaid with interest and therefore does not represent a benefit to the Yukon or Canada.[14]

BENEFITS TO THE UNITED STATES

An analysis of the Pipeline Agreement would not be complete without a brief review of the benefits which the United States stands to gain from it.

Two of these have already been mentioned: a southern rather than a northern route in the Yukon and a ceiling on the pipeline's tax liability. Another important benefit is timing. Article 2(c) of the agreement states that

> Both Governments will take measures necessary to facilitate the expeditious and efficient construction of the Pipeline, consistent with the respective regulatory requirements of each country.

The agreement indeed provides a timetable specifying the start of both main line pipe laying in the Yukon (January 1, 1981) and operation (January 1, 1983), dates which have now receded as a result of the delays the pipeline suffered in 1978 and 1979. Canada's agreement to these deadlines was an important concession to the United States, given the lack of a land claim settlement and the amount of work necessary to gauge the pipeline's environmental impact. There was no reciprocal obligation upon the US to meet these deadlines.

The most important benefit the United States will derive from the agreement is unquestionably the savings that will accrue to American consumers from the construction of an overland pipeline. Alcan's superiority over El Paso in transportation costs was estimated at $.17 per thousand cubic feet by the White House task force. Over the first twenty years of pipeline operation, this difference yields a $6 billion saving to the United States. But that already considerable figure may be low. As already noted, the Federal Power Commission calculated Alcan's advantage over El Paso at $.30 per thousand cubic feet (mcf). The group of American pipeline companies that will build the eastern leg of the Alcan system placed the difference at $.45/mcf.[15] Should it be right, the aggregate transportation savings to the United States over twenty years would amount not to $6 billion but to $15.8 billion. These rents, generated by the use of Canada as a land-bridge to carry an American resource from one part of the United States to another, will be appropriated exclusively by the US.

It is instructive to contrast the benefits both countries will collect under the Pipeline Agreement from the construction of an overland pipeline. The last qualification is an important one as it excludes the economic benefits which the US will gain from receiving the gas itself, benefits which El Paso could have supplied.[16] The utilization of this country as a corridor to deliver American gas will generate four flows of revenues: those stemming from the construction and operation of the pipeline in Canada; the Yukon Property Tax; the savings on the future transportation of Delta gas via a Dempster route; and the rents created by the cheaper overland route.

The NEB estimated the present value of the first flow at $1.68 billion; although the Yukon Property Tax has a gross present value of $250 million, it is not clear whether it will yield any net benefits; the value of the transportation savings on Mackenzie Delta gas is entirely dependent on whether and when a Dempster pipeline is built and is therefore uncertain; the value of the rents from the cheaper route using the White House's conservative $6 billion estimate discounted to the present at 5% annually is over $1.5 billion. Although Canada will collect the first three revenue flows, it will not collect the fourth. Assuming that the Yukon Property Tax just covers the socio-economic costs of the pipeline and that a Dempster lateral is not built, the latter not being an unreasonable expectation at this time, it is possible that Canada will reap only half of the economic benefits resulting from the pipeline's construction through this country. It is important to reiterate that this simple calculation does not take into account the enormous benefits the US will gain from receiving Alaskan gas.

The Americans got everything they wanted from the negotiations: an overland route, an expeditious construction schedule and well-defined limits on every aspect of potential liability. In the long run, these gains are likely to be surpassed by the benefits flowing from a greater degree of Canadian-American co-operation in energy policy, an evolution to which the Pipeline Agreement added a powerful impetus. Among the benefits Carter listed in his report to Congress following the pipeline negotiations were the enhanced security in present Canadian gas exports, the probability of new exports, the stimulation of the Canadian gas industry and the opportunity for further collaboration on a variety of other energy issues such as oil exchanges, pipelines and strategic oil reserves. Taken together, these developments amount to a *de facto* continentalism.

CHAPTER NINE

THE PHANTOM PIPELINE

The Pipeline Agreement between Canada and the United States represented an extraordinary triumph for Foothills and Northwest. Their Alaska Highway pipeline had been conceived, designed, modified and approved in record time, defeating overwhelming odds in the process. In the euphoria that lingered after the successful completion of the pipeline negotiations, Blair could be forgiven for boasting that "business has never been so great." But, if for Canada and the US the Pipeline Agreement was the culmination of their policy efforts regarding the transportation of northern gas, for Northwest and Foothills it was only the end of the beginning. The herculean tasks of financing and building the line still lay ahead. These would soon prove as daunting as the battle against Arctic Gas and El Paso had been.

Canada and the US had chosen the Alaska Highway pipeline over its competitors essentially because they had deemed it the least undesirable of the three alternatives to carry Prudhoe Bay gas. They had also made this choice on the basis of incomplete information and under great time pressure. It was inevitable then that a critical re-examination of the pipeline after the exhilaration surrounding the Pipeline Agreement had waned would reveal many unanswered questions about its viability. Those related to the marketability of Prudhoe Bay gas and therefore the financing of the line were the most disturbing: would there really be a market for Prudhoe Bay gas when the pipeline would begin operations? And if there was, could the pipeline be financed without government guarantees?

These questions re-emerged soon after the signing of the Pipeline Agreement in the protracted congressional debate over the de-regulation of American natural gas prices. The bill over which Congress deliberated for eighteen fractious months between April 1977 and October 1978 was part of the ambitious energy legislation Carter had proposed as his first major initiative after taking office. The section of the legislation dealing with natural gas prices was essential to the construction of the Alaska Highway pipeline for two reasons. First, it set a well-head price for Alaskan gas. Because Prudhoe Bay gas was "new" gas that had never moved in interstate commerce, the Federal Power Commission, which until recently set interstate prices, had never determined what would be its fair price. The FPC could have held public hearings to establish that price but this would likely have been a time-consuming process. This is why the Carter Administration, hoping to save time, asked Congress to approve a price. Without one, Prudhoe Bay gas could not be bought or sold and the Alaska Highway pipeline could therefore not be built.

The natural gas bill was just as important to Northwest for a second reason: it allowed the expensive Prudhoe Bay gas to be "rolled in" or blended with cheaper existing supplies. The costs of bringing Alaskan gas to market were so high that unless they were averaged with those of "lower 48" sources, Prudhoe Bay gas would not be marketable. From an economic standpoint, the fact that Prudhoe Bay gas would have to be sold below cost immediately raised the question of whether the pipeline was premature. If consumers were unwilling to pay the high Alaskan prices, did it not indicate that cheaper energy supplies were available?

Because the answer to that question was almost certainly yes, Northwest and Foothills had an immense vested interest in making sure that Congress passed at least the two pricing provisions related to Alaskan gas. Without them, prospective purchasers of Alaskan gas could not negotiate contracts with Prudhoe Bay producers; without purchase contracts, Northwest and Foothills could not arrange to finance the pipeline. Without a resolution of the pricing question, not only could there be no financing, but there was little incentive for either Northwest or Foothills to continue doing expensive engineering design work on the pipeline. Since there was no slack in their timetable of pre-construction activities, it was inevitable that the pipeline would be delayed the longer Congress debated the gas bill.

THE NATURAL GAS POLICY ACT OF 1978

In the vigorous debate over the rate of increase in American gas prices, however, the pipeline loomed very small. There were much greater stakes than a pipeline, tens of billions of dollars, depending on how quickly natural gas prices were allowed to rise. The oil and gas industry and producing states, such as Louisiana and Texas, argued for a steep increase in prices to stimulate exploration. They pointed to the steady decline in reserves and to growing shortages as evidence that American gas prices—which had been regulated since 1954—should be allowed to rise freely with market forces. Consumer groups and states, on the other hand, advocated just as strongly the continuation of price controls on the premise that de-regulation would not uncover new reserves and would only lead to windfall profits for the oil industry. The resulting stalemate paralyzed progress on the gas bill for a year and a half and was almost fatal to the Alaska Highway pipeline on three separate occasions.

In the early fall of 1977, the House of Representatives approved a watered down version of the natural gas bill which would have kept prices low. In October, the Senate, however, passed a version of the bill which would have de-regulated prices completely after two years. As is usual in a similar impasse, the House and Senate appointed a Joint Conference Committee to attempt to bridge their differences. The conferees haggled for five months before achieving a tentative agreement in May 1978. It was an enormously complex proposal which incorporated all the worst features of a compromise. The reconciliation of diametrically opposite viewpoints and the accommodation of numerous parochial interests had yielded an improbable agreement which featured twelve, seventeen or twenty-six categories of gas prices, depending on one's interpretation of the bill. As it was, this unwieldy compromise was accepted by the House conferees only by the narrowest of margins. The difference of one vote would have killed the compromise, imperilled the gas bill and put the pipeline in limbo.

This was an outcome that the Carter Administration simply could not afford. Having declared the energy crisis "the moral equivalent of war", Carter had staked his political prestige on the enactment of his energy legislation. The White House, therefore, spared no efforts in trying to influence votes. New York Democrats were told for example that the passage of a bill providing aid to the financially beleaguered New York City would be made much more difficult if they did not support the natural gas compromise.

The closeness of the House conference committee vote—thirteen to twelve—foreshadowed the many difficulties that still lay ahead for the natural gas bill. The next step was to translate the compromise into legislative language. The result, released in July 1978, was a 171-page document which, inevitably, did not correspond with what some conferees remembered having signed two months earlier. Once more, the fate of the bill hung in the balance as these conferees hesitated to ratify the compromise. Once more, the White House resorted to arm-twisting. Republican Senator James McClure of Idaho signed the conference report only after Schlesinger promised administration support for an expanded research effort on the breeder reactor with most of the money to be spent in Idaho. The Speaker of the House, "Tip" O'Neill, who vigorously lobbied recalcitrant congressmen, confessed later that this had been "the toughest thing I have ever had to face. I hope I will never have to do it again." [1]

Carter himself set the tone for his administration's efforts in pushing the gas bill and the rest of his energy package through Congress when he told a group of visiting state governors that

> The entire world is looking at our government to see whether we have the national will to deal with this difficult challenge. If this legislation is

> not enacted, it will have a devastating effect on our national image, the value of the dollar, our balance of trade and inflation.

Believing that action spoke more loudly than words, Carter joined the fray personally in lobbying congressmen, even in the midst of the Middle East summit at Camp David with President Sadat and Prime Minister Begin. Carter also enlisted the support of large corporations for his energy legislation. The day he lectured the state governors, he called a conclave of 125 business leaders from across the US to deliver the same message. The reaction of one of them captured their ambivalent response. "The bill may be an abomination but it's the only abomination in town."[2] As the final showdown on the floors of both the Senate and the House approached, the administration's message became more shrill: congressmen were told that if they voted against the gas bill and gas shortages materialized in a few years because the Alaska Highway pipeline had not been built, they would have to bear the blame—and the political consequences.

Still the opposition to the bill remained strong. An unlikely alliance of left wing and right wing senators—the former thinking that the bill went too far and the latter not far enough—vowed to filibuster the bill when it reached the floor of the Senate. Time was now becoming critical. If the bill was not passed by both houses before Congress rose in October for the mid-term elections, it would die on the order paper. The bill would then have to be reintroduced and debated all over again. In the alternative, the Federal Energy Regulatory Commission (FERC)—the FPC's successor—could be asked to set the price of Alaskan gas. This, however, would necessitate public hearings, which might well last a year. In either case, the pipeline would be delayed again, its costs would escalate and the ability of its sponsors to finance it would be reduced, if not precluded altogether.

In mid-August 1978, the bill was finally reintroduced in the Senate. A motion to send it back to committee was defeated with the help of undecided senators who were swayed at the last minute by Carter's success in establishing a framework for peace in the Middle East during the Camp David summit. The Senate passed the bill on September 27 and sent it to the House.

To reduce its opposition in the lower house, the gas bill was tied to other less controversial parts of the energy package. On October 13, in a last attempt to defeat it, opponents of de-regulation tried to separate the gas bill from the rest of the energy legislation. If they had succeeded, the bill would have died and, with it, plans to build the pipeline in the early 1980s. They lost by one vote, 207 to 206. Two days later, in the early hours of Sunday morning, October 15, 1978, the House passed the energy legislation moments before it recessed for the elections.

THE US GAS BUBBLE

The pipeline had survived—but just barely. Its construction had been delayed by nine months, to the fall of 1983, since no one wanted to sign a contract for Alaskan gas until its well-head price and the conditions of its sale were known. Both Northwest and Foothills had reduced their level of spending on preconstruction engineering design. Costs had moved upward as a result of the pipeline's postponement and now stood at over $12 billion. Of greater concern to Northwest was the fact that the pipeline had lost much of its momentum. The dubious economic foundation of the entire project—made evident in its need to roll in Prudhoe Bay gas—had led critics of Carter's energy policy proposals to ask during the congressional gas debate why the pipeline should be built when the price of the gas it carried would exceed its market value. The Carter Administration had been able to cajole reticent congressmen into supporting roll-in pricing by arguing that the pipeline could not be privately financed otherwise and that the pipeline was desperately needed to ensure the security of American energy supplies. The emergence of a gas bubble in the United States in 1978 was therefore enormously embarrassing to the Carter Administration. A few months earlier, it had pronounced the worsening gas situation the United States' most acute energy problem. Now that there was a surplus, many congressmen began to question the competence of the President's energy advisers, including Schlesinger.

The American gas bubble, paradoxically, had its roots in the pervasive shortages the United States had suffered since 1973. Industrial gas consumers, whom the Federal Power Commission had classified as low priority users since many of them had the ability to switch to other fuels during emergencies, had had to bear the brunt of these shortages. After the disastrous winter of 1977, many large plants did not revert back to natural gas but continued burning oil instead. Depressed prices for industrial grades of oil encouraged other companies to switch to oil. Industrial gas demand declined, oil imports rose and a domestic gas glut was created. Meanwhile, the drilling boom taking place at the same time was increasing supply even before the passage of the natural gas bill. There was yet a second reason for the gas bubble. The natural gas bill allowed the surplus of intrastate gas that had developed over the years (because intrastate gas prices were not regulated) to move into the interstate market, resulting in a sudden surge in supply.

The first indication of the metamorphosis in the gas outlook was that none of the crippling shortages that had plagued the United States in 1977 were repeated in 1978 although the winter had been almost as cold. In 1978, even Northwest, whose quest for new gas supplies had led it to sponsor the Alaska Highway pipeline, was forced to reduce its imports of Canadian gas because it could not sell all the gas it had under contract.

To many critics of the Carter Administration, the sudden emergence of a gas glut was evidence of the lack of direction in American energy policy. The administration's response to the gas surplus reinforced this belief. In November 1978, Schlesinger announced that henceforth the government would ask utilities to continue using gas, reversing the administration's longstanding commitment—embodied in the Natural Gas Policy Act for which it had lobbied so vigorously—that they be made to convert to coal. Schlesinger's explanation—"We wish to burn all the gas that we can in the short term to hold down oil imports"[3]—was a logical one given the tightening international oil supply situation as a result of the Iranian crisis, but it nevertheless lost the administration much credibility at a time when that credibility was becoming indispensable to the progress of the Alaska Highway pipeline. The administration's dire warnings of worsening shortages if Alaskan gas was not developed quickly and its strong-arm tactics on the pipeline's behalf during the natural gas debate were now backfiring.

Experts remain divided on the duration of the American gas bubble, although most agree that it will last at least three or four years. If Canada's experience is any indication, it may be longer-lived as the gradual de-regulation in natural gas prices encourages the development of previously uneconomic reserves. This, of course, is what the White House Pipeline Task Force had predicted in its report to Carter in July 1977 (See Chapter Seven).

THE CANADIAN GAS SURPLUS

If the American gas bubble had provided ammunition to the opponents of de-regulation during the congressional debate over gas prices, the rising Canadian surplus becoming evident at the time and the news of large Mexican discoveries had led them to question the need for the Alaska Highway pipeline altogether: why build a $12 billion pipeline, they asked, when the United States could import gas more cheaply from Mexico and Canada? This was an argument which would lead the Carter Administration to adopt a policy of rejecting any new imports that did not contribute directly to the Alaska Highway pipeline's construction (i.e., only those imports using the pipeline would be allowed). The American government's commitment to the pipeline was now leading to further commitments, an incremental process similar to the Canadian government's northern pipeline policy of the early 1970s.

The emergence of a large Canadian surplus in 1978 was perhaps less extraordinary than the American gas bubble but nonetheless quite remarkable in itself. The Canadian oil and gas industry had made the transition from scarcity to abundance with dizzying speed. In 1977, large segments of the industry had still warned of impending domestic shortages. Only a year later, many of the same companies which had previously urged the construction of a frontier pipeline began clamouring for large increases in exports. Canada's gas outlook had gone full circle in only eight years, from a surplus in 1970 to a deficit in 1974 to a surplus again in 1978. Through this entire period, the industry's forecasts of natural gas supply and demand had evolved in perfect symmetry with the projects it was advocating. When industry had pressed for exports in 1970, it had argued that gas supply would grow rapidly and demand slowly; when it had promoted a northern pipeline in the mid-Seventies, its forecasts had shown declining supplies and accelerating demand; finally, after the pipeline had been approved, supplies were once again described as abundant and demand as sluggish, allowing industry to support new export proposals.

The evident error in the National Energy Board's 1977 forecast and the increasing industry pressure to allow new gas exports led the NEB in the fall of 1978 to conduct new hearings on natural gas supply and demand. For the board to review its forecast made only the year before during the pipeline hearings was as explicit an admission of its misjudgement as could have been given. The purpose of the 1978 gas hearings, of course, was not to expose the unsound foundation of the government's pipeline decision. For the NEB, self-criticism, much less criticism of government policy, is not a much-practised indulgence. On the contrary, the gas hearings, like their forerunner three and a half years earlier, were designed to gather evidence which would set the course of future gas policy. Just as the 1974-75 hearings had provided it with a platform to explain how Canada had drifted from a position of surplus to one of shortage, the 1978 gas hearings gave industry a welcome opportunity to present its case.

This case is marked by an extraordinary circularity of reasoning. The industry claims that, without new exports, its revenues will not increase rapidly enough to sustain a vigorous exploration effort; without such an exploration effort, the future rate of gas discovery will drop and become too low to meet Canadian domestic requirements. This logic makes exports essential to the satisfaction of future Canadian demand even though it was excessive exports which, in 1975, threatened the fulfilment of domestic needs. As natural gas is a finite, non-renewable resource, the argument that domestic supplies would, in effect, be "created" as a result of a vigorous export policy is one which demonstrably breaks down in the long term. In the short term, it ignores that there exist other means (such as tax incentives) of ensuring that exploration and development keep pace with domestic requirements.

The experience of recent years suggested that the NEB assess the large additions to reserves being recorded in Alberta cautiously since it was unclear whether they meant that Canada's potential was greater than previously thought, as industry claimed, or merely being discovered more quickly than before. In its report released in February 1979, the NEB chose to be both conservative and adventurous. It revised its forecast of the date when frontier gas would become needed domestically to 1992, a date which would undoubtedly have receded further into the future had the board taken fuller account of the reserves being discovered in Alberta and the potential for energy conservation.

If the NEB could not be faulted for erring on the side of caution in estimating supply and demand, given its previous unhappy experience at forecasting, it is difficult to interpret as charitably the board's relaxation of its export formula. In the past, the board had set aside an arbitrary volume equal to twenty-five times the fourth year of demand (the so-called 25A4 formula) for domestic requirements and allowed the rest to be exported. This had proved a profoundly unsatisfactory method of guiding export policy: it did not deal with the question of why Canada should export at all and what the costs and benefits of various export levels would be. It also failed to consider the rate at which gas could be produced (deliverability): a large stock of reserves, as Canadians discovered in 1975, did not necessarily guarantee that production levels would be adequate to cover requirements.

The board therefore proposed in its 1979 gas report a more sophisticated export formula taking into account both the stock of reserves in the ground and their deliverability. This new formula, on the NEB's own admission, however, lowered the volume of reserves set aside for domestic requirements, an extraordinary reform at a time when the international oil situation was and remains unstable. The effect of liberalizing the export formula was to create an exportable surplus where none would have existed under the old formula.[4]

PRE-BUILDING OF THE ALASKA HIGHWAY PIPELINE

As the sponsors of a pipeline that would deliver gas to the American market at a cost several times greater than that of Alberta supplies, Foothills and Northwest were vitally affected by the NEB's determination of Canada's exportable surplus. The existence of a gas surplus in Canada, particularly the inferred presence of a "deep basin" in the Alberta foothills which might contain up to 50 trillion cubic feet of gas at current prices—almost as much as Alberta's present proven reserves—represented a formidable threat to the Alaska Highway pipeline. Large-scale exports of Canadian gas could well delay the American need for the project and make it singularly unattractive in the short term. The NEB's conclusion that Canada's exportable surplus in early 1979 was only 2 trillion cubic feet was therefore good news to Northwest and Foothills because it invalidated the proposition that the United States could defer the development of Prudhoe Bay gas in favour of greater Canadian imports.

But if the Alaska Highway pipeline was potentially threatened by large new Canadian exports, it paradoxically also depended on them for part of its financing. In its 1977 report on the northern pipelines, the NEB had suggested that excess Alberta production could be exported to the United States on a short-term basis if there were an "ironclad" guarantee that it would be replaced later with equivalent volumes of Alaskan gas. Such a swap proposal would have seen the southern portions of the Alaska Highway pipeline built earlier than otherwise necessary to accommodate the increased Canadian exports. To Canada, the chief advantage of a swap would have been to delay the date when frontier gas had to be connected to market. To Foothills and

Northwest, the pre-building of up to a third of the pipeline offered an earlier cash-flow, a lower risk of cost overruns and the promise of an easier financing of the whole project. Given the enormous costs of the pipeline, these were considerable advantages indeed. As the pipeline became delayed in the United States and its costs began to mount, the pre-building plan evolved gradually from a helpful fillip to the pipeline's progress to an absolutely essential—if insufficient—prerequisite to its success.

In a period of only a year, the pre-build plan underwent several transformations which underscored its growing importance to the viability of the Alaska Highway pipeline. The swap provision was dropped; the proposed term of the export licences was lengthened from six to fifteen years. In order to rally support behind the pipeline, Northwest made a condition for the importation of Canadian gas that any American company that wanted to buy gas flowing through the pre-built segments of the Alaska Highway line first join the consortium Northwest was heading. This condition was designed not only to reduce competition to the pre-build scheme but also to attract more companies into sponsoring the Alaska Highway line.

The gas export application Foothills initially advanced through Pan Alberta Gas—Pan Alberta is a subsidiary of Alberta Gas Trunk Lines—was the biggest ever filed before the National Energy Board: 4.9 trillion cubic feet, representing a 50% increase in authorized exports at the end of 1978. This, of course , was a greater volume than the NEB had found was surplus to Canadian needs. Pan Alberta was therefore put in the curious position of arguing in Canada that the NEB had underestimated the exportable surplus at the same time that Foothills and Northwest insisted in the United States that Canadian gas imports could in no way be seen as delaying the need for the expeditious construction of the Alaska Highway line. It is ironic that whereas Arctic Gas had once proposed to piggyback Mackenzie Delta gas on Prudhoe Bay gas, Foothills was now proposing to piggyback Prudhoe Bay gas on Alberta gas.

The reason why Pan Alberta was forced to propose such a large export—over 1 billion cubic feet a day— was simple: designed to carry up to 3.6 bcfd of Prudhoe Bay and Mackenzie Delta gas, the Alaska Highway pipeline would be a large diameter pipeline which would be prohibitively expensive to operate at a small fraction of capacity. In order to reap the advantages inherent in pre-building the southern sections of the line, Foothills would have to fill it to the maximum extent possible. Even at 1.04 bcfd, however, there was no question that the transportation of Alberta gas through the Alaska Highway pipeline would be economically inefficient.

It is not surprising then that several Alberta gas producers—all of whose gross revenues are calculated by deducting transportation costs from the selling price for gas—opposed the pre-build plan and preferred instead to ship their gas through TransCanada Pipelines. Concerned that if Pan Alberta's export application was approved, they would end shouldering part of the cost of pre-building the Alaska Highway pipeline, a consortium of at first ten gas producers, growing to thirteen, put together in 1978 a competing export proposal under the name of ProGas. ProGas proposed to export at least 767 billion cubic feet (about half of Canada's annual consumption) by looping TCPL and taking advantage of the spare capacity in its system. ProGas' plan was thus strongly reminiscent of the Maple Leaf and early Alcan applications which had also relied on the use of spare capacity in existing pipelines to minimize the length of new line to be built.

It was ironic and fitting therefore that ProGas' manager should have been none other than Bob Blair's old nemesis Vern Horte, who in his previous incarnation as CAG's president had not only warned that Canada was running short of gas but had also repeatedly ridiculed Blair's plans to build "spaghetti pipelines". In 1978, the two adversaries again confronted each other, this time each promoting virtually the antithesis of his former position.

Horte, however, was now the underdog. As the two tcf the NEB had found surplus to Canadian needs was considerably less than the volume Pan Alberta hoped to export, let alone the sum of the eleven export applications that had been submitted by the spring of 1979, it was clear that few proposals would be accepted. Pan Alberta in this regard enjoyed a major advantage that none of its competitors shared: it was part of a project that both the Canadian and American governments had endorsed as being in their national interest.

In spite of the delays the Alaska Highway pipeline had encountered as a result of the congressional debate over the Natural Gas Policy Act, the Carter Administration remained firmly committed to the project. Indeed, because of these delays and growing skepticism about the pipeline's economic viability, top officials in the US government, including James Schlesinger, had reaffirmed publicly their support for the line on several occasions. Believing that Alaskan gas had to be developed quickly and convinced that without new government initiatives the pipeline would continue to flounder—by now the pipeline had been delayed another twelve months, the Carter Administration decided to help Northwest by disallowing any new gas imports into the United States that did not assist the project directly. The only imports that qualified, of course, were those associated with the pre-built sections of the line. This strategy, unstated at first, was revealed when the United States turned down large imports of Mexican gas at a price substantially below that of Alaskan gas. Although Mexican prices would have risen in step with international oil prices, they nevertheless constituted an attractive alternative in the short term. The administration's policy of coercing any company wishing to acquire supplemental gas supplies to join the Northwest partnership illustrated two facts: the Alaska Highway pipeline was in deep trouble and the American government was determined to do everything in its power short of extending financial guarantees to rescue the project.

The American government's efforts at shoring up the Alaska Highway pipeline received a powerful boost from Prime Minister Trudeau's trip to

Washington on March 3, 1979 to meet with Carter. This was Trudeau's fourth visit to Washington in two years. Its main purpose was to discuss the pipeline's lack of progress.

Trudeau's visit was humiliating, a forceful reminder of the unequal relationship between Canada and the United States. The Alaska Highway pipeline was an American project. Canada shared no blame for the delays it had encountered so far, having legislated its approval of the pipeline in early 1978 and established a Northern Pipeline Agency to oversee the pipeline's construction. Yet, it was Trudeau who was going to Washington to ascertain "what intentions...they have of proceeding with the pipeline project" and what could be done to help it. Once again, Canada was assuming the role of suitor towards the United States; once again, it was indicating its dependency by doing so.

After their meeting, Carter and Trudeau re-stated their "strong commitment" to the Alaska Highway pipeline. They agreed to explore ways "whereby any additional Canadian gas exports...could facilitate the timely construction" of the project. In this statement, Trudeau was reversing what Energy Minister Gillespie had said in the House of Commons only two days before following the release of the NEB gas report. At that time, Gillespie had stated that the exportable surplus the NEB had found should be used to support the development and expansion of markets in Quebec and the Maritimes by helping to defray the cost of new pipeline facilities to eastern Canada. As a result of Trudeau's trip to Washington, the government changed its position and announced its willingness to consider how this same exportable surplus could be used for an entirely different purpose, the construction of a pipeline to serve American needs.

The American government's strong support of pre-building and the Canadian government's inclination in its favour constituted an unmistakable warning to the companies competing with Pan Alberta for the right to increase gas exports: unless they were prepared to move their gas via the southern sections of the Alaska Highway pipeline, they faced the risk of losing the lucrative export market altogether. It took less than two months following Carter and Trudeau's meeting for Trans Canada Pipelines and Consolidated Natural Gas to announce they would submit a joint export bid with Pan Alberta. TransCanada's support in particular was both startling and "a tremendous boost for the entire project" in John MacMillian's words.

AGTL and TCPL had spent the better part of the 1970s at loggerheads. It would be no great exaggeration to describe the recent history of Canadian natural gas policy as the evolution of the antagonism between the two companies. In 1970, both had proposed competing Mackenzie pipelines. In 1971, AGTL had created Pan Alberta explicitly to break TransCanada's monopoly over gas purchases in Alberta. The rivalry between the two seemed to grow in the aftermath of the spectacular duel between Arctic Gas and Foothills. In the mid-Seventies, both sponsored studies on the transportation of liquefied natural gas by tanker from the High Arctic and proposed to build pipelines to eastern Canada. In 1977, at the prodding of the NEB, which was concerned that the Foothills partnership be strengthened, TransCanada and Foothills negotiated for a few months TCPL's possible participation in the Alaska Highway pipeline. These negotiations broke down in April 1978 with some bitterness when TransCanada decided to sponsor its own export proposal over Foothills' pre-build plan.

It would be difficult to imagine two companies that had clashed more often in a period of eight years. TransCanada's announcement on April 25, 1979, that it would make common cause with Pan Alberta and "join in a maximum effort to support construction of the entire Alaska Highway Pipeline Project"was therefore electrifying. AGTL and TCPL's dramatic reconciliation was the direct result of Dome Petroleum's purchase in August and September 1978 of a controlling interest in TransCanada (which it increased substantially in May 1979). Canadian-owned, a large gas producer and the only company drilling in the deep waters of the Beaufort Sea, Dome had a direct interest in the success of the Alaska Highway pipeline. If the pipeline was not built, Dome would find it increasingly difficult to continue attracting the funds it needed to maintain its expensive exploratory effort. A Dempster alternative to move Beaufort Sea gas would no longer exist. The defeat of both Foothills and, before it, Arctic Gas would set the cause of northern pipelining back for years and might well delay Beaufort Sea production. As the Alaska Highway pipeline remained stalled, Dome therefore decided to intervene.

Dome did not share the history of animosity that was dividing AGTL and TransCanada. Indeed, Dome Chairman "Smilin'" Jack Gallagher explained the purchase of TransCanada stock in part by offering that

> ... we may be able to assist in the relationship between Canada and the Alberta government, TransCanada and Alberta Gas Trunk. Instead of having these confrontations, maybe we can work things out together.[5]

Dome's influence in TransCanada made itself felt quickly. In January 1979, Schlesinger told Dome that the United States was not interested in importing Canadian gas unless it helped to build the Alaska Highway pipeline. Three months later, Dome withdrew from ProGas, which it had helped to create, and brought TransCanada into the Foothills camp. Under the agreement reached with AGTL, TransCanada agreed to support Pan Alberta's export proposal and announced that it was prepared to acquire a 49% interest in the Saskatchewan segment of the Alaska Highway pipeline and a 35% interest in the connecting 1,100-mile Northern Border segment to Illinois. The latter in particular, represented an important commitment towards helping finance the entire Alaska Highway pipeline.

Consolidated Natural Gas, another export applicant, joined Pan Alberta at the same time as TransCanada. Together, the three companies were requesting the export of 5.85 tcf, a volume equivalent to almost a quarter of the Prudhoe Bay reserves. Pre-building was now gathering an increasing momentum. In June, ProGas agreed to have the Northern Border pipeline carry its export when it came into service, rather than TransCanada. Sulpetro, a small Canadian producer—on whose board of directors sits Marshall Crowe—followed by giving Pan Alberta the option of carrying part of its requested export through the pre-built facilities of the Alaska Highway pipeline.

The concentration of export applications in the spring of 1979 carried several implications: it reduced the risk of protracted adversary hearings before the National Energy Board; it effectively decreased the number of competing applications and, hence, the range of policy options open to the NEB; finally, it substantially enhanced the probability that pre-building would occur. It is significant in this respect that both the Canadian and American governments were instrumental through their gas export and import policies in effecting the rapprochement between Alberta Gas Trunk and TransCanada. As had been the case nine years earlier through the publication of its northern pipeline guidelines, the Canadian government was playing a key role in lessening competition in the oil and gas industry in order to achieve more rapid resource development.

The pre-building of the Alaska Highway pipeline, however, also raised several major policy issues. The dedication of Canada's exportable gas surplus to the Alaska Highway line rather than the Quebec and Maritimes pipeline, for example, could make the latter more difficult to finance and thus delay its construction. The most important issue pre-building raised was not so much this as the risk that the northern two-thirds of the Alaska Highway pipeline would be postponed indefinitely. The duration of Pan Alberta's export request—fifteen years—made it clear that Foothills wanted to amortize as much of the Alaska Highway pipeline as possible by selling Alberta gas to the United States. This in itself was an indication that the pipeline was proving difficult to finance. It was not inconceivable then that after they had pre-built the southern sections of their project, Foothills and Northwest would be forced to abandon the rest of the pipeline.

In this eventuality the pre-built sections of the line would become nothing more than an export pipeline. Worse, it would be an uneconomic pipeline since it would operate at less than half of capacity. Who then would rescue the project? Alberta producers through lower profits? American consumers through higher prices? Pan Alberta? Foothills? The Canadian government? Unless there was an explicit and firm assurance that Prudhoe Bay gas would flow through the pipeline on schedule, there was a risk that Pan Alberta would have to come back to the NEB for even greater exports merely to make the pre-build financially solvent.

In order to assuage these concerns, Pan Alberta began to consider in mid-1979 the possibility of depreciating the pre-built sections of the Alaska

Highway pipeline entirely on the export of Canadian gas. A "stand alone" pre-build was the logical last step in the evolution the proposal had undergone since the NEB had first advanced it in 1977. The pre-build's latest version indeed ensured that it would not falter financially if the rest of the pipeline continued to be delayed. At the same time, it removed any incentive Foothills might have had of completing the whole pipeline.

This was a profoundly troubling prospect for the Canadian government. It had approved the Alaska Highway pipeline to stimulate the economy, create jobs and provide access to the Mackenzie Delta. If building the easiest segments first meant that the most difficult ones might not get built, the bulk of the benefits associated with the project evaporated. Canada could only lose by approving large new gas exports without ensuring beforehand that northern gas would be available when needed. If this fact had not been perfectly clear earlier, Trudeau was advised by Carter and Schlesinger during his visit to Washington that the Canadian government would be "damn fools" if it allowed pre-building without ensuring that the rest of the pipeline would follow.

Not surprisingly, then, the Canadian government took a hard line on pre-building in early 1979. Testifying before a House of Commons committee, Allan MacEachen, the minister responsible for the pipeline, said

> It is the policy of this government that we will insist upon a guarantee that the total line be built, that the financial arrangements for the building of the entire line be in place before we give the green light for going ahead with the pre-build.[6]

This, indeed, is what Section 4 of the Pipeline Agreement stipulates. Before it can begin construction on any segment of its pipeline, Foothills must demonstrate that it has obtained the financing necessary to complete the whole pipeline (Northwest must do the same in the United States). This is a standard clause in National Energy Board certificates designed to ensure that a project which has been found in the public interest will in fact be built in its entirety.

In mid-1979, Foothills was forced to admit that it could not meet this requirement and proceed with the pre-build on schedule. This was because Foothills would not be able to prove it could finance the pipeline until the NEB and the Federal Energy Regulatory Commission in the US had ruled on a number of matters affecting the line's rate of return and tariffs. As the delays experienced in the United States until then indicated, it could be some time until Foothills would be in a position to approach financial investors. If it waited until it could do so, it would set back pre-building by several months and perhaps kill it altogether since, by then, it would be ready to build the entire line.

Foothills' admission created a conundrum of monumental proportions for the Canadian government. If it stuck to its position, pre-building would be put into jeopardy; if it relented, it had no assurance that the whole line would be completed. It did not have the option of approving other gas exports to appease the oil and gas industry since American policy disallowed imports in that country that did not help the pipeline. This conundrum was complicated by the fact that it was not at all clear that Foothills would be able to finance its portion of the Alaska Highway pipeline without pre-building. Its intention to amortize the southern sections of the line entirely on the export of Alberta gas testified eloquently to the difficulties financing was creating.

But these difficulties, however considerable, were dwarfed by the problems Northwest was facing in the United States. Obviously, if Foothills succeeded in financing the Canadian portion of the line and Northwest failed for the American section, there would be no pipeline. In considering the risks posed by pre-building, the Canadian government therefore had to be concerned about the possibility that the pipeline could not be financed privately in the US. And in the two years since the signing of the Pipeline Agreement, the evidence that Northwest would need government guarantees had been mounting.

Throughout 1978 and the first half of 1979, Northwest claimed in the United States that, unless specific actions were taken favouring an Alaska Highway pipeline, the project's private financing would be precluded. This was an effective war of nerves to wage against a government that was both deeply committed to the pipeline and strongly opposed to extending federal loan guarantees.

Northwest first made its claim during the congressional debate over the Natural Gas Policy Act, repeated it when the Federal Energy Regulatory Commission proposed its draft incentive rate of return for the pipeline, stated it again after the American government released draft stipulations on environmental and construction performance and reiterated it once more when Northwest requested the State of Alaska to commit $500 million in equity to the project by June 1979. Northwest's admission in January 1979, furthermore, that it was then "experiencing difficulty in obtaining the necessary financial backing in the private sector due to a lack of visible government support of the project."[7] reinforced the growing body of evidence that the Alaska Highway pipeline was facing serious financial difficulty.

FINANCING

The spectre of government guarantees has hovered over the northern gas pipeline projects since the early 1970s. Arctic Gas was the first to recognize the need for guarantees in financing its Mackenzie pipeline. For its part, El Paso hoped to rely on American government subsidies to build a fleet of LNG (liquefied natural gas) tankers. The third competitor in the race,

Northwest, also agreed at first it would need some government support. Testifying before the Federal Power Commission in September 1976, Northwest's chief financial adviser declared: "I believe that if this question were to be decided in the light of conditions such as they exist today, the answer would be yes. I believe public support is needed."[8]

In early 1977, Northwest, however, began to claim it could finance the Alaska Highway pipeline without government guarantees. This politically opportune promise was a major factor behind the Canadian and American governments' selection of the Alaska Highway pipeline over its alternatives. Indeed, government financial involvement in the northern pipeline was so abhorrent in the United States that Congress stated explicitly that it would not extend any federal guarantees when it ratified Carter's decision in the fall of 1977. Whether Northwest had been in a position to assure American authorities it would not need government guarantees, by this decision it became committed by law to financing its pipeline privately—unless, of course, Congress reversed itself.

What are guarantees?[9] Seventy-five percent of the pipeline's cost will be raised in the form of debt, that is, it will be borrowed from lenders. Since the sum each lender will be asked to advance will constitute a major share of his overall investment portfolio, he will demand explicit and comprehensive assurances that his money will be returned with interest according to a prearranged schedule. There must therefore exist a credit-worthy backer who can provide these assurances and guarantee the pipeline debt. A guarantor need not spend any money on the pipeline if everything goes well. He must, however, be ready and willing to rescue the project if it runs into difficulty.

The Alaska Highway pipeline sponsors cannot provide these guarantees because the pipeline's cost—now at least $14 billion—exceeds their assets. Therefore, they intend to finance the pipeline entirely on the strength of the revenues it will earn over its twenty-five year economic life. These revenues will have to be sufficient to cover all operating costs, interest on the pipeline's debt, the retirement of the debt, a return on equity and ultimately a return of the sponsors' equity itself. It is because there is a risk that the pipeline may cease to generate revenue before its debt has been fully repaid that institutional lenders are demanding guarantees before investing in the project. The risks the pipeline faces include non-completion (if, for example, cost overruns were to outstrip the financial resources of the pipeline sponsors and cause the project's abandonment), interruption or diminution of service (if, say, technical problems at Prudhoe Bay were to reduce or halt gas production) and abandonment (which changing market circumstances might dictate if Alaskan gas could no longer be sold). Admittedly the probability of any of these events occurring is extremely small. Institutional lenders, however, cannot afford to take any risks when the stakes are so high. A Wall Street investment banker puts it this way. In the Alaska Highway pipeline,

> you have all the financing problems of a construction project in the Arctic multiplied by a number of times. Remember, this is the largest single project ever undertaken by anybody in private industry. For every institution that takes part in it, it will be the largest investment they ever made in anything. No one will move an inch until every single inch of this is screwed down every step of the way. You can't have any loose ends flapping around.[10]

Lenders, in other words, will not commit any money to the project until some credit-worthy party has assumed the responsibility of repaying the debt and interest on schedule under any and all circumstances. Who then can provide these guarantees?

The US Department of the Treasury has maintained ever since 1975, when it began looking into the problem, that the financial participation of the pipeline's beneficiaries—the Prudhoe Bay producers, the State of Alaska and the natural gas transmission industry—would provide the guarantees lenders seek, thereby obviating the need for government involvement. It was on that basis that the Carter Administration concluded that government guarantees were not necessary and should not be given. An analysis of Treasury's position—the premise upon which all arguments on the feasibility of private financing rest —reveals that it relies as much on wishful thinking as on an assessment of the interests of the North Slope producers, the State of Alaska and the gas industry.

The Prudhoe Bay Producers

The three major Prudhoe Bay producers, Exxon, Arco and Sohio, are most often treated as a homogeneous group whose interests can be expected to overlap considerably if indeed they are not already identical. This common assumption, however, masks significant differences in the share of North Slope oil and gas production each controls and their respective financial resources.

Sohio owns 53% of the oil at Prudhoe Bay but only 27% of the gas. Exxon and Arco, on the other hand, each own 20% of the oil but 36% of the gas. As the oil and gas are associated in the same reservoir, the production of one will affect the production of the other. If a trade-off had to be made in the future between accelarating gas or oil production, the interests of the three companies would be expected to diverge substantially. Sohio, for example, would most likely resist any increase in the rate of take for gas that might lower oil recovery. Thus, although it can be said that it is to the advantage of the three producers to sell their gas, their stakes in the construction of an Alaska Highway pipeline are far from equal.

The financial capabilities of the three companies also vary greatly. Exxon, the largest oil company in the world (assets at the end of 1976: $36.3 billion), could conceivably build most of, and perhaps even the entire, pipeline if it was so inclined. With assets only a quarter those of Exxon, Arco has more limited clout. Sohio is even smaller. Indeed, Sohio indebted itself to such an extent to finance its share of the $9 billion Alyeska oil pipeline that it cannot at this time pursue any further substantial obligations—such as guaranteeing an Alaska Highway pipeline debt—even if it wanted to: the indenture covenants on its Alyeska bonds do not allow it. As it is, the three companies will have to spend several billions of dollars over the next few years to maintain oil production at Prudhoe Bay. They do not see therefore their involvement in a gas pipeline as a priority.

But there are even more compelling reasons why the Prudhoe Bay producers do not want to help finance the Alaska Highway pipeline. American anti-trust legislation forbids them from acquiring any equity in the pipeline (Canadian anti-combines law places no similar restrictions in Canada). They have therefore little incentive in guaranteeing pipeline bonds since they would never be able to control the project and would only repay debts if it ran into difficulty. Buying pipeline bonds, on the other hand, would provide them with a lower return on their investment than they would earn elsewhere.

For these reasons, Exxon, Arco and Sohio have consistently and vehemently stated over the years that they wanted no part in the financing of any gas pipeline from Prudhoe Bay.

The State of Alaska

The State of Alaska is in a different position. In 1976, it offered to help finance the El Paso project which it strongly supported. Two years later, Northwest suggested that the state transfer its allegiance to the Alaska Highway pipeline and issue $1 billion in tax-exempt bonds (which would require a congressional amendment to the Internal Revenue Code) and $500 million in convertible debentures. During the summer of 1978, the state legislature dutifully passed a bill to create an Alaska Gas Pipeline Financing Authority to do just that, providing Northwest could demonstrate it had assembled a capital pool of debt and equity funds equal to at least 150% of the estimated pipeline cost.

By early 1979, however, the state's pledge was no longer sufficient for Northwest. In February, John McMillian wrote a letter to the state government in a tone that was both urgent and demanding:

> Last year we informed you that it was important, but not critical, that the state provide financial support to the Alaska Highway gas project. Today, the financial advisers of the project inform me that such support by the state is not only a prerequisite to private financing, but must be

> obtained during the current session of the Alaskan legislature... Financial commitments from the State of Alaska must be made in 1979, and must take the form of a definite commitment that Alaskan funds will be available unconditionally, subject only to completing the remainder of the financial plan and obtaining final FERC approval.[11]

This time, the state's legislature refused to accede to Northwest's extraordinary and unreasonable request. Alaska has good reasons to be cautious. Its income already depends overwhelmingly on Prudhoe Bay oil. To commit general funds or future oil revenues to a gas pipeline which would also start at Prudhoe Bay would sharply increase its exposure to any accident involving oil production on the North Slope. Technical difficulties in the field or an explosion at the Alyeska pipeline terminal at Valdez, for example, would reduce both oil and gas production. An investment in the gas pipeline would therefore only multiply the consequences of these adversities.

In any event, it is not clear whether a less ambitious involvement than that for which Northwest is pressing, such as state guarantees for the pipeline's debt, would be credible to major institutional lenders. These lenders already hold large amounts of Alyeska pipeline bonds. If the gas pipeline were to run into difficulties and Alaska had to help in its rescue, it is reasonable to expect that the state would try to recoup its losses by increasing taxes on oil production or the Alyeska pipeline. The major institutional lenders would therefore justifiably interpret any state guarantee of a gas pipeline's debt as merely a shift of risks from the gas pipeline bonds they are being asked to buy to the oil pipeline bonds they already hold.[12]

Gas Transmission Companies

Paradoxically, there are fewer transmission companies in the Northwest partnership than used to belong to Arctic Gas. Several very large companies such as Columbia Gas (1976 revenues: $1.7 billion), Texas Eastern Transmission (1976 revenues: $1.5 billion) and Michigan-Wisconsin ("Mich-Wich"), which used to be members of Arctic Gas, have so far refused to join Northwest. Some, like Columbia Gas, do not feel they have to participate, even though they have signed agreements to buy Prudhoe Bay gas, because the Alaska Natural Gas Transportation Act of 1976 gives any company the right to buy gas without having to join the Alaska Highway pipeline partnership. Others, such as Peoples' Gas of Chicago, hold reservations about the pipeline's financeability: "We have serious questions as to the financing of the pipeline, and until we have a firm fix on that we don't think we should make an investment", Joe Wells, Peoples' vice-president declared to the *Washington Post* in November 1978.

Others still find themselves sponsoring projects that are competing with the Alaska Highway pipeline, at least in the short term. That category includes companies such as Mich-Wich, Texas Eastern and Tenneco who have signed contracts to buy gas from ProGas. Mich-Wich and Tenneco's attempt to obtain gas supplies that were not contingent on the pre-building of the Alaska Highway pipeline led an exasperated McMillian to accuse them in February 1979 of "fighting our project like a mad dog", an accusation which reveals more about Northwest's precarious position than the character of these companies.

The reasons why the Northwest partnership has remained small—the American gas bubble, the high cost of Alaskan gas, the existence of cheap alternative supplies, the pipeline's uncertain financeability—have already been mentioned. They are all of particular concern to gas transmission companies who would have to sell Prudhoe Bay gas. Some projections of American gas demand suggest that the pipeline's entire throughput might not be marketable even in the late 1980s.[13] Part of Carter's energy program which Congress passed in 1978 were indeed specifically designed to restrict future industrial and thermal gas demand. The confusion remaining over the size of the American gas market in the 1980s helps to explain why, eight months after the passage of the Natural Gas Policy Act of 1978 which Northwest claimed would result in the prompt negotiation of sales contracts for Prudhoe Bay gas, only three had in fact been signed.

It is important to remember that American natural gas transmission companies are all regulated utilities. Their profits are controlled and they therefore are seldom compelled to assume high risks. Until the fate of the Alaska Highway pipeline has been settled, few of them will feel much urgency to share Northwest's pre-construction costs.

The American Department of the Treasury's conclusion in 1977 that the Prudhoe Bay producers, the State of Alaska and the American gas transmission industry would enthusiastically join in the financing of the Alaska Highway pipeline was naive if not self-deceiving. These beneficiaries did not rush to Northwest's succour when the pipeline began to flounder. On the contrary, common sense and their own self-interest dictate a continuing greater degree of circumspection than Treasury seemed willing to assume.

The reasons why the pipeline will need government guarantees were analysed incisively by Dr. Arlon Tussing and Connie Barlow in a series of reports commissioned by the Alaska state legislature after it had agreed in principle in 1978 to help finance the pipeline. Tussing, of course, is the same man Blair credits with convincing him to sponsor the Alaska Highway pipeline in early 1976. His role in forging the Foothills-Northwest partnership and his long-standing familiarity with Alaskan oil and gas transportation issues made him an ideal candidate to review the financing difficulties faced by the pipeline. His final report, released in April 1979, was unequivocal in its main conclusion:

> The Alaska Highway gas pipeline cannot be financed and built unless

> the United States government guarantees at least part of the project debt. This judgement, which the authors related in an earlier report to the Alaska Legislature, is held almost unanimously by the natural gas transmission industry, Alaska gas producers, investment bankers, lending institutions, state and federal regulators and concerned members of Congress. The only significant dissent we encountered in more than six months of investigation came from a few top officials of the United States Department of Energy (DOE) and from Northwest Alaskan Pipeline Company (Northwest), the project's principal sponsor.[14]

Two months earlier, McMillian had denounced Tussing's work in angry tones that implied that Tussing had hit home.

> Tussing is an academic intellectual. If he had financed a used Volkswagen I think he would have had more credibility when he had written his report. He is a college professor. He is just a solid fourteen-carat gold nut running around loose. That is one of the nicest things I can say about him.[15]

Not withstanding this churlish attempt at discrediting Tussing, the fact that the Alaska Highway pipeline will need government guarantees can hardly be disputed. James Schlesinger himself seemed to signal a shift in the position of the Carter Administration when he testified before a congressional committee in January 1979. Asked what Congress could do to help the pipeline, Schlesinger answered, "Congress will not wish to reject out-of-hand the possibility of loan guarantees for the pipeline". He added, when prodded, that a figure of $2 to $3 billion for the Alaska section of the line "might be in the right ball park".[16]

THE POLITICAL IMPASSE

Northwest, however, will not find it easy to obtain guarantees from the American government. The report of the Senate Energy Committee accompanying the congressional resolution endorsing Carter's pipeline decision suggested some of the difficulties Northwest will encounter:

> While the committee has reservations about the ability of the Alcan project sponsors to secure the necessary private financing, we are recommending approval of the President's decision based upon the unqualified assertions made by the Administration and Alcan officials.
>
> It is essential for the project sponsors to proceed with their financing arrangements as promptly as possible. The State of Alaska, the producers, and most of all the project sponsors should bear in mind that the

> door to the Federal Treasury has not been left open to them. We have taken the Administration's and sponsors' assurances at face value and are placing our reliance upon them.
>
> The Committee cautions the Administration and sponsors against taking a back door approach to Federal financing.... We intend to monitor the project's progress closely and caution that financial "gimmicks" involving consumer risk taking via the Federal Treasury or via special tariffs will not be tolerated by the Congress.[17]

This blunt warning was repeated a year later, in the fall of 1978, when Congress was considering the roll-in pricing provision for Prudhoe Bay gas as part of its debate over the Natural Gas Policy Act. At that time, the House and Senate conferees felt compelled—perhaps because of the considerable pressure Northwest and the administration put on them—to restate that "roll-in pricing is the only Federal subsidy, of any type, direct or indirect, to be provided for the pipeline".[18] Congress clearly intended to take Northwest at its word and force it to live with the consequences of its undertaking.

If, under these conditions, Northwest had scored what could only be described as a Pyrrhic victory, it did its cause much harm in the two years following the Pipeline Agreement by continuing to assert emphatically that it could finance the Alaska Highway pipeline privately. Undoubtedly, Northwest had much to lose by admitting the need for government guarantees. It perhaps even believed its own claim. Nevertheless, as time went by, and Northwest obstinately maintained that it would be able to raise the money needed for the pipeline in spite of all the contrary evidence, its credibility suffered perceptibly. The very strategy it followed—demanding concessions purportedly designed to obviate the need for guarantees—not only earned Northwest much resentment for its abrasive style but was also bound to fail. Indeed, it began backfiring almost immediately. During the congressional gas debate, Northwest claimed for example that passage of the Natural Gas Policy Act would lead to the prompt negotiation of Prudhoe Bay sales contracts which, in turn, would lead to the pipeline's private financing. When sales contracts took considerably longer to materialize than Northwest had implied, several congressmen began to feel that they had been misled.

The Carter Administration also failed to deal with the financing issues openly and realistically. Having selected the Alaska Highway pipeline, and therefore sharing a stake in the project's success, it apparently felt obliged to promote it regardless of changing circumstances. Thus it continued to warn of worsening gas shortages if the pipeline was not built and maintained that Northwest would not need government guarantees, even after both claims had become suspect. Its later strategy of denying all gas import applications that did not directly assist the pipeline—because it remained unstated at first—succeeded only in underlining the web of mutual obligations binding it to Northwest.

This web is indeed remarkable. McMillian used to be a member of the Democratic National Committee National Finance Council. He is a good friend of Bob Strauss, Carter's chief trouble shooter (he has successively handled international trade negotiations, the fight against inflation and Middle East negotiations) and a former chairman of the Democratic National Committee. In 1977, McMillian gave $10,000 to Democratic organizations. The following year, he headed Citizens for Tax Reform in 1978 Inc., a volunteer group lobbying for Carter's tax reform proposals. The group was headquartered in Northwest's Washington office. McMillian also fought energetically for Carter's gas bill at a time when it had little congressional support.[19]

McMillian was able to capitalize on his Democratic connections in the last months before the pipeline decision. In February 1977, for example, he was invited to the state dinner Carter gave at the White House for Trudeau during the Prime Minister's visit to Washington. He was the only representative of the three pipeline applicants in the United States to be there. During the dinner itself, McMillian sat at a table with Don Jamieson, the Canadian Secretary for External Affairs, and Walter Mondale, the American Vice-President. One month later, McMillian saw Trudeau again, this time in Aspen, Colorado, at the ski chalet of a mutual friend, Senator Mike Gravel from Alaska (a Democrat). Although it is not known what the three men talked about, the cause of an Alaska Highway pipeline could only be helped by such an encounter.

McMillian, of course, owes much to the Carter Administration: the selection of his project over those of his more powerful rivals, the roll-in of Prudhoe Bay gas to make the pipeline economic, the numerous reaffirmations of support in 1978 and 1979 after the pipeline began to flounder, even the elimination of potential competitors. Carter and McMillian owe each other large debts and these help to explain why the two may have been reticent about acknowledging the true nature of the pipeline's difficulties. Tussing noted in early 1979 that

> Both parties are damned if they do and damned if they don't: the project is essentially stalled, but if the sponsors now admit that the line might not be built without government help, many members of Congress will believe (as indeed they may already believe) that Northwest and the President deliberately and systematically misled them about the need for federal support.[20]

Any political fight over guarantees promised to be highly charged. Guarantees would require congressional approval which, given the history of the issue, would not be granted easily. The administration would find it difficult to reconcile its 1979 policy of budgetary austerity with the extension of guarantees to members of an industry that is more publicly vilified than perhaps any other. Mostly, the administration would have to explain convincingly why none of the arguments it advanced against guarantees in Carter's 1977 *Decision and Report to Congress on the Alaska Natural Gas Transportation System* still applied. At that time, the administration rejected guarantees on the following grounds:

1. Serious questions of equity result from the transfer of risks to taxpayers, many of whom are not gas consumers and will not receive additional gas supplies as a result of the Alaska project.
2. Federal financial support substitutes the government for private lenders in the critical risk assessment function normally performed by private lenders.
3. A subsidy in the form of lower interest rates yields an artificially low price for gas.
4. The incentive for efficient management of the project is reduced.
5. The government is placed in conflicting roles as guarantor and as regulator of the project.

It was unrealistic to expect, barring an extraordinary event, that Congress would debate reasons for overriding these arguments and resolve what kinds of guarantees to extend to the pipeline and under what conditions before November 1980, the date of the next presidential election.

Circumstances made another scenario improbable. First, Northwest, whose enemies are many, would seek to protect its interests as the leading American sponsor of the pipeline. This would mean retaining the support of the administration. Northwest had much to lose by admitting to the need for guarantees prematurely and forcing a President, whose popularity at several times during his term of office had plunged dangerously low, to deal with a politically embarrassing issue. On the contrary, it would be to Northwest's advantage to prolong the charade until the very end. Northwest could therefore continue to demand regulatory concessions on the pretext that they were needed to ensure the pipeline's private financing. If granted, these concessions could only help. If refused, Northwest would have a ready-made scapegoat to blame for its troubles.

If the pace of events which prevailed in the first half of 1979 were maintained, it was unlikely Northwest would be able to approach institutional investors with a financial package before 1980. All the evidence suggested that this financing plan would be found wanting. Northwest, nevertheless, could undoubtedly claim to have fulfilled all its obligations and could maintain, with some justification, that bureaucratic inertia and intransigence was responsible for the delays and escalations in the cost of its project.

If this scenario held, Congress would likely not address the question of government guarantees until 1981, which would push the pipeline's completion back another two years to 1986. Although continued delays are costly to

Northwest and may yet prove fatal, they should enhance the attractiveness of the Alaska Highway pipeline. Already, the 60% increase in international oil prices imposed by the Organization of Petroleum Exporting Countries (OPEC) in the first half of 1979 was heightening American concern to achieve energy self-sufficiency. It is ironic that the only good news Northwest should have received in the two years following the Pipeline Agreement would have come from Iran, a country halfway around the globe. If the Shah's overthrow had not disrupted the world's flow of oil and precipitated the OPEC price jump, no one would have seriously expected the pipeline to be in operation before the end of the 1980s at the earliest. At the very least, the Iranian situation should enable Northwest to anticipate a more favourable reception from Congress to a request for government guarantees.

The fact that the troubles that have afflicted the pipeline have been concentrated almost entirely in the United States to date does not exclude, of course, the possibility that the Canadian government too will be called upon to shore up the project. Although the pipeline is to be built and owned by different companies and will cross several jurisdictions, it remains a single entity. Canada stands to be one of the pipeline's main beneficiaries and will therefore come under tremendous pressure from the United States to help rescue the project. Indeed, Congress might well demand the involvement of all the pipeline's beneficiaries, including Canada, before agreeing to guarantee its debt. The reasons why Canada should refuse are self-evident. They are the same as those Carter listed in his report to Congress. Furthermore, the pipeline is an American project. By helping in its financing, Canada would be subsidizing American consumers of Alaskan gas. Most important perhaps is the fact that Foothills faces fewer obstacles in Canada than Northwest does in the United States. Foothills, to be sure, cannot proceed with the Canadian sections of the pipeline until it has been assured that the American sections will be built. But once it has received this assurance and signed contracts to deliver gas across Canada, it will only be providing a transportation service against whose risks it can protect itself better than Northwest. Foothills, therefore, might not need government guarantees although it has already requested and expected to receive special treatment from both the National Energy Board and the Northern Pipeline Agency.

This was not to say, however, that Foothills, too, despite its protestations, would not some day request guarantees. The pipeline saga, it was clear, would continue to unfold in unexpected ways. Already, Foothills, a company which was initially dedicated to carrying Mackenzie Delta gas to Canadian markets and then became the sponsor of a pipeline to carry Alaskan gas to American markets only to concentrate its efforts in 1979 on building a pipeline to carry Alberta gas to American markets, had undergone a greater metamorphosis than could have been imagined in 1975. It would be rash to expect future developments to become more predictable. On the contrary, the events of the Seventies indicated that it was the unimaginable that would continue to occur with greater regularity than the commonplace.

CHAPTER TEN

THE NORTHERN PIPELINE AND CANADIAN ENERGY POLICY

When it is finally built, the Alaska Highway pipeline will be the most important natural gas pipeline in North America. The Canadian government's decision in 1977 to approve its construction was without a doubt one of the most far-reaching this country has made in the last decade. The pipeline will not only exert a determining influence on the development of Canada's western Arctic and its hydro-carbon resources but will also stimulate greater Canadian-American cooperation in the field of energy policy.

In the two years after the signing of the Pipeline Agreement, the number of oil and gas transportation projects proposed in the North multiplied—Dempster and Polar gas pipelines, an Alaska Highway oil pipeline, possible Mackenzie Valley gas and oil pipelines, year-round navigation of oil and liquefied natural gas ice-breaking tankers through the North-West Passage. As a result we must reflect upon the nature of the decision-making process which led to the selection of the Alaska Highway pipeline in order to draw lessons for the future. Two questions in particular need to be asked: First, what does the pipeline decision tell us about the way in which we deal with complex issues involving the national interest? Second, what is likely to be the legacy of ten years of northern pipeline planning?

Retrospective

A review of the policy effort which culminated in the approval of the Alaska Highway pipeline and the approval in principle of the Dempster pipeline highlights a number of distinctive elements in the decision-making process which are worth underlining. The list that follows is not meant to be comprehensive. There exist too many ways of cataloguing and analysing individual facets of the pipeline decision—many of which remain shrouded in secrecy to this day—for an all-inclusive balance sheet to be drawn up. Nevertheless, even incomplete, this list is illuminating.

1. COMPLEXITY What perhaps makes the northern pipeline decision most unique is its complexity. More interests were affected, more issues were involved and therefore more government departments included, than with any other decision made at the federal level in recent years. The issues the government had to confront in choosing which pipeline to approve, if any, fell into two broad categories: those that had a direct bearing on the individual pipeline projects themselves, such as cost, environmental and social impacts, and those that defined the policy context in which the government had to make its decision, such as Canadian-American relations, the pace of northern development and the government's own political fortunes.

These issues interacted in a highly dynamic environment. First, the pipeline proposals kept changing; Arctic Gas modified its route, Foothills proposed the Alaska Highway pipeline. Second, the relative importance of some issues evolved over time. Early concern about a pipeline's impact on the Canadian economy was assuaged by subsequent analysis. The risk and consequences of cost overruns, on the other hand, became recognized only in the wake of the construction of the Alyeska oil pipeline, that is, not long before the pipeline decision. Third, the policy context itself underwent continuous transformation. The roller-coaster forecasts of natural gas supply and demand represent the most striking instance of the shifting ground upon which the analysis of the pipeline projects had to take place. Fourth, the American deadline created enormous time pressures which compounded the difficulties created by all these changes.

This already bewilderingly complicated equation was made even more so by political factors. Public perception of the issues raised by the northern pipeline—as culled in the Goldfarb polls—helped to establish a hierarchy among them which, not surprisingly, did not always correspond to their intrinsic importance. Widespread apprehension over the North's "fragile environment" and the survival of the caribou, for example, conditioned public acceptance of the Berger Report and thus influenced the government decision. Although a legitimate concern, the environmental impact of the pipeline proposals arguably ranked below their long-term effect on the integration of Canadian and American energy policies, an issue which faded from the public eye in the mid-Seventies.

Given the complexity of the pipeline decision, the broad public acceptance of the Pipeline Agreement demonstrates how skillfully the government succeeded in reconciling the competing demands of industry and native people, American gas users and nationalists, developers and environmentalists. At the time of its release, the Pipeline Agreement was widely hailed in newspaper editorials as a practical compromise which minimized environmental and social disruption while it assured the overland delivery of Alaskan gas and did not foreclose the eventual development of Canada's reserves in the Mackenzie Delta. A good compromise, of course, does not necessarily make good policy.

2. DRIFT The pipeline decision-making process was characterized by a continuous drift in assumptions, in events and in authority. In a period of only eight years, the government supported in turn a Mackenzie Valley oil pipeline, a Mackenzie Valley gas pipeline and ultimately an Alaska Highway gas pipeline. When the latter was delayed, the drift continued. The southern portions of the pipeline might carry at first Alberta gas only. It was also possible that an Alaska Highway oil pipeline would precede the rest of the gas line. To react to opportunity is one thing, to be guided by it another. One may well ask what each of the projects the government successively endorsed have in common other than the trans-shipment of American resources across Canadian territory and the stimulation of the Canadian economy. Whatever it is, the momentum towards pipeline development generated by several years of expectation and industry lobbying seemed to transcend any changes in the economic and energy environments.

The drift in assumptions was perhaps caused by a drift in events. In spite of the scale of its efforts, the government never quite succeeded in controlling the flow of events. With telling frequency, it was forced to react to external developments: the trips of the *Manhattan*, AGTL's desertion of Arctic Gas, the worsening gas balance, the Alaska Highway pipeline application, the American timetable, the Berger Report, all imposed new demands and constraints to which the government did not always know how to respond. Indeed, to the end, the government seemed undecided about its proper role. Should it act as passive regulator, overseeing but not guiding the competing pipeline applications? Or should it take a more interventionist stance aimed at removing the initiative from the private sector? This latent conflict endured, unresolved, through most of the period. It helps to explain the puzzling circumspection which followed in 1975 the government's previous aggressive promotion of Mackenzie pipelines, or the careful orchestration of events in mid-1977 just prior to the pipeline negotiations after a period of almost laissez-faire.

To these two kinds of drift must be added a third, the drift in authority. Perhaps because the issues were so complex and government policy largely reactive rather than anticipatory, it was not always clear how decisions were made, on what grounds and sometimes even on which authority. The May 1970 meeting of deputy ministers which led to the promulgation of the pipeline guidelines, for example, was an important milestone in pipeline planning. Yet, the guidelines' exact purpose was never explicitly revealed, the basis on which they were drawn was highly questionable and the decision to formulate them seemed to emerge spontaneously from within the civil service. The reasons behind the delay in appointing the Lysyk Commission remain obscure. Berger, in the end, played a much greater role in the pipeline decision than the government had intended when it established his inquiry. The National Energy Board's selection of the Alaska Highway pipeline over Arctic Gas was based on criteria that cannot all be found in its pipeline report.

Is it little wonder that Cabinet ministers would claim throughout this period that they had not prejudged the pipeline issue? Their authority over pipeline matters was being constantly eroded.

3. FRAGMENTATION The drift in pipeline policy was maintained by a fragmented decision-making process which made a thorough appraisal of the pipeline's purpose and impacts difficult. A commission of inquiry was named to investigate the environmental and socio-economic impact of the Mackenzie pipeline; a first phase socio-economic inquiry then studied the Alaska Highway pipeline while a different panel assessed in a preliminary way its impact on the environment; the National Energy Board pored over the engineering design, financing and economic effects of both a Mackenzie and Alaska Highway pipeline; internal government task forces produced analyses on the many aspects of the northern pipeline; public opinion polls were commissioned to gauge political variables. There was no framework in which to integrate all these studies, no criteria to measure the trade-offs that would have to be made among them. The pipeline issue was splintered into various elements for the purpose of examination, on the implicit premise that its total impact could be ascertained by the sum of these discrete evaluations. The interrelationships among the elements were thus obscured, their cumulative effects hidden and a complete view of the project pre-empted.

By statute, the NEB should have traced these interrelationships and reached a recommendation based on a comprehensive analysis of the pipeline proposal. The NEB's pipeline hearings were, it is true, the longest the board had ever held. They were mostly devoted, however, to determining not whether a pipeline should be built nor indeed what the advantages and disadvantages of building a pipeline might be but rather how to build one. In doing so, the NEB did not merely surrender to the engineers who dominate its staff. It translated a fundamental policy question into little more than the analysis of nuts and bolts.

The national importance of the issues demanded exacting standards in assessing the pipeline applications as the consequences of underestimating any of the apprehended impacts of the proposed projects could potentially be devastating. Moreover, the unprecedented magnitude and long-term implications of each of the pipeline applications dictated a regulatory review so scrupulous that it could bear the closest public scrutiny. The NEB failed on both counts.

In retrospect, the creation of the Lysyk and EARP (Environmental Assessment and Review Process) hearings appears almost as an afterthought. Their late appointment not only leads one to ask what role they were intended to play but indeed when the goverment first began to consider the

Alaska Highway pipeline as a serious alternative. A partial answer to the first question is obtained in the Pipeline Agreement itself. The agreement gives no indication that the conclusions of either inquiry influenced the Canadian negotiators. The fact that the recommendations Lysyk and EARP made were almost completely ignored suggests that, from the very beginning, the Yukon hearings were seen as marginal to the pipeline decision.

The assessment of the Alaska Highway pipeline option undoubtedly suffered from its late filing by Foothills but at least as much from the skeptical reception which the government gave it. It should have been apparent before the summer of 1976 already that the well-entrenched assumption of "Arctic Gas or nothing" was no longer valid—if indeed it had ever been. Yet, the government not only waited until the eleventh hour before taking the politically obvious step of naming the Yukon panels, but it also failed to develop its own internal expertise on this alternative until early in 1977. When the government became concerned with the issue of cost overruns in the fall of 1976, for example, and asked a Toronto consulting firm to conduct a quick study of the risks involved, it limited its terms of reference to the Mackenzie Valley. When Treasury Board analysed the costs and benefits of the various pipeline options as part of the Northern Pipeline Study Group report to Cabinet, it did not include the Alaska Highway pipeline.

In spite of years of work, the government in 1977 was still not fully prepared to make a final determination of the issue. Although the pressure of the American timetable was unquestionably responsible in part, the government's own approach to the problem was equally at fault.

4. EROSION OF OPTIONS The government's conduct of its northern pipeline policy exhibited a curious inconsistency in one key area. On the one hand, the government sought arduously to retain the greatest degree of latitude possible as it approached the pipeline decision; on the other hand, it circumscribed several of its most important options by making premature commitments. Into this latter category falls the government's vigorous promotion of Mackenzie pipelines in the early 1970s. This policy eventually compromised Canada to such an extent towards the United States that the government effectively lost the right of rejecting an overland pipeline to carry Alaskan gas. The only latitude it retained—and that too was relative—was to choose which pipeline route to sanction.

The signing of a pipeline treaty precluding Canada from taxing Alaskan gas in transit (unless it imposed similar taxes on Canadian pipelines) represented an obligation which would later reduce its bargaining leverage during the pipeline negotiations. It is true that Canada had little choice but to agree to a pipeline treaty. At the time Canada began negotiating the treaty—although not when it first expressed an interest in it—domestic natural gas shortages appeared imminent. The only solution to these shortages, short of unilaterally abrogating export commitments, was thought to lie in a joint frontier pipeline with the United States, one which the US would not approve without the prior assurances of a pipeline treaty. In any event, it would have been unreasonable for Canada to expect to be able to tax Alaskan gas in transit with impunity when 40% of the energy it consumes crosses the United States.

This explanation, however, merely underlines the restricted scope of Canadian energy policy. Canada's pursuit of closer energy ties with its neighbour during the 1950s and 1960s not only led to large increases in gas exports but also to the construction of pipelines crossing American territory which, of course, were built without the safeguards the US would later demand for its own frontier pipeline. The over-commitment to the gas export market and the existence of "hostages" in the US later reduced the perimeter within which Canada could set its northern pipeline policy and gave the US an influence from which it was able to derive benefits worth several billions of dollars.

The government's consent to the gradual erosion of its options at one level—whether to build a pipeline—contrasts with the obsessive care it showed on another to control the situation. Thus, it gave the commissions of inquiry it appointed only the authority to determine under what conditions a pipeline should be built, not to conclude that the adverse impacts of development might make it unacceptable. When Berger resisted this interpretation of his mandate, the government tried to intimidate him by threatening to change his terms of reference, withhold documents, make a decision before his report was ready and limit his budget. Similarly the government orchestrated public opinion by selectively releasing information and restricting the channels available for public participation. At times, the government seemed to show greater concern for the political repercussions of its decisions than for the consequences of the decisions themselves.

5. RESTRICTED PARTICIPATION The government's attitude towards public participation during the years of the pipeline decision-making process was at best ambivalent. Several Cabinet ministers, for example, did not hesitate to claim credit for the earth-shaking precedent which the Berger Inquiry established. Several others, however, also criticised it for allegedly exacerbating popular opposition to a Mackenzie pipeline. The government, of course, cannot have it both ways. Either it creates an independent inquiry which fosters effective public participation and accepts the consequences, or it appoints one with reduced powers to create the illusion of full consultation while retaining a tight rein over the final decision. In spite of its ostentatious tributes to the Berger process, the government later opted for the second alternative as the strictures imposed upon Lysyk demonstrated.

Those members of the public who did not live in the Mackenzie Valley or along the Alaska Highway and still wanted to express their views on the various pipeline proposals faced a number of barriers that discouraged all but the most insistent. The first of these was the government's indifference, if not hostility, to the principle of public participation. The government refused to provide public interest groups and individuals with the means of articulating alternatives to pipeline development; it denied them funding to challenge Foothills' and Arctic Gas' arguments before the National Energy Board; it also denied them access to much of its own information gathered, one must point out, at the taxpayer's expense. As a result, the public interest groups that did participate remained for the most part small, under-financed, poorly organized and ineffective.

The second biggest barrier to public participation was the absence of readily available channels through which the public could present its views. These channels consisted essentially of two major public hearings, both long and complex and headquartered in Yellowknife and Ottawa respectively. The confrontation between the five most active public interest groups before the National Energy Board—the Committee for an Independent Canada, the Committee for Justice and Liberty, the Canadian Wildlife Federation, Energy Probe and the Work Group on Canadian Energy Policy—on the one hand and Foothills and Arctic Gas on the other seldom rose above the level of an absurd comedy. Arctic Gas was spending millions of dollars presenting its application and was represented by a phalanx of lawyers. Lined up behind the pipeline applications was a host of oil and gas interests, large industrial gas consumers and manufacturing and service companies standing to profit from northern development. The combined resources of the public interest groups amounted to roughly one-tenth of one percent of CAG's expenditures during its five years of existence. These groups could not afford legal representation and were indeed unable to attend the hearings full time. In a league where Foothills spent more than one million dollars in legal fees, the public interest groups were hopelessly out-classed.

Only one environmental group appeared before the Berger Inquiry—the Canadian Arctic Resources Committee—and its intervention was made possible only as a result of Berger's decision to provide limited funds to parties who would not have been able to participate otherwise. Even so, however, CARC almost went bankrupt when it incurred debts of $40,000, an absurdly small sum when one considers that Foothills spent almost twice as much on NEB transcripts alone.

But, if the pipeline companies faced no meaningful opposition to their initiatives from the public, the government faced little opposition in Parliament either. The manner in which the pipeline decision was reached provides a sobering insight into the failure of the parliamentary process.[1] In the entire period since 1968, the government faced no effective challenge to its policies, even during its short interlude in a minority during 1972 and 1974. This lack of opposition derives in part from the fact that the Liberals and the Conservatives have exhibited over the years a political bi-partisanship on most issues affecting the oil and gas industry—an eloquent tribute to the effectiveness of this lobby. As a result of their bias, the Conservatives tended to question rather than debate the government on the northern pipeline. They restricted their opposition in large measure to conditional rather than absolute considerations; in other words, under what conditions would a pipeline be acceptable rather than should one be built? Hampered by government secrecy and limited research capability, the issues the opposition parties raised during this period were often parochial and of secondary importance. The lack of expertise at their command handicapped them further by inhibiting them from stating their own position, as was the case in early May 1977 when the Conservatives turned down the NDP's challenge to reject a Mackenzie pipeline.

However else one may characterize the government's handling of the pipeline issue, it is not by openness, accessibility—or accountability.

6. DEVELOPMENT PARTNERSHIP Surely one of the most remarkable characteristics of the pipeline decision-making process has to be what can only be called the symbiotic relationship which prevailed between government and industry. In 1972, government pressure helped to persuade Gas Arctic and Northwest to merge. In 1979, government policy favoured the realignment of gas export applications behind Pan Alberta. In the former case, the most powerful alliance of oil and gas interests ever forged in this country was created; in the latter, the government backed itself into a corner by contributing to the momentum behind pre-building without receiving any of the assurances that the rest of the Alaska Highway pipeline would follow.

The government-industry partnership in large resource projects, of course, is not just a recent phenomenon in Canada. In the late 1950s, the government helped TransCanada Pipelines by building the most expensive section of the pipeline north of Lake Superior and leasing it to the company; in the Sixties, the government came to the rescue of small independent companies exploring in the High Arctic by forming Panarctic Oils of which it owns 45%; in 1975 the government helped to keep Syncrude alive by investing hundreds of millions of dollars in it. The government's role as a developer, while it has undoubtedly fostered economic growth, has also been of direct economic benefit to large resource companies. Moreover, it has led to a confusion of interests, the government's function as the protector of the public good being tempered by its association with the companies it ostensibly regulates.

7. BIAS The strongest bias of all was the government's attitude towards resource development. Throughout the 1970s, the question of whether to exploit the Mackenzie Delta reserves was never asked: the only question was always when and how. (Arctic Gas executives never doubted they would have won had 15 trillion cubic feet of gas been found in the Mackenzie Delta rather than 5.1.) This is a policy by rote of growth for growth's sake. It helps to explain how the government was able to shift its support so effortlessly

from pipeline proposal to pipeline proposal. Each in the end meant the same thing: faster development, more jobs, more exports, more wealth.

The policy of developing everything as quickly as possible is not one which helps to keep Canada's energy options open as its authors will sometimes claim. On the contrary, it requires such a single-minded investment of capital, technological and human resources that it effectively forecloses the pursuit of alternative policies, such as those towards conservation and renewable energy. This, too, is a cost of blindly accelerating northern development.

It can come as no surprise that those who believed that other values were as equally important as the rapid exploitation of natural resources saw the monolithic co-venturing between government and industry in the North as conspiratorial.[2] The elaborate decision-making process created by government for the disposition of the pipeline applications was anything but impartial and thorough. On the contrary, it distinguished itself mostly for its ad hoc nature and its political expedience. The proliferation of public inquiries of limited scope in response to political demands was an arresting symptom of the government's neglect in formulating comprehensive policies. Is it really absurd to ask what would have occurred had an Alaska Highway pipeline, rather than a Mackenzie pipeline, been proposed in 1974 and Judge Berger named to investigate its impact? Would a Mackenzie pipeline then have been conceived as an eleventh hour alternative and received regulatory approval because it did not suffer from the same flaws that would have become apparent after two years of examination of the Alaska Highway pipeline?

The haphazard nature of the Canadian process stands in sharp contrast to the direction the United States established in 1973 and successfully preserved thereafter. In spite of the separation of powers between the executive and legislative branches of government, the US maintained a far greater continuity in policy than Canada where power is more concentrated. The 1973 law approving the TransAlaska Pipeline System specifically instructed the American government to assess the feasibility of an overland gas pipeline and determine Canada's willingness to allow its construction. Congressional and administrative action thus led to the signing of the pipeline treaty and yielded the Department of the Interior study in December 1975 which helped to revive interest in the Alaska Highway pipeline.

The Alaska Natural Gas Transportation Act was the logical successor to the Trans-Alaska Pipeline Authorization Act. It did more than set a timetable for the American pipeline decision. It established as well a framework for making that decision: it stated the roles and duties of each decision-maker, the factors that each would have to consider in assessing the pipeline options; it defined provisions for public participation and appeals and specified legislative review of the President's decision. By contrast, the Canadian Cabinet itself largely chose the boundaries of the decision-making process, that is, its terms of reference and those who would be involved; it did not elaborate criteria publicly for making or justifying its decision other than to indicate that it would serve the national interest; it kept much of the work done for it secret; it effectively curtailed public participation by accelerating the decision-making process; holding a majority in the House of Commons, the government only faced token parliamentary review of its decision.

The contrast between the Canadian and American resolution of the pipeline issue reveals more than a difference between the political cultures of the two countries: it shows the extraterritorial impact of American legislation; it demonstrates Canada's willingness to accept a project of enormous consequences before it was fully understood. The government may not have prejudged the pipeline issue by acceding to the American deadline but it did prejudge its ability to make a thorough decision.

The Canadian government, it is now clear, muddled through the ten years it spent on the northern pipeline. It made precipitous commitments which often precipitated further undertakings. It responded to external "crises" with ad hoc solutions. It gradually altered the objectives the pipeline was to serve better to justify its construction. Thus, though the problem kept changing, the solution always remained the same.

Drifting with events seldom yields optimum decisions. In the Alaska Highway pipeline, Canada ended up with a project it does not need, that is to be built according to a timetable that may or may not reflect domestic priorities. Most of the issues the pipeline raised, those dealing with energy policy, Canadian-American relations, industrial strategy and northern development, for example, remain outstanding. Canada is no closer to their urgent reassessment than it was in 1970. Worse, perhaps, the government's ability to grapple with these issues does not seem to have improved measurably in the interval. The best evidence that the government would repeat the mistakes of the past, having been unable to learn its lessons, is provided in Trudeau's announcement of support for an Alaska Highway oil pipeline during the 1979 election campaign.

The Alaska Highway oil pipeline, like the Kitimat and TransMountain pipelines before it, was proposed to carry excess Prudhoe Bay oil that cannot be marketed in California to the American Midwest (the so-called Northern Tier states). Foothills began developing the concept of an Alaska Highway oil pipeline in 1977, before the gas pipeline decision—in case it lost, one wonders?—and after the Kitimat and TransMountain proposals had encountered heavy political opposition. The Alaska Highway oil pipeline, as its name implies, would parallel the gas line for most of its route, linking up to existing oil pipelines in northern Alberta.

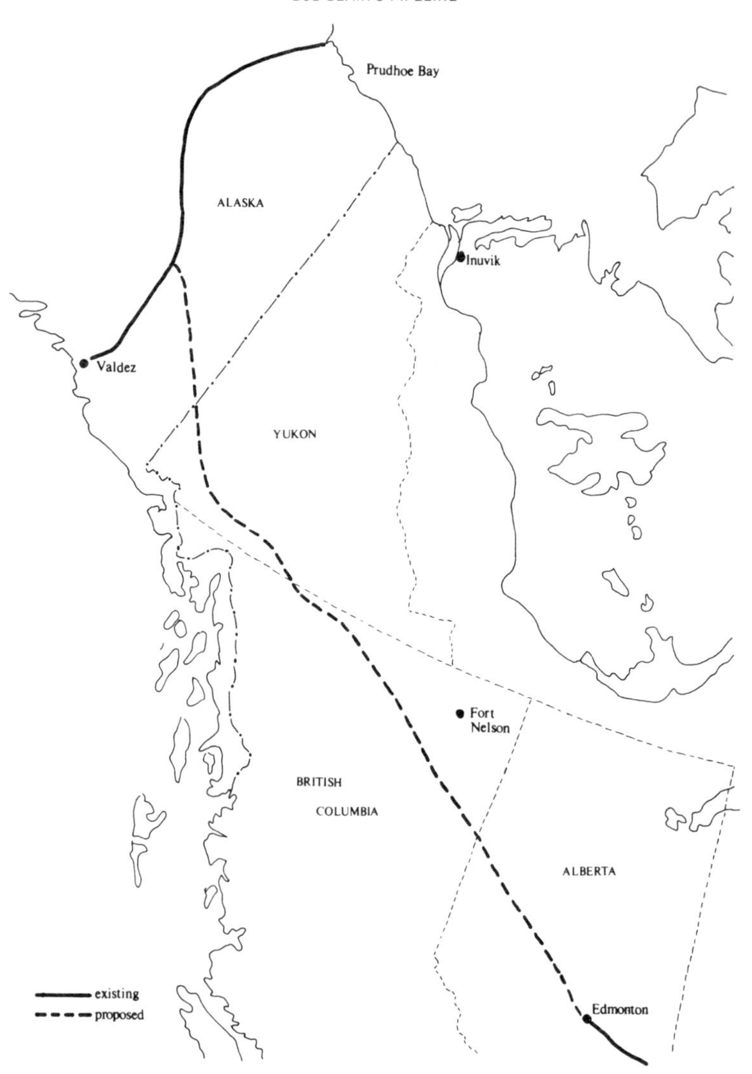

ALASKA HIGHWAY OIL PIPELINE

On April 10, 1979, as he was addressing the Petroleum Club in Calgary, Trudeau declared:

> Now parallel to that, there is the question of the oil pipeline. The United States, in March, asked us to express our views on how they would be able to get the oil efficiently from Alaska, from Prudhoe Bay into the United States, into the Midwest. And as you know, there are many projects, some of which don't involve Canada and some of which do. But even those which don't involve Canada have created environmental concerns, justifiable concerns. About spills on the high seas and the

> effect on our coast, our fisheries, and so on. So after looking at all the various projects, and in response to the United States' request for our views, the Canadian government has officially decided that not only would we reject the Kitimat approach which is rather well known, but that we would opt for the Foothills route, one of the two, either the all land route parallel to the gas pipeline, or the pipeline plus tanker from Valdez, pipeline from Valdez to Skagway, pipeline from Skagway to Whitehorse and then down the same route to Edmonton. Now that is calculated to be about one billion dollars. I don't know if the United States will take that option, but obviously the pipeline and the gas and oil pipeline along the same route would not only be good economically, and one would help the other, but it would be good environmentally. And we are officially, today, indicating to the United States that that is our preference. Of course, we want to see what their response is on that oil pipeline. But here again, just in terms of payroll if it proceeds, that billion dollar project would be in the order of $148 million payable just for Alberta and British Columbia.

The announcement came as a complete surprise. Senior officials at both the Departments of Indian and Northern Affairs and Energy, Mines and Resources had not known in advance about Trudeau's statement. Indeed, a little over a year earlier, on February 24, 1978, Trudeau had rejected the Kitimat pipeline in words that implied government opposition to the transshipment of Alaskan oil across Canada:

> If it's just for the Americans, you know, my offhand attitude is why don't they build a port on their West Coast if they want to bring oil for themselves. We would be interested in considering it only if we needed a port for ourselves but, as I say, that hasn't been demonstrated.[3]

After Trudeau's emphatic rejection of the Kitimat pipeline, however, Gillespie had written Schlesinger a letter suggesting that Canada and the United States study the Alaska Highway oil pipeline as an alternative. Gillespie's letter, like Trudeau's Calgary speech, offered some painful parallels to the Canadian government's pipeline policy of the early 1970s. In April 1972, also in Alberta, Trudeau had announced the construction of a Mackenzie Valley highway, without any prior environmental studies and without the advice of senior civil servants. A month later, Donald Macdonald had written to the American Secretary of the Interior, Rogers Morton, inviting the US to re-examine a Mackenzie Valley oil pipeline, an invitation Gillespie was extending six years later for the Alaska Highway oil pipeline. In his letter, Macdonald had claimed that the environmental damage caused by a Mackenzie Valley oil pipeline would be acceptable since a Mackenzie Valley gas pipeline would probably be built in any event. Trudeau was repeating the same argument in his speech, this time for the Alaska Highway. As the government had done in 1977 after the release of the Pipeline Agreement, Trudeau was underlining the economic benefits of the pipeline construction without reference to its adverse environmental and social impacts.

This case of *deja vu* does not stop here. In 1978, after it had first announced its interest in the oil pipeline, Foothills reaffirmed on several occasions its prior commitment to the gas line—a reaffirmation reminiscent of the days when Foothills claimed it wanted to build the Maple Leaf line before the Alaska Highway line. In 1979, as a result of the delays incurred by the gas line, Foothills began to acknowledge that the oil pipeline could, and then should, be built before the gas line. The American Congress in late 1978 passed a law, modeled on the Alaska Natural Gas Transportation Act, setting a deadline of early December 1979 for a presidential decision on an oil pipeline. Once again, Canada was going to have to compress its own consideration of the issue if it wanted to meet the American timetable (three of the four alternatives cross Canadian territory). Once again, the native people and the environment were likely to suffer the most from the speed with which a decision was made. Although the new Clark Conservative government was not bound by a Liberal electoral promise, it had to face the expectations its predecessor may already have engendered in the United States.

If it needed demonstrating, the government's handling of the oil pipeline issue reveals that political opportunism can erase any lessons that ten years of sometimes arduous consideration of the northern gas pipeline could have been expected to yield. This is a discouraging prospect indeed when decisions on Dempster and Polar Gas pipelines—and perhaps even now Mackenzie pipelines—are pending.

THE PIPELINE'S LEGACY

"Pipelines", says Bob Blair, "do great things for the places they go to ultimately as markets and something for the places they come from, but they are of strictly limited benefit to the places they go through".[4] This is particularly true in the case of the Alaska Highway pipeline where the delays already experienced and the prospect of new ones have sharply reduced the present value of the economic benefits it was supposed to bring. Neither the Canadian nor the American government, it is true, anticipated the delays the pipeline would encounter when they signed the Pipeline Agreement. Whenever both countries undertake other joint projects, however, it will be prudent to remember how tenuous some of the benefits of these undertakings can become.

The Alaska Highway pipeline's most enduring and, without question, most important legacy will be the stimulation of closer energy ties between Canada and the United States. When the pipeline is to be built is, in this context, of secondary importance as the approval itself demonstrates a political commitment which, if not carried through soon in the Alaska Highway pipeline, will be manifested in other endeavours. It is ironic that Carter and Trudeau should have ratified the Pipeline Agreement which their negotiators had just reached during the latter's official visit to Washington in September 1977 to witness the signing of the new Panama Canal Treaties. The fact that it was setting the stage for an arrangement many would regard as similar to the one from which Panama was finally extricating itself seemed to be lost on the Canadian government. Yet, the parallels are there. The northern pipeline will constitute a land-bridge of undeniable strategic value to the United States.

In 1975, a prominent Canadian businessman asked:

> Without being nationalistic at all, is it really desirable, considering sovereignty in the long, long term, for one country to establish one of its most critically important and permanent energy service corridors across some 1,600 continuous miles of another country?[5]

Two years later, the same businessman argued that "it may be good for Canadian purposes to achieve something sought by the United States . . . to satisfy an American purpose".[6] The speaker on both occasions was Bob Blair. The startling evolution in his position, of course, owed much to Foothills' transition from sponsor of the Maple Leaf project to that of sponsor of the Alaska Highway pipeline. Blair reconciles the seeming contradiction in sentiment between the two statements by explaining that the Canadian portion of the Alaska Highway pipeline will be designed, operated, built and controlled by Canadians whereas a Canadian Arctic Gas Pipeline would have entailed a substantial foreign component. This is a singularly unconvincing argument. Both ends of the pipeline will be in the United States. It will carry only American gas initially and may never carry Canadian gas. Under the terms of the Pipeline Agreement, the U.S. retains significant control even over Canadian portions of the line: Canada, for example, cannot raise the Yukon Property Tax over a certain limit; contracts for the pipeline's components must be submitted to competitive bidding, reducing the government's ability to enforce Canadian content regulations. The pipeline's very construction, its rate of expansion and its financing will all be determined to a greater or lesser extent in the United States. Although its ownership will be Canadian, it can hardly be described as fulfilling a Canadian purpose.

Security of supply has traditionally played an important role in guiding American energy policy. The construction of an Alaska Highway pipeline will give the United States a stake in Canadian territory and politics greater than has ever existed before. A dramatic reminder of this fact was provided in the fall of 1978 when civil disturbances in Iran sharply curtailed that country's large oil exports. American energy officials approached Northwest almost immediately to ascertain how quickly the southern portions of the

Alaska Highway Pipeline could be installed under the pre-building plan. The American initiative was undertaken, of course, before the Canadian government had decided to release new gas exports from this country.

But once again, the government had engendered powerful expectations which were circumscribing Canadian policy options. Immediately after the Pipeline Agreement, Schlesinger announced that Canada had informally agreed to increase gas exports. Canada had done no such thing but the growth of the Alberta gas surplus, the industry's eagerness to export and the government's own evident desire to develop the North had led the US to expect new gas supplies from this country, an eloquent testimony to the status Canada holds vis a vis the United States.

On this occasion, as on previous ones, Schlesinger showed greater foresight than his Canadian counterpart. The discussion of increased gas exports was not the only instance of closer Canadian-American cooperation in energy policy after the signing of the Pipeline Agreement. In his report to Congress on the pipeline decision, Carter had noted that an overland gas pipeline from Alaska would lead to enhanced energy ties with Canada. Indeed, in 1978 and 1979, a joint strategic oil storage programme, a more closely integrated electricity grid, oil swaps, the use of excess Canadian refinery capacity to refine American oil, a new oil pipeline to carry surplus Prudhoe Bay crude, a joint research agreement on the development of the tar sands, increased exports of electricity and the export of liquefied natural gas from the High Arctic were all discussed or implemented. What will be their cumulative opportunity costs? Will a succession of similar projects further erode Canadian sovereignty?

The Pipeline Agreement underlines Canada's growing "Finlandization". Although not formally a satellite of the United States, Canada is so imbued with American values, so dependent on American goodwill, so economically tied to the health of its neighbour and so exposed to possible retaliation that its ability to act independently is being circumscribed. The implicit premise that has underlain much of Canada's policy towards its neighbour, and was brought into sharp focus during the pipeline negotiations, is that a favour rendered today will be returned tomorrow. Although it may be too early still after the Pipeline Agreement to assess the validity of this belief, it does not seem to have governed Canadian-American relations since September 1977. The "fish war" between the two countries in the summer of 1978 is one example which suggests that the US is unlikely to make concessions to Canada on a quid pro quo basis.

At best, Canada's faith in earning favours from the US is naive. It does not allow for the often curious and parochial manner in which American foreign policy is developed. The consideration given by Congress of retaliatory measures for Canada's treatment of American border TV stations is a case in point. It is also important to underline that Canada's better neighbour policy contains many pitfalls as it forces trade-offs between issues that are not directly comparable and leads to accommodation where the costs and benefits of such a policy cannot be evaluated.

At worst, however, this doctrine is tragically wrong. Canada may prosper economically by collecting such IOUs from its neighbour—if they are returned—but will it prosper an an independent nation? In the modern world, the interdependence of countries may not only be inevitable but desirable as well. In the case of countries of vastly unequal power and wealth, however, this interdependence can lead only too easily to a confusion in national priorities in the smaller country.

More and more, the objectives of Canadian energy policy are taking an American colouration. In February 1979, following the shut-down of Iranian oil production, Don Jamieson, the Secretary of State for External Affairs, would declare that Canada "would not allow Americans to freeze in the dark". This was a charitable position to take but hardly a realistic one, since Canada relied on Iran until then for a greater share of oil imports than did the United States.

Yet the attitude that Canada must help the United States solve its energy problem is deeply ingrained. In June 1979, the president of Dome Petroleum, Bill Richards, summarized the views of many of his peers when he said:

> Surely the export of oil and gas surplus to Canada's needs is nothing more than enlightened self-interest. We have the potential in Canada to make a material contribution to North America's energy needs. The Western world is faced with the prospect of an oil and gas shortage. If this shortage, in fact, occurs, it could result in a world-wide depression. Canada as a great trading nation can hardly expect to prosper when all its neighbours and trading partners are suffering from a depression.[7]

Even the "nationalistic" Bob Blair would argue in November 1978 for the development of Mackenzie Delta gas in the mid 1980s—though Canada by his own calculation would not need frontier gas until the late 1990s —"because I believe that in the North American supply situation there will be an absolute deficiency of natural gas supply overall at a point in time before 1985".[8] As Alastair Gillespie put it, "It is only reasonable for our trading partners who are energy deficient to expect us to export energy which is surplus to our own needs".[9] But at what cost?

At the cost of building frontier pipelines before they are needed? Or of risking irreversible environmental damage, such as the decimation of the Porcupine caribou herd, an occurrence many biologists fear if the Dempster pipeline is built and the Dempster Highway open to unrestricted use? Or, of sacrificing native interests? An internal memorandum of the Federal Office of Native Claims, dated November 1977, states that "The government of Canada is prepared to extinguish native land claims, if necessary by legislation, to support its international word and commitment but will only do so in a way that represents the fairest possible settlement to those involved". A cynic might claim that the Canadian government was already predisposed towards legislating the extinguishment of native claims. Whatever the validity of this claim, there can be little question that the Pipeline Agreement imposes a formidable constraint on the aspirations of the Yukon's native people.

There are other costs, of course, some of which are extremely difficult to measure. At a time when the weakness of Canada's manufacturing industries is widely deplored, is it desirable to invest tens of billions of dollars in frontier development to create a new industry to export raw materials? What may be the foreign policy costs of being perceived as a resource hinterland to the United States? Should there be another Arab oil embargo against the US, will Canada be automatically included? Although the skewed structure of the Canadian economy is not a matter which may worry many Canadians, are we not being short-sighted by measuring the success of national policies on the degree to which they raise our standard of living in the short term?

Are these the costs Canadians are willing to pay to help solve energy shortages in the United States, shortages which, it is important to emphasize, are partly the result of waste and mismanagement? Canada could not satisfy American energy needs even if it wanted to; its resources are too small and American demand too great. This fact is undisputed. Yet, most of the Canadian oil and gas industry continues to argue that large-scale energy exports to the US are both feasible and desirable.

It is fitting that the last word in this chronicle of the northern pipeline should go to Bob Blair. In August 1977, after the government had endorsed the Alaska Highway pipeline, Blair declared with unthinking irony that "as well as hewers of wood and drawers of water, one of the other trades in which Canadians have world class qualification is the trade of building pipelines".[10] Blair, of course, is right.

Yet it is not at all clear that this is an achievement which is in the Canadian national interest. It may be that Canadians must succeed in being more than hewers of wood and drawers of water, more than pipeline developers, if this country is to be independent, secure, and prosperous.

CHAPTER ELEVEN

PREBUILDING THE PIPELINE

What shall it profit Canada if we gain a pipeline, and lose a nation's soul? What shall it profit the people of Canada, if we gain a thousand pipe-lines, and lose Parliament?

—Stanley Knowles during the 1956 Pipeline Debate

In March 1979, James Schlesinger had told Prime Minister Trudeau that Canadians would be "damn fools" to approve the prebuild without first obtaining a guarantee from the United States that the entire Alaska Highway pipeline would be completed on schedule.[1] In July 1980 the Canadian government approved the prebuild anyway, without having received any binding US assurances regarding the pipeline's completion.

In making this decision, the government not only ignored Schlesinger's advice but it indeed repudiated its own previously-stated policy. The sixteen months separating Schlesinger's warning and the prebuild decision provide, as a result, an important insight into Canada's policy-making process. They reveal the preeminent, if largely unseen, role of bureaucrats in making policy. They underline the growing interdependence of Canada and the United States in energy matters. Most of all, they highlight the government's inability to arrest the erosion of its policy options over time. In this regard, the government's evident reluctance to choose between the alternatives that remained open to it in July 1980 testified eloquently to the predicament into which it had allowed itself to drift.

The dilemma which the government faced in July 1980 was the following. If it approved the prebuild and its associated gas exports, Canada would lose its lever to force the United States to complete the rest of the pipeline on schedule. Further delays in the pipeline's completion would expose the country to several risks. First, the economic benefits of building and operating the whole pipeline would recede into the future. Second, the prebuild would perhaps have to be kept full even after the authorized exports had terminated, as Canada would be subject to intense US and industry pressure for more exports if there were energy shortages in the United States and an empty pipeline ran from Alberta to Chicago. Third, Canada would no longer be able to gain access to its own reserves in the Mackenzie Delta since the construction of a Dempster pipeline to these reserves is contingent upon the completion of the Alaska Highway system. Canada would thus be increasing its gas exports as it lost one of its options to meet its future domestic needs.

If, on the other hand, the government postponed the prebuild for a year or more while it waited for US guarantees that the pipeline would be completed, it would defer large economic benefits, among them an estimated $17 billion in export revenues; it would adversely affect the domestic gas industry, reduce exploration, and probably bankrupt several small Canadian-owned producing companies; it would also alienate Alberta, which supported the prebuild, just as the two governments were resuming their laborious negotiations over an oil-pricing and revenue-sharing agreement; finally, it would irritate the United States, which had been led to expect that the prebuild would be approved.

Neither alternative was attractive but the first entailed future risks whereas the second involved immediate costs. Given this trade-off, it is not altogether surprising that the government made the choice it did.

The prebuild decision was admittedly the most difficult the new Liberal government had to face after its return to office in the February 1980 election. What made it difficult was the convergence of several distinct issues, among them, Canada's gas export policy, the pricing of these exports, the risks Canada should assume in assisting in the Alaska Highway pipeline's completion, and the relations between the Alberta and the federal government. The prebuild provided the nexus for all these issues, forcing the government to weigh the achievement of an objective in one area against the sacrifice of one in another. The government could not, for example, both please Alberta by approving the prebuild exports and eliminate the prebuild's risks. Nor could it increase exports without losing some latitude in setting the export price. This equation was further complicated by the prebuild's dual nature: although it constituted an independent project, being financed separately from the rest of the pipeline (hence the term "stand-alone prebuild"), it nevertheless was also intended to become an integral part of it at some future date. It was important for legal as well as political and economic reasons that the government resolve this ambiguity.

The Northern Pipeline Act, which Parliament passed in 1978 to give force to the Pipeline Agreement between Canada and the United States, provided the legal basis for proceeding with the prebuild. Though there was nothing in the Act to prevent the Alaska Highway pipeline from being built in stages and from exporting Canadian gas in the process, the prebuild had to be shown to be a part of the overall pipeline or it would not fall under the Act's authority. Condition 12 of Schedule III of the Act was designed to supply this test. Condition 12 required Foothills to demonstrate that it had financed the entire Canadian portion of the pipeline before it could build any of its segments—including the prebuild. But because the pipeline had been delayed in the United States, Foothills was unable to meet this condition. To allow the prebuild to proceed, the government amended Condition 12 and, to protect Canada against the risk that the pipeline's northern portions would never be built, sought and obtained assurances from the US that the pipeline would be completed by 1985. These assurances, however, were substantially less than what the Canadian government had deemed essential at first. Whether they were legally sufficient to meet the requirements of the Northern Pipeline Act became the subject of a suit launched in the B.C. Supreme Court by Ian Waddell, the New Democratic Party's federal energy critic.

The legal basis for the prebuild decision fuelled the political storm which surrounded the project. It provided an inviting target for Opposition attacks in Parliament and attracted considerable editorial criticism in Canadian newspapers. The prebuild decision would have been contentious in any event because of its very nature. It is a symptom of the Canadian condition that pipelines have become metaphors for all that is considered admirable and deplorable in this country's economic and political evolution. In this regard, the controversy surrounding the prebuild decision echoed many of the themes of the 1956 "Great Pipeline Debate."

THE CREATION OF THE IMPASSE

In mid-1979, the Alaska Highway pipeline faced an uncertain future. It could not be financed under the terms of the Presidential Decision and its completion date had already slipped by two years. As further delays in the Alaskan sections of the project were inevitable, Foothills and Northwest began devoting an increasing proportion of their efforts to prebuilding the southern sections of the line. To be economically viable, the prebuild needed exports. An application was therefore filed before the National Energy Board by Pan-Alberta Gas, a sister company of Foothills, to export 4.9 trillion cubic feet over fifteen years. This term implicitly belied Foothills' claim that the rest of the pipeline would be completed expeditiously. Foothills, it was clear, was not prepared to assume the risk that the pipeline would be delayed and was hence seeking to finance the prebuild on the export of the Alberta gas rather than the transportation of Alaskan gas. The National Energy Board consolidated the Pan-Alberta application with twelve other export applications and began hearings on July 10, 1979.

In order to maximize the chances for success, Pan-Alberta "packed" the hearings. It sent form briefs to each of its gas suppliers asking them to intervene in support of its application. The tactic proved effective, though somewhat *gauche:* 135 of the 182 interveners explicitly supported the prebuild, but several small producers filled out their sample briefs incorrectly, some even forgetting to delete the instructions on them!

If Pan-Alberta's ploy was amusing in its transparency, its effect on the hearings themselves was disquieting. As a result of Pan-Alberta's tactics and the political constraints under which Pan-Alberta's competitors found themselves (in early 1979, Schlesinger had said that the US government would not be interested in importing gas from Canada if such imports did not support the construction of the Alaska Highway pipeline), and a number of other factors,[2] the export hearings were among the most one-sided in memory. Not only did Pan-Alberta face no effective opposition but the argument for large new exports itself went largely unchallenged.

It is revealing that the National Energy Board did not feel an obligation to redress the lopsided nature of its hearings. The government had declared the Alaska Highway pipeline to be in the public interest. A few months earlier, in its February 1979 report on Canadian Natural Gas Supply and Requirements, the Board had concluded that a gas surplus existed. Accordingly, the Board staff was instructed not to prepare any cross-examination that challenged the desirability of exporting gas.

This was a shocking instruction, and one that said a great deal about the Board's perception of its role. As fashioned by the Board, this role is to accept rather than to challenge the status quo, to change policy incrementally rather than chart bold new directions; above all, it is to avoid conflict, a tendency reinforced by Jack Stabback's chairmanship of the export panel. Stabback is, by nature, a compromiser and the Board's report, released on December 6, 1979, reflected his spirit of accommodation. The report sought to reconcile the competing demands the Board had had to adjudicate during the hearings: the demand for a greater volume of export than the surplus calculation would allow; and Pan-Alberta's demand for favoured treatment among all applicants in accord with its role in promoting the prebuild.

In its report, the Board calculated that the exportable surplus had more than doubled to 4.25 trillion cubic feet in the ten months since the last surplus estimate had been made. Although this was a dramatic increase, it was plainly insufficient to approve all the exports requested. Rather than reject any, the Board reduced each one in line with the surplus it estimated would exist year by year.[3] The Board thus approved a total of 3.75 Tcf in new exports, almost half of which were allocated to Pan-Alberta.

Having already found the Alaska Highway pipeline to be in the national interest, the NEB determined that "to the extent prebuilding would contribute to the financing and completion of the whole project, prebuilding would also be in the public interest." It would take the Board three more months to conclude that prebuilding by itself, independent of the rest of the pipeline, was also in the public interest. In December 1979, however, the Board was not convinced of the merits of a stand-alone prebuild and the need therefore for long-term exports if, as Foothills continued to maintain, Alaskan gas was to start flowing in the fall of 1984. Thus, even though the NEB had cut Pan-Alberta's application by 25 per cent annually starting in 1984, Stabback was absolutely convinced that the export decision was "supportive of the pipeline."[4]

Unfortunately for Foothills, the decision was not at all supportive of a stand-alone prebuild. The volumes Pan-Alberta had received could not justify the prebuild for the simple reason that Foothills, notwithstanding its public pronouncements, could not predict with certainty the date when Alaskan gas would start to flow. This is why Foothills had proposed, and needed, a stand-alone prebuild, one which could be financed entirely on the export of Alberta gas. For political reasons, however, Foothills had not felt it could admit to the reality of what it was proposing. Indeed, throughout 1979, Foothills had publicly insisted that "it is not and has never been intended in the Canadian sections that the pre-build is a stand-alone."[5] It thus invited the NEB to take it at its word and accept the assurance that the entire Alaska Highway pipeline would be completed by 1984. In a sense, Foothills had fallen prey to the "CAGPL syndrome." It no longer had sought to tailor its project to the national interest but rather to fit the national interest to its project. Because, in the fall of 1979, the two were perceived as diverging, Foothills was forced to redesign its prebuild proposal extensively. This feverish rescue attempt would span seven months and would conclude with the reversal of both the NEB's and the government's previously-held positions.

Foothills' opening salvo was to schedule a press conference in Calgary on December 13 to respond to the NEB decision. In order to forestall the adverse publicity that was sure to follow — the prebuild's delay or cancellation would anger Alberta as well as the gas industry — Bob de Cotret, the Conservative minister responsible for the pipeline (the Conservatives had replaced the Liberals in power in the 1979 election) issued a statement at noon restating the Canadian government's commitment to the entire pipeline and its support for the prebuild.

The Conservatives, however, were unwilling to commit themselves to a stand-alone prebuild. De Cotret had stated in November:

> We will not move on the prebuild until we have assurances the financing of the rest of the project is in place and it is in a position to move ahead expeditiously.[6]

De Cotret was thereby echoing a similar statement made by Allan MacEachen in March when the Liberals were still in office. On this issue, the three major parties were of one mind.

This unity nevertheless did not prevent the Liberals and the NDP from using strong language to criticize the government's acceptance of the NEB recommendation. Marc Lalonde, the Liberal energy critic, for example, denounced the export approval as perhaps "one of the greatest sellouts we have seen." In a statement that would come back to haunt him, he added:

> In our view, exports of natural gas to the United States should be authorized only on the basis of, first of all, an ironclad commitment regarding the building of the whole Alaska Gas pipeline. Everything has to be signed, sealed, and delivered, particularly the financing plan and the financing guarantees, before we start exporting one cubic foot of gas out of this country to the United States.[7]

At its Calgary press conference, Foothills announced that it could no longer meet its scheduled start-up dates of November 1, 1980 for the western leg of the prebuild and November 1, 1981 for the eastern leg. With a note of self-pity, Foothills added that the NEB decision to grant ProGas an export licence had "hurt our partners from a psychological standpoint" and that it was therefore necessary to "await a more coherent arrangement for overall implementing of previous decisions of the two national governments."

Foothills received two more blows in quick succession. In the evening of December 13, the Conservative government fell after having lost a vote of non-confidence in Parliament. As a result, the prebuild's regulatory difficulties were compounded by political uncertainty. At the end of January, the government announced a 30 per cent increase in the gas export price to bring it in line with world oil prices. This increase, making Canadian gas among the most expensive in the United States, led some of the prebuild's American customers to reconsider their purchase of Alberta gas.

The gas export price increase marked the nadir of the prebuild's fortunes and led an exasperated Bob Blair to state in February 1980:

> If we were looking afresh at that project today, its possible downsides and its rather strictly limited upside, its regulatory overlays and its confusions of unexpected interventions from the US government side particularly, then we know that our bright guys with pencils would say "pass on it" relative to other opportunities. All we are doing at best is help furnish the US energy economy a utility service and the effort/risk has become hardly worth putting more investment out front.[8]

A SOLUTION EMERGES

If, at the time, it seemed that the NEB export report had dealt a fatal blow to a stand-alone prebuild, the pipeline sponsors could nevertheless ill afford to abandon the prebuild now. As a result of the pipeline's continued inertia in the United States, the completion of the Alaskan portions of the project had been pushed back another year, to 1985. The cost of the entire project, including the gas processing plant at Prudhoe Bay, had climbed to a staggering $23 billion. Foothills had placed itself at considerable financial risk in its promotion of the Alaska Highway pipeline, having already spent close to $140 million — an investment on which it would receive no return if the prebuild was killed. Baldly put, the prebuild was Foothills' and Northwest's only hope to start generating revenue from a pipeline whose completion date neither of them could predict.

Paradoxically, the seeds of a solution to the impasse which the NEB report had created were to be found in the report itself. The Board had hinted that not all of Canada's gas surplus had been approved for export. If it was possible to obtain this unallocated gas and divert some of the already approved exports through the prebuild — in particular the ProGas volumes — a stand-alone financing of the prebuild might become feasible.

The first step was to ascertain whether an unallocated surplus indeed existed. Accordingly, on December 31 Bob Blair wrote the NEB to describe the difficulties the Board's decision had created and to outline the minimum conditions needed to proceed with the prebuild. He also invited the Board to reiterate its support for the prebuild. The Board's reply was sent on January 4, 1980. In it, the Board confirmed that some 500 billion cubic feet of unallocated surplus gas existed. As it had been requested, the Board reaffirmed that it had "found that prebuilding of the Foothills pipeline system is in the public interest."

The second step was to develop a financing plan for the prebuild that would be acceptable to both the National Energy Board and the Northern Pipeline Agency (NPA) which had been created by Parliament in 1978 to oversee and expedite the pipeline's construction. This plan would dictate, in addition to new exports and the diversion of already approved volumes, a much higher rate of depreciation to allow the prebuild to stand alone and be amortized on the basis of Alberta gas rather than Alaskan gas. Such a plan would necessarily involve modifications to previous NEB decisions regarding exports and the pipeline's tariffs and would therefore have to be presented to new hearings. It would also require that Condition 12 be amended so that the prebuild could be financed independently from the rest of the pipeline.

Foothills would need a forum in which to present and defend that plan as a prelude to having regulatory authorities accept or reject it. On January

7, the National Energy Board announced it would give Foothills that forum at a hearing to start in February. Foothills was asked to lead evidence on whether it could finance the prebuild "under present known conditions" and, if not, to "identify the minimum changes needed to achieve financeability." The NEB's decision to call a hearing on the financing of the prebuild—rather than on the financing of the entire pipeline, as it had originally intended—represented a major breakthrough for Foothills. It implicitly legitimized a stand-alone prebuild and gave Foothills the opportunity to gain institutional support for it. It also showed the influence the NEB exerted, not only on Foothills' fortunes, but also in determining policy. If it concluded that a stand-alone prebuild was both feasible and desirable, it would force the government to reconsider its opposition in principle to the concept.

As there would be no reprieve from an adverse regulatory decision, Foothills could take no chances. It had to develop a financing plan that would satisfy both Canadian regulatory requirements and its own exigencies. In seeking to meet these two objectives, Foothills held a number of meetings with officials of the National Energy Board and the Northern Pipeline Agency to discuss ways of proceeding with a stand-alone prebuild. Bob Pierce, Foothills' president, Bob Blair (now chairman of the company), and Scotty Cameron, Pan-Alberta's president, led the Foothills side. Mitchell Sharp, the Northern Pipeline Commissioner, represented the Agency and Geoff Edge, the NEB's vice-chairman, represented the Board.

The meetings in which Geoff Edge participated covered a number of areas that went to the heart of both the prebuild's financing and the new export hearings. These areas included the discussion of the effects of previous Board decisions on the prebuild; information on the progress of financing negotiations concerning the American sections of the pipeline; procedural matters relating to the form of application and the timing of new hearings (e.g., exports); changes in Condition 12 of the Northern Pipeline Act to allow a stand-alone prebuild; and, increases in the gas export price.

Edge's active involvement in this process raised disturbing questions about the fairness of the upcoming hearings: would he now sit as a judge of a financing plan and an export application he had helped to develop? Indeed, had he already indicated his support for them? Edge denies that he had but his commitment to seeing the pipeline built—a commitment some have described as an obsession—was well known. It was Edge who had decided to call separate hearings on the prebuild financing. Edge would also soon name himself to chair the gas export hearing on Pan-Alberta's application for the unallocated surplus. He was therefore playing a crucial role in determining whether and under what conditions a stand-alone prebuild would be allowed to proceed. His willingness to meet

Foothills officials privately before these hearings began may not necessarily have indicated prejudgement but could only have helped the company formulate its plans.

On February 12, Pan-Alberta filed its new export application. Moving with uncommon dispatch, the Board gave its staff only one day to review the supporting documents before setting down a hearing to start on March 18. Edge chose to step down from the export hearing panel but continued to chair the financing hearings, his meetings with Foothills having become public knowledge. These hearings, in any event, were the more important: if the Board found, at their conclusion, that the prebuild could only be financed on the basis of new exports, Pan-Alberta's application would become nothing more than a formality.

In its meetings with Edge, Foothills had made it clear that the prebuild could not proceed under the conditions the Board had imposed. The choice the Board faced therefore was to soften these conditions or delay and perhaps even kill the prebuild. The latter, however, was not a burden the Board was prepared to accept because the stakes were simply too high: the prebuild not only represented an estimated $17 billion in export sale revenues but also the first stage in a project which had the full support of both the Canadian and American governments. The prudent regulatory course was to change the conditions Foothills judged as unacceptable and let Cabinet decide whether these changes had gone too far.

The prebuild financing hearings began on February 19, one day after the Liberals had been returned to power in the 1980 general election. Edge delivered the Board's findings at 3:00 p.m. on March 11. The Foothills lawyers were apprehensive. The list of changes they had requested was long and every one of the changes was needed if the prebuild was to succeed. In previous rulings concerning tariff matters, Edge had tried to push Foothills to the limit. Edge understood perfectly well that the changes Foothills was demanding were leading to a stand-alone prebuild, a project different from what the export decision had envisaged and far different from what the northern pipeline decision had suggested. Though Edge did not like the concept of a stand-alone prebuild, he was more concerned with the consequences of delaying the prebuild. Only three months earlier, the Board had found additional exports to be in public interest. Should it now hold back on the means to move these exports to market? And if it did, what would be the consequences for independent producers with shut-in reserves? Should the Canadian gas industry be penalized for Foothills' and Northwest's inability to guarantee the date when Alaskan gas would start to flow? Edge thought not and therefore, on March 11, he agreed to almost all the changes Foothills had demanded.

The questions troubling Edge were all valid but they illustrated the circularity of reasoning to which the Board's commitment to the pipeline was leading. In December, the Board had approved gas exports to justify the prebuild because the prebuild was in the public interest. Now that the exports had been found in the public interest, they were used to warrant a stand-alone prebuild. The exports and the prebuild, in other words, lived in perfect symbiosis, neither being able to proceed without the other and each justifying the other's existence.

The importance of Edge's concurrence with Foothills cannot be overemphasized. The Board's stamp of approval gave the stand-alone prebuild a legitimacy it had lacked until then. Foothills would now use it in arguing that Condition 12 be changed. It also established the framework for the gas export hearings beginning a week later. Their outcome was now foregone and, indeed, the Board approved Pan-Alberta's application on April 30.

The Board's findings on the prebuild financing and its subsequent export decision represented a considerable retreat from the conditions imposed in the December report. This was a retreat directed largely by Edge, who was effectively running the Board in the wake of Stabback's decision to retire. The NEB's rapid shift in policy towards a stand-alone prebuild reflected Edge's equally rapid ascendancy within the Board.

The change in Foothills' fortunes was as abrupt as it was remarkable. Although the prebuild still faced a number of hurdles, it had gained new momentum. The main obstacle that remained was Condition 12. It was all that separated the first stage of the Alaska Highway pipeline from a simple gas export pipeline.

THE INTERNAL DEBATE

The pipeline's delays in the United States had vastly increased Condition 12's importance to Canada. It was the "stick" to the exports' "carrot." It was the means to ensure that the whole pipeline would be completed once the prebuild had been approved. In short, it was the key to the early realization of the benefits Canada had sought in the Pipeline Agreement.

There was consequently a great deal of opposition within government to changing Condition 12. That opposition was centered mainly within the Departments of Finance and Energy, Mines and Resources, which underlined in their briefing memoranda the risks of a stand-alone prebuild: the risk of open-ended exports; the risk of further delays in the northern sections of the pipeline; the risk of losing one option for the transportation of Canadian frontier gas; the risk of increasing American dependence on Canadian gas imports, particularly since Canadian gas continued to be cheaper than Alaskan gas.

If the prebuild counted many critics, it also knew its staunch advocates in the National Energy Board and the Northern Pipeline Agency. The NPA's mandate, as given in the Northern Pipeline Act, was principally "to facilitate the efficient and expeditious planning and construction of the pipeline." These were hardly the detached regulator's terms of reference and it comes as no surprise then that the NPA should have quickly become the prebuild's most enthusiastic booster within government. Senator H.A. (Bud) Olson, the Minister responsible for the pipeline and Alberta's sole representative in the new Liberal Cabinet, also felt a deep commitment to the project. He would spend a great deal of his time between March 3, when he was appointed, and July 17, when the Canadian decision was made, lobbying on its behalf. A member of the Priorities and Planning Committee of Cabinet, Olson was able to apply his influence at the highest political levels.

Olson, Edge, and Sharp all agreed on the desirability of amending Condition 12. If this was a simple enough procedure requiring no more than an Order-in-Council, there existed legal constraints on the degree to which Condition 12 could be changed. The constraints arose from the Northern Pipeline Act itself which authorized the construction of one pipeline only—the Alaska Highway pipeline. If no assurances could be given that the prebuild in time would become integrated into an Alaska Highway pipeline, the Act itself, rather than just Condition 12, would have to be amended. An amendment to the Act would require parliamentary approval and would thus politicize the complex of issues surrounding the prebuild. It would become a major embarrassment to the government by challenging the very underpinnings of its approval of the Alaska Highway pipeline three years earlier.

The key to amending Condition 12, therefore, lay in obtaining credible assurances from the United States concerning the building of the northern portions of the Alaska Highway pipeline. These assurances would have to satisfy both the legal requirements of the Northern Pipeline Act and the Canadian government's political needs. They would have to refute the charge that Canada was "selling out" its gas—the charge that Marc Lalonde had made only a few months earlier in Opposition—and protect Canada against the risk of proceeding with a stand-alone prebuild. The problem Canada faced in early 1980 was that the United States was not able to provide any meaningful assurance concerning the date of the pipeline's completion, let alone an "ironclad commitment."

THE FINANCING NEGOTIATIONS

What Canada needed was proof that the pipeline could be financed. There existed a great deal of skepticism regarding Northwest's ability to raise the funds it would need to build its project. The problems the pipeline faced had been analyzed incisively in the reports Arlon Tussing had prepared for the Alaska legislature in early 1979. These reports had been circulated widely in Canada and contributed to the uneasiness many felt about amending Condition 12.

That uneasiness was increased by the lack of progress evident in the United States. The Carter Administration acknowledged this problem and periodically tried to revitalize the pipeline. In one of these efforts, in July 1979, President Carter publicly rebuked the Prudhoe Bay producers, Exxon, Arco, and BP/Sohio, for dragging their feet in coming to the pipeline's aid. He instructed James Schlesinger to discuss with them the role they could play in helping to finance the pipeline. These discussions proceeded at a glacial pace. It was not until October 26, three months later, that Exxon presented a first financing plan with producer involvement. It took until March 18, another five months, for the producers and the pipeline sponsors to meet face to face for the first time! A non-binding agreement stating the producers' and Northwest's intention to develop a financing plan for the pipeline would take another three months to reach. This imperceptible rate of progress testified eloquently to the financing difficulties the pipeline faced. It had the unfortunate effect of reducing Canada's expectations both of what American assurances would be forthcoming and what might be acceptable as a *quid pro quo* for softening Condition 12.

The major financing issues the producers and the pipeline sponsors were debating fell into seven broad categories:

1. Cost. There was no definite cost estimate for the entire pipeline. Having suffered the consequences of Alyeska's massive cost overruns, the producers were refusing to commit themselves to a project whose cost, too, might escalate significantly.

2. Overrun Pool. In order to finance the pipeline, money-lenders would have to be assured that cost overruns could be covered. Who would provide this overrun pool?

3. Completion Guarantees. What assurances could the pipeline sponsors provide that they would complete the pipeline and repay its debt on schedule?

4. Nature of Producers' Involvement. The 1977 Presidential Decision which had approved the pipeline prohibited the Prudhoe Bay producers for antitrust reasons from owning any equity in the project. The producers were reluctant to join the sponsors in assuming the very expensive engineering design costs ($500 million) without any assurance that they would have the right to participate in the pipeline's management during its construction and operation.

5. Gas Conditioning. It would cost $3.5 billion to build a conditioning plant at Prudhoe Bay to process and clean the gas before it could be carried. Who would pay for the plant?

6. Alaska Participation. The State of Alaska had the choice of taking

one-eighth of the gas produced at Prudhoe Bay in kind and was interested in establishing a petro-chemical industry. Could Alaska help in financing the pipeline?

7. Regulatory Uncertainty. Several regulatory issues remained outstanding. Their resolution would colour the producers' and the sponsors' perception of their financial participation in the pipeline.

In an attempt to bridge the chasm between the sponsors and the producers, the U.S. Department of Energy appointed Martin Lipton in late 1979 to act as mediator. Lipton found his assignment a particularly thankless one. Neither side was willing to compromise; Northwest relied on the Presidential Decision to safeguard its position and minimize the producers' role; the producers, for their part, insisted on certain regulatory changes (concerning the treatment of conditioning costs, for example) before they agreed to participate. In complete frustration, Lipton circulated a memorandum on January 30, accusing Northwest's John McMillian of refusing to negotiate the details of a financing plan. Lipton went on to recommend a drastic solution—that the producers build the Alaskan portion of the line and then sell it to the American government. The bitter recriminations which ensued threatened to set the whole project back once again. The proposal was dropped and Lipton left two weeks later.

This was undoubtedly the pipeline's darkest hour. In the United States, the financing negotiations had seemingly reached an impasse. In Canada, Foothills was still struggling to keep the prebuild alive in the wake of the National Energy Board's gas export decision. At this critical juncture, the Northern Pipeline Commissioner, Mitchell Sharp, intervened and asked Pierre Trudeau to write President Carter a letter underlining the risk that the whole project was in danger of collapsing unless greater efforts were made to expedite matters.

Trudeau heeded Sharp's advice and wrote Carter in March soon after being returned to office. The letter had its desired effect. McMillian used it in his bargaining with the producers and, on March 18, in the office of Energy Secretary Charles Duncan (James Schlesinger had resigned in the fall of 1979), a draft agreement was reached on the sharing of the $500 million in pre-construction design costs.

Because the Canadian government would come to rely on this agreement as one of the assurances from the United States that the Alaska Highway pipeline would be completed—and would use it therefore to justify its approval of the prebuild—it is important to define its scope carefully. The agreement only allowed the pipeline sponsors to proceed with the necessary pre-construction engineering work on schedule. It did not constitute a financing plan for the pipeline. This would have to be the subject of a second agreement (these two agreements became known as the Phase I and Phase II agreements respectively). Even though the scope of the Phase I agreement was extremely narrow, the producers and the sponsors gave themselves yet another month, to April 15, to finalize the first agreement and identify their differences on Phase II.

GAS EXPORT PRICING

Having just overcome one obstacle in the United States, the prebuild was immediately confronted with another, this one involving the export price of Canadian gas. The price increase that had taken effect in February had already led two of the American buyers of prebuild gas, United Gas Pipe Line and Panhandle Eastern Pipe Line, to reconsider their purchases. Another price increase might lose these sales, endanger others, and thus threaten the prebuild itself. The U.S. government, too, was concerned about the price of Canadian gas exports, both because of its direct effect on US energy costs and also because such pricing might influence Mexico and Algeria to raise the price of their gas exports.

On March 24, accordingly, US Energy Secretary Duncan went to Ottawa to negotiate a set of principles which might guide future Canadian export pricing. The two countries agreed after the meeting that Canada would continue to base its export price on the international oil price but would henceforth give three months' notice of any price increase. By mid-April, the world oil price had risen again and the Department of Energy, Mines and Resources prepared itself to announce an increase of 27¢ per thousand cubic feet in the Canadian export price of natural gas.

Having learned that such an announcement was imminent, McMillian wrote a personal letter to Prime Minister Trudeau requesting a delay in the increase. He argued that a rise in the Canadian price would "result in termination of the prebuild project because of the fragile status of the project in the marketplace." He then warned that if the prebuild was terminated, it would cause "a severe psychological blow as well as significant practical set-backs to the overall project and...would result in significant delays." By raising its gas export price, Canada would therefore not only endanger the prebuild exports but indeed the entire pipeline.

Concerned that they might lose their export sales, some Canadian gas producers wrote Lalonde, the Minister of Energy, Mines and Resources, at the same time, also asking for a delay in the export price increase. This concerted pressure was successful. On April 15, only three weeks after having reasserted Canada's policy to peg its export price to the international oil price, Lalonde announced a postponement of the price increase. He cited as the reason the "adverse psychological impact that an early increase might have on the initiatives now under way to get the Alaska Highway Gas Pipeline started."

Canada did not raise the gas export price any further in 1980. The price freeze was an indication that the United States was gaining new leverage on the prebuild issue. Canada, with a mounting surplus, needed to export but the US was in the middle of a gas glut and did not have an urgent need for new imports. The continuing record level of activity in Alberta was creating a severe marketing problem which underlined the importance of the prebuild exports. If these were delayed, the Canadian gas industry would face a major crisis. As the prebuild decision approached, this factor would come to restrain Canada's insistence on American guarantees that the pipeline be completed on schedule.

Canada's decision not to increase its gas export price represented one major concession; amending Condition 12 would be another. How far was Canada to go in helping the pipeline? This was the crux of the issue as a decision on the terms of Condition 12 approached.

AMENDING CONDITION 12

The dilatory pace of the financing negotiations between Northwest and the Prudhoe Bay producers carried ominous implications for the prebuild. It was politically and legally impossible for Canada to approve the prebuild without some assurance from the United States that the rest of the pipeline could be financed. Foothills, however, was facing increasingly difficult time constraints in meeting its November 1 completion target for the prebuild's western leg. It had already succeeded in extending the deadline for a government decision by purchasing long lead-time items for its pipeline, but it could not do so indefinitely because it faced a summer-only "construction window" for a 22-kilometer section of line in British Columbia.

The Northern Pipeline Agency was acutely aware of these time constraints. Mitchell Sharp indeed had already proposed that Condition 12 be amended on at least two separate occasions. His recommendation had been rejected both times because Cabinet feared that such a change would be interpreted in Washington as a softening of the Canadian position. The awkward compromise that was reached was for the NEB to amend Condition 12 subject to Cabinet approval and hold hearings on the financing of the pipeline as though the amendment had been accepted. This compromise was designed to satisfy both the hard-liners who had opposed changing Condition 12 until the US had guaranteed the pipeline's completion and the supporters of the prebuild who wanted to prevent a delay in the project.

The new Condition 12 no longer required Foothills to obtain financing for the entire pipeline before building any section of it, but to show it could finance the prebuild. The amendment also called on Foothills to "establish to the satisfaction of the Minister and the Board that financing of that portion of the pipeline, other than the prebuild sections...can be obtained to enable the pipeline to be completed before the end of 1985... ."

Two matters of particular importance need to be underlined here, one procedural and one substantive. First, the Board was holding a hearing to enable Foothills to demonstrate that it could meet the weaker Condition 12; it was not holding a hearing to determine what the risks and benefits of various amendments might be or whether, indeed, to amend Condition 12 at all. The Board deemed these questions to have been answered by its determination that the prebuild was in the public interest. Second, the Board was asking Foothills to establish that it *could*, not *would*, finance the pipeline in order to complete it by 1985.

This distinction was more than semantic for, if Foothills could establish that the whole pipeline might be completed in 1985, it certainly could not guarantee completion. Even in its watered-down version, therefore, the new Condition 12 did not ensure that the northern sections of the pipeline would be built expeditiously. As if to underline the point, Cyrus Vance, the US Secretary of State, would say on his visit to Ottawa on April 23 that he "could give no commitment at this time that the funds [for the pipeline] could be raised."[9]

The Condition 12 hearings which began on April 29 were thus entirely symbolic. They were not intended to test the level of protection Foothills could provide against the risk that the pipeline would be delayed indefinitely but merely to give the appearance that such protection existed. The nineteen days given to interveners to prepare for the hearings indicated that the NEB was more concerned with haste than thoroughness. At the opening of the hearings, indeed, the Board rejected three motions seeking a postponement and a broadening of the scope of the hearings.

Even so, Foothills was unable to demonstrate during the short hearings that it could meet the new Condition 12. Rather than rule on the matter, and kill the prebuild, Edge, who was chairing the hearings, chose to release a statement outlining the four issues which, in his view, remained to be resolved before Condition 12 was met. Of course, in following this unusual procedure Edge was doing more than indicating to Foothills what it still had to do. He was giving the prebuild yet another chance, underscoring in the process the Board's continuing role as the pipeline's mentor. Indeed, Edge now believed that "the prospect of a significant delay in the pre-building of the Eastern Leg could be prejudicial to the pre-build project and to the whole of the Alaska Natural Gas Transportation System."[10] This was the same warning that McMillian had delivered in his letter to Prime Minister Trudeau. The NEB had thus come to accept that the prebuild was not merely a useful fillip to the pipeline's financing but a prerequisite to its scheduled completion.

The circle had now closed: under Condition 12, there could be no prebuild without the whole pipeline following; as a result of financial realities, however, there might be no pipeline without the prebuild going ahead first. The government now had to decide which would come first: the chicken or the egg.

THE CANADIAN LOBBY

With the release of the NEB's statement on Condition 12, Canada had taken every step it could, short of Cabinet approval, to enable the prebuild to proceed in 1980. The NEB had recommended additional gas exports, approved a stand-alone financing plan for the prebuild, amended Condition 12 (subject to ratification by Cabinet), and listed the issues on which it would require more evidence before it could rule on the pipeline's financing. It was now up to the United States to deliver the assurances Canada was seeking.

It was in order to find out what assurances Canada could expect that Bud Olson went to Washington on May 12 accompanied by Sharp and Edge. Olson's mission was made considerably more difficult by the government's inability to formulate a clear list of pre-conditions that the United States would have to meet before Canada approved the prebuild. The absence of such a bottom line reflected the government's own internal split between the prebuild's critics and its advocates who could not agree on how hard Canada should press the United States. This irresolution was costly for it was eroding Canada's options. By May 12, indeed, it had become virtually impossible for the US to give Canada meaningful guarantees concerning the pipeline's completion—such as a Congressional commitment to help finance the pipeline if necessary—in time to allow the prebuild to meet its year-end start-up schedule. As a result, the assurances Canada sought became a function more and more of what it could obtain from the US in the few weeks remaining than of the protection it needed against the risk of delay or non-completion.

This strategy, of course, was one to which Olson, Sharp and Edge were all predisposed. As the prebuild's strongest supporters in Ottawa, they were not inclined to jeopardize its construction by being intransigent with the Americans. Olson, nevertheless, recognized that the Phase I agreement which the producers and the pipeline sponsors had negotiated, but still not signed, would not alone provide a politically acceptable basis for Canada's approval of the prebuild. A more comprehensive level of protection would be needed. During his discussions with American congressmen and officers of the US Department of Energy, Olson began developing the concept of putting in place "a framework of agreements" to ensure the pipeline's completion. This framework was to consist of three principal elements: a reassertion of the Administration's support for the pipeline and its readiness to sponsor any Congressional waiver to the Presidential Decision that would be necessary to finance the pipeline; a statement by the Prudhoe Bay producers that they were committed to the pipeline and that they intended to participate in its financing; and an undertaking from Congressional leaders that they would seek quick approval of any financing plan the producers and the sponsors reached.

Although Olson returned from Washington with the outline of such a compromise, his visit had not succeeded in impressing upon his American hosts the urgency of Canada's demands and the consequent need for prompt action. The prebuild simply did not loom as a large issue in Washington and, it being an election year, the attention of American politicians was focused elsewhere.

The lack of visible progress over the month following Olson's trip made for a stormy meeting of the Priorities and Planning Committee of Cabinet on June 17. The Committee was already in a belligerent mood as a result of the US Senate's continued unwillingness to ratify the Canadian-American Fisheries Treaty, which was essential to the welfare of Canadian fishermen. If the US government could be stymied by a recalcitrant Congress on this issue, what assurance did Canada have that a similar stalemate might not be repeated some day over the pipeline? Indeed, what assurances did Canada have regarding the pipeline itself? The Cabinet Committee had a draft letter from President Carter reaffirming his Administration's support for the pipeline. It had the Phase I financing agreement between the US sponsors of the line and the Prudhoe Bay producers. A draft Phase II agreement existed but it fell far short of binding the producers to help finance the pipeline: all they would agree to was to "work with Alaskan Northwest in an effort to develop its financing plan." If the producers, who stood to earn well in excess of $40 billion in gas sale revenues, were still unwilling to commit themselves to completing the pipeline, why should Canada accept the risk of prebuilding its southern portions?

These assurances were not deemed to be enough. They did not remove the pipeline's financing obstacles in Canada or in the United States and therefore did not ensure that the project in its entirety would be completed by 1985. Cabinet was becoming militant as time was running out. Foothills had once again stretched its schedule but would be able to do so no more: since the Flathead Ridge in southeastern British Columbia had to be crossed in August to complete the Canadian portion of the western leg in 1980, July 15 was the last day until which a decision could be delayed. As it was, it would already be too late if winter were to come early.

Cabinet's willingness to press the United States more strongly was a sign of its dissatisfaction, of course, but also of its distance from the issue since the February election. It had allowed policy-making to slip into the hands of others, principally those of the NEB and the NPA. It was Edge and Sharp who had moulded Canada's strategy, who had judged a stand-alone prebuild to be in the national interest, and who had dropped

Canada's insistence for an ironclad commitment to the pipeline from the United States. Sharp would later argue that the members of the Priorities and Planning Committee had been poorly briefed about the issue and and that their debate therefore had been emotional and uninformed. It would probably be equally true to state that Cabinet's newly-found militance reflected considerable frustration. It had boxed itself in by neglecting the issue and now had to pay the consequences.

The absence of any meaningful US assurances concerning the pipeline's completion was particularly galling for Marc Lalonde. He had stated his party's (and his own) position only six months before in uncompromising terms. Intensely proud, he now had to endure taunts almost daily in the House of Commons about the nature of the "ironclad commitment" the United States would deliver. Having let the prebuild issue drift this far, Lalonde tried personally to press the United States. His opportunity came four days later, on June 21, during the economic summit of the seven leading industrialized nations held in Venice. Lalonde spent seven hours with US Energy Secretary Duncan and John Sawhill, the Under-Secretary, discussing gas export pricing and the prebuild. Lalonde reaffirmed the need for Congressional action to change the Presidential Decision to allow Foothills to finance the Canadian section of the pipeline.[11] What Lalonde was requesting, however, could no longer be done because time was too short. Lalonde resuscitated the concept of swapping the prebuild exports for equivalent volumes of Alaskan gas once the Alaska Highway pipeline was operating. Although the swaps had once provided the rationale for the prebuild, they had proved an impractical concept to implement and had thus been dropped. As all forecasts showed that Canada would not need frontier gas until the turn of the century, the swapping proposal may have been intended more to cover Lalonde's retreat from his previous position than to secure immediate advantages to Canada.

Prime Minister Trudeau, too, tried to press the Canadian position during the Venice summit, in a half-hour meeting with President Carter. Carter, however, had not read his briefing notes and was therefore unable to answer Canada's concerns. Trudeau was irritated by this incident which showed all too clearly the indifference with which the United States viewed the issue. As Canada could not, and would not, approve the prebuild on the strength of the assurances it had received already, the prebuild was once again on the verge of collapse. In a last-ditch rescue attempt, Bud Olson went once again to Washington.

His first visit had not met its objective. In the six weeks since, almost nothing had happened. The Prudhoe Bay producers and the pipeline sponsors had finally signed their two-phase financing agreement which only bound them to keep the pipeline alive for one more year. However unsatisfactory this agreement was to the Canadian government, it was clear that the producers would go no further. Olson therefore decided to concentrate on the third element of the strategy he had developed in May — a Congressional assurance.

At 7:30 a.m. on June 27, Olson began a breakfast meeting with Charles Duncan, Henry Jackson, the chairman of the US Senate Energy Committee, John Dingle, the chairman of the House Energy Committee, the minority and majority leaders of both Houses of Congress, and senior officers of the Federal Energy Regulatory Commission and the Economic Regulatory Agency. He outlined what assurances Canada needed and why. He reminded his audience of Canada's experience with the Fisheries Treaty and the requirement therefore for a Congressional as well as an Administration commitment to the pipeline. He described the consequences of a year's delay: Foothills and Northwest would wind down their operations and would not commit further sums to the project until they had obtained every single regulatory approval that they needed. Further delays would be inevitable. But if he obtained the assurance he was seeking, Olson promised to recommend Cabinet approval of the amendment to Condition 12.

Olson emphasized he was making no threats; this low-key approach worked. Sharp had already discussed with key Congressional leaders the text of statements they would be asked to make. To Sharp and Olson's surprise, the Americans proposed something more: a joint Congressional resolution in support of the pipeline. The resolution was drafted that morning, Olson reviewed it, and the Senate passed it unanimously that afternoon with the House of Representatives concurring three days later, on July 1.

The Congressional resolution had an enormous effect, not so much for what it said, but rather for what it represented. The resolution itself was quite modest. It stated only that "it is the sense of Congress that the System [Alaska Highway pipeline] remains an essential part of securing this nation's energy future and, as such, enjoys the highest level of Congressional support for its expeditious construction and completion by the end of 1985." Such an expression of support cost little to make since it did not commit Congress to any specific course of action. Canadian officials had approached Senator Jackson in the spring to discuss the possibility of having a much more ambitious resolution introduced in the Senate. They were told that any resolution which would approach the level of commitment Canada was seeking would prove too controversial to be passed in the time available and the idea had therefore been dropped.

If the resolution was largely devoid of substance, it nevertheless was of great symbolic importance. It represented the third assurance Canada had been seeking. It had been passed unanimously and in record time. Sharp and Olson would now argue that Canada would insult the United

States if it delayed the prebuild after having sought and obtained such an expression of support.

Only one piece was missing to the puzzle: a resolution of the issues the NEB had identified on May 9 in its statement on Condition 12. On June 27 the Board, "recognizing that some movement on the four issues has occurred in the time since the statement was made," wrote "to know if any concerns Foothills (Yukon) might have had on the four issues... have been met." The procedure the Board was following was extraordinary, for Foothills, with a large vested interest in proceeding with the prebuild as quickly as possible, could not be expected to give anything but an affirmative reply (which it did on July 7). That Foothills be satisfied that it could finance the Canadian sections of the Alaska Highway pipeline was, of course, a necessary precondition to any Board finding on Condition 12. But, if all the Board needed was Foothills' word for it, there had been little point in holding a public hearing in the first place.

THE GOVERNMENT DECISION

The task facing the Priorities and Planning Committee of Cabinet when it met on July 9 to consider the prebuild decision was a most unenviable one. In Prime Minister Trudeau's words, "the sole purpose of the government at this time is to ascertain whether we have these guarantees or not. This is a judgment call."[12] It was a judgment call complicated by the government's inability, over the spring, to formulate criteria by which it could assess the "guarantees" it had received from the United States. As the date for a decision approached, Cabinet ministers indeed offered divergent public interpretations of what these criteria should be. Trudeau would say in Parliament that "we will be weighing the evidence to make a decision as to whether a prebuild will prevent the building of the whole thing or, on the contrary, will encourage it."[13] Olson, on the other hand, would be quoted as saying that "what's more important now is not the guarantees from the United States but whether or not Canadians living in Alberta want it done."[14] What made these statements striking at the time was not so much the disagreement they illustrated but rather the implicit readjustment in the government's objectives. The government was no longer seeking an ironclad commitment from the United States. On the contrary, it had tailored its objectives to the assurances provided by the United States. All along, the government's approach under Sharp's pragmatic guidance had been to obtain what was possible. It was a flexible strategy with no bottom line and no precise definition of what would constitute an adequate level of assurance.

That level of assurance was arguably no greater on July 9 than it had been on June 17 when the Cabinet Committee had judged it to be insufficient. The only new element was the joint Congressional resolution whose importance loomed out of all proportion to its true substance. Indeed, the government's eleventh-hour attempt at obtaining a firmer assurance from the US had backfired by yielding a modest result which compromised Canada nevertheless for having sought it. Cabinet now had to reconcile the high expectations it had engendered with the meagre assurances it had received.

The prebuild decision had narrowed to the choice between two options: Canada could reject the US assurances as being insufficient and postpone the prebuild for at least a year or it could accept them and let the prebuild proceed. The costs in choosing the first option were high: a deferral in large export revenues, a slump in the gas industry, Alberta's further alienation on the eve of oil-pricing negotiations, and Washington's displeasure. The second option, too, implied some costs but few that would be immediate. It is true that some American irritants would remain: the withholding of import permits for the non-prebuild gas exports that Canada had already authorized, and the continued American resistance to Canada's gas export pricing policy. But the risks associated with a stand-alone prebuild would not materialize for a few years, and perhaps never.

The immediate costs were mostly political. The prebuild had few public supporters and many critics. The New Democratic Party attacked the government relentlessly for bypassing Parliament in making a decision which, it claimed, violated the intent of the Northern Pipeline Act. This charge won editorial backing in several newspapers and won Tory support as well. Joe Clark, for example, accused the government of making an "ironclad flip-flop." The Conservatives, indeed, sensing a division in Liberal ranks, began to mount an increasing barrage of criticism of their own. Cabinet was taken aback by the unexpected strength of the Conservative attack. Although Cabinet was ready to approve the prebuild, it was reluctant to assume the entire political costs of an unpopular decision, particularly when those who stood to benefit the most from the prebuild, the same Alberta constituencies which the Conservatives represented, seemed unwilling to support it publicly. On July 9, therefore, the Priorities and Planning Committee of Cabinet deferred making a final decision until its political consequences could be gauged more accurately.

Once again, Bud Olson took the lead in rallying support to the prebuild. He went to Calgary to urge Albertans to lobby for the project and to launch a letter-writing campaign in favour of the prebuild. The stratagem was effective. The Conservatives were silenced and the Liberals received the public show of support for which they had hoped. The full Cabinet met in the morning of July 17 for an hour and a half to discuss the prebuild and again at 5:00 p.m. that day. At 8 o'clock, Marc Lalonde rose in the House of Commons to announce that "the government has taken a decision to approve in principle the construction of the Alaska pipeline." It was fitting that the confusion that had surrounded the prebuild from the beginning should have endured even in the government's announcement of its decision. Lalonde, of course, had meant to refer to the prebuild and not the entire pipeline project.

CONCLUSION

The main issue confronting Canada in July 1980 was not whether the prebuild would help the pipeline's cause, as Prime Minister Trudeau suggested — the prebuild cannot do otherwise — but whether the entire pipeline would be built on schedule. In this respect, the prebuild did not resolve any of the financing problems the pipeline faced: it did not remove the obstacles to financing created by the Presidential Decision; it did not clarify the role of either the Prudhoe Bay producers or the State of Alaska in covering cost overruns or providing completion guarantees; and, of course, it did not eliminate the possible need for government financial backstopping. This last issue remained very much unanswered when Cabinet made its decision. Diane Hall, a Foothills Vice-President, would unwittingly provide ammunition to the prebuild critics only days before the final decision by declaring that "we don't know in the end whether there will have to be an American government guarantee for the Alaska portion"[15] of the pipeline. The assurances Canada received from the United States addressed these financing problems but did not remove them, forcing Canada to make its "judgment call" about the risks a stand-alone prebuild presented. The uncertainty that remained concerning these problems, of course, was the main reason why it was impossible in July 1980 to state categorically when the pipeline would be completed.

Because the prebuild decision involved other issues besides the pipeline, other criteria must also be used in assessing it. In the spring of 1980, for example, Ottawa considered using the prebuild exports as a lever in its negotiations with Alberta over oil-pricing and revenue-sharing. That approach was eventually rejected, in part because it was felt there were too many issues already dividing the two governments to add another. The depth of this division, of course, was later dramatically revealed in the reaction which Ottawa's National Energy Program and its constitutional proposals provoked not only in Alberta but in the West as a whole. If one of the government's objectives in approving the prebuild was to placate Alberta, it plainly did not succeed.

It is ironic that the Canadian government was unable to find the time necessary to obviate the risks of a stand-alone prebuild although Schlesinger had warned Trudeau of these risks sixteen months before the final decision. The reason was, of course, that the government not only addressed the prebuild issues too late — after the NEB export report — but it also conformed to the tight deadlines Foothills imposed. Although these deadlines were extended repeatedly, they never gave the government more than a few weeks at a time in which to plan. As a result, a perpetual state of crisis surrounded the prebuild issue and the government never took full advantage of the six and a half months which ended up separating Foothills' first deadline from the final decision.

It is instructive to contrast the government's drift on this issue with the initiative it took in the fall of 1980 concerning the Cold Lake heavy oil project in Alberta. When Esso threatened to wind down its Cold Lake operations because of the federal-provincial stalemate over domestic oil pricing, the government invested $40 million in the project to keep it alive for a further six months. The government could, of course, have applied the same principle to the prebuild. There, too, it could have purchased extra time to resolve outstanding issues. That time would have allowed the government to formulate a clearer position and might have yielded a more concrete American commitment to the pipeline.

The government's failure to assess and make full use of the time it had was critical. It effectively foreclosed the opportunity of demanding firm assurances from the United States, since the US would not have enough time to deliver them. It forced Canada to content itself, not with a Congressional waiver of certain sections of the Presidential Decision affecting the pipeline's financing, but with the promise merely that such a waiver would be considered at some undetermined date in the future.

It is true that the two federal elections in 1979 and 1980 diverted the attention of Canadian politicians from the prebuild issue. But this fact, in itself, does not provide a satisfactory explanation for the absence of a more clearly defined Canadian strategy to obtain a higher lever of US commitment to the pipeline. Both the Liberals and Conservatives, after all, had been essentially united in their demand for unequivocal American guarantees regarding the pipeline's completion. The key to understanding the prebuild decision can be found in the role taken by the National Energy Board and in the mandate and autonomy of the Northern Pipeline Agency.

The NPA, as has been pointed out, had quickly interpreted its mandate as one of advocacy. Mitchell Sharp, for example, believed that the risks of not approving the prebuild far outweighed the risks of proceeding without an ironclad commitment from the US. If the prebuild was postponed, Sharp feared that the whole pipeline would suffer a body blow and would perhaps recede indefinitely into the future. If the prebuild was approved, he was not particularly concerned that the northern portions of the line might be delayed a year or two, because Alberta gas would still be flowing and amortizing the prebuild's facilities. Sharp therefore was not going to place the prebuild in jeopardy if, in Geoff Edge's words, all the US could offer were "reasonably firm assurances, but not complete assurances"[16] that the rest of the pipeline would be built on schedule.

The NPA's promotion of a stand-alone prebuild ran directly counter, of course, to the policy which both the Liberals and Conservatives had publicly espoused. That the NPA was able to win the prebuild battle in spite of this conflict reveals an extraordinary influence and autonomy which is fundamentally the result of Sharp's role as Northern Pipeline Commissioner. A former senior Cabinet minister and a former colleague of many of the members of the Trudeau Cabinet, Sharp was more used to making policy than implementing it. Shortly after the prebuild decision, Marc Lalonde chided Sharp for usurping ministerial prerogatives by making policy decisions without consultation or government approval.[17] The prebuild provides an outstanding example of how policy can be made by non-elected officials who then present politicians with a virtual *fait accompli*.

If the prebuild decision must be scrutinized both for the risks to which it exposes this country and for what it reveals about the policy-making process, it must also be evaluated for the questions it raises about the government's approval of the Alaska Highway pipeline. In 1977, the government justified this approval on essentially two grounds: an impending domestic need for frontier gas and the sizeable economic benefits of building and operating the pipeline. The prebuild and its associated gas exports reaffirm what was becoming apparent in 1977, namely, that Canada will not need frontier gas for many years — perhaps not until after the year 2000 if recent forecasts are accurate. That argument, already suspect in 1977, thus became completely untenable in 1980.

The second argument for approving the pipeline was economic. The pipeline's construction and operation will yield very large economic and industrial benefits. The value of these benefits, however, depends entirely on the timing of the pipeline's completion: the more it is delayed, the less the expected benefits are worth today. Indeed, the pipeline's continued delay raises the very real risk that it will compete for scarce labour and capital resources with other energy projects scheduled for the mid-1980s, among them the $7 billion Alsands tar sands plant, the $11 billion Cold Lake heavy oil project, and the $4 billion Hibernia field development. The overlap of several such projects would almost certainly lead to labour shortages in specific trades and intensify inflationary pressures in some sectors of the economy.

Unfortunately, the Pipeline Agreement does not include a provision penalizing either party for delays. Although such a provision would undoubtedly have proven contentious to enforce, its absence has meant a deferral for at least three years, without compensation, of the economic benefits Canada was to earn from the pipeline. As these benefits were one of the reasons the government gave for approving the pipeline, its inability to use the prebuild as a lever to obtain firmer US assurances regarding the pipeline's completion must be seen as a major shortcoming in the prebuild decision.

The government's approval of the prebuild illustrates how the pipeline's bi-national character had blurred the distinction between Canadian and American interests. In approving the prebuild, Canada was accepting a substantial risk, essentially to advance an American purpose — the construction of the Alaska Highway pipeline. Mitchell Sharp justified this risk by arguing that "it is very much in the interest of Canada to get this line built if only to reduce the dependence of the United States on Canada."[18] The paradox in seeking to reduce American dependence on Canadian gas by increasing exports captures the historic ambiguity in Canadian energy policy. It has never been clear whether one objective of this policy is to achieve greater Canadian integration with the United States in the energy field — the cumulative effect of past decisions — or to promote increased Canadian independence. The prebuild decision demonstrates that the ambiguity remains very much unresolved.

FOOTNOTES

Chapter 1

1.Katherine Govier, "Radical Sheik" in *Canadian Business*, February 1979

2.Ibid

3.Ian McDougall, "The National Energy Board: Solving American Problems, Creating Canadian Dilemmas", in *The Canadian Forum*, August 1977, Vol. LVII, no. 673.

4.Published by J.J. Douglas Ltd. in 1977. Foothills had no editorial control over the contents of the book.

5."Application to the National Energy Board and Supporting Material of Foothills Pipelines (Yukon) Ltd. Regarding its Tariffs, Tolls, Financing and Other Related Matters" Vol 1, April, 1979: Summary of consulting expenses as at Dec. 31, 1978, p 6-39.

6.Quoted in "Ed Phillips", a profile by John Schneiner, in *Kanata*, May-June 1979

7.William Kilbourn: *Pipeline* (Clarke Irwin, 1970, Toronto) pp vi, vii

Chapter 2

1.See Robert Douglas Mead, *Journeys down the Line* (Doubleday and Co. Inc., Garden City, New York, 1978) pp 80-85.

2.Several excellent accounts exist of the government's policy towards northern petroleum development during this period. I am particularly indebted to Edgar J. Dosman, *The National Interest* (McClelland and Stewart, 1975, Toronto); David Crane, "What's Behind Canada's Energy Crisis", a five part series in the *Toronto Star*, October 11, 1975, to October 18, 1975; Robert B. Gibson, "The decision-making process", in the Workgroup on Canadian Energy Policy, *A Case for Delaying the Mackenzie Valley Natural Gas Pipeline*(1974)

3. Edgar Dosman, *op. cit.*[1], p 24

4. See Richard Rohmer, *The Arctic Imperative* (McClelland and Stewart, 1973, Toronto), Chapters 4 to 7 for a longer account of these events.

5. Dosman, *op. cit.*[1], p 24

6. Dosman offers a more detailed account of this meeting in *ibid.*, pp 71-75

7. Text of an address by the Hon. J.J. Greene, Minister of Energy, Mines and Resources to the Mid-year Meeting of the Independent Petroleum Association of America, Denver, Colorado, May 12, 1970.

8. F.K. North, "Oil and Gas Resources: Delusion or Deception?" in *The Calgary Herald*, November 28, 1972

On June 2, 1971, J.J. Greene would make his now famous claim that "Canada's total oil reserves were 469 billion barrels at the end of 1970 while total natural gas reserves were 725 trillion cubic feet. At 1970 rates of production, these reserves represent 923 years' supply for oil and 392 for gas".

9. Address by the Hon. Jean Chretien, Minister of Indian Affairs and Northern Development, to the Society of Petroleum Engineers, Dallas, Texas, March 10, 1971

10. *Toronto Star*, March 20, 1971

11. Crane, *op. cit.*[1], October 14, 1975

12. Ibid

13. Dosman, *op.cit.*[1], p 107

14. Transcript of remarks by the Prime Minister to a public meeting, Sportex Hall, Edmonton, April 28, 1972, p 9

15. Minutes of Proceedings and Evidence of the Standing Committee on Indian Affairs and Northern Development, April 13, 1972. Quoted in *The Mackenzie Valley Highway*, Pollution Probe, October 19, 1972

16. Dosman, *op. cit.*[1], p 99

17. Department of Finance: "A Northern Canadian Gas Pipeline: Evaluation of the Impact on the National Economy" October, 1972; reprinted in *The Canadian Forum*, June-July 1973, Vol. 53, numbers 629 and 630

18. Eric Kierans, March 1971; quoted in Pollution Probe's Mackenzie Pipeline Information Package No. 8, "Economic Consequences"

Chapter 3

1. *Financial Post*, April 1972; Stephen Duncan, "Northern Vision, 1972 style, Dief's Dream has Escaped"

2.See the testimony of Dr. R. Page to the Mackenzie Valley Pipeline Inquiry in Martin O'Malley *The Past and Future Land* (Peter Martin Associates Ltd., 1976), Toronto pp 55-68

3.*Toronto Star*, August 14, 1970. Quoted in McCullum and Olthuis, *Moratorium* (Anglican Book Centre, 1977, Toronto) p 71

4.Speech notes for Hon. Jean Chretien, Minister of Indian and Northern Affairs, at legislature dinner on the occasion of the opening of the 51st session of the Council of the Northwest Territories in Yellowknife, January 18, 1974

5.Transcript of St. Lawrence Centre town hall meeting, Toronto, January 24, 1973

6. Quoted in D. Peacock, *People, Peregrines and Arctic Pipelines* (J.J. Douglas Ltd., 1977, Vancouver) p. 63

7. Quoted in *Maclean's*, July 25, 1977

8. *Globe and Mail* interview, December 31, 1977

Chapter 4

1.*Globe and Mail*, January 15, 1974

2.*Financial Post*, February 9, 1974

3.*Globe and Mail*, October 4, 1974

4.Testimony before the Senate Commerce Committee and the Senate Committee on Interior and Insular Affairs, February 17, 1976

5.See "The National Energy Board: Economic Jurisprudence in the National Interest or Symbolic Reassurance?" by Ian McDougall in *The Alberta Law Review*, Vol. IX, No. 2, July 1973

6.Minutes of Proceedings and Evidence of the Standing Committee on Natural Resources and Public Works, March 13, 1973, pp 14-15

7.Department of Energy, Mines and Resources: *An Energy Policy for Canada* (Phase 1) (Information Canada, 1973), p 97

8.See Murray Edelman, *The Symbolic Uses of Politics* (University of Illinois Press, 1964, Urbana)

9.Confidential memorandum from C.G. Edge to National Energy Board chairman, December 18, 1974

10.John Helliwell: "The National Energy Board's 1974-1975 National Gas Supply Hearings", in *Canadian Public Policy*, 1:3, Summer 1975

11.*Globe and Mail*, February 18, 1975

12.Minutes of management committee of Gas Arctic/Northwest Project Study Group, January 22, 1975

13.Law Reform Commission of Canada: *The National Energy Board* (1977), p 37

14.*Ibid*, p 40

15.R.D. Howland: "Principal Requirements for Northern Pipelines", speech given to the Canadian Northern Pipeline Research Conference, February 2-4, 1972. *Proceedings*, p. 195

16.On April 26, 1977, during the second round of the NEB pipeline hearings, Crowe addressed a meeting of thirty representatives of Canadian banking and financial institutions at a luncheon sponsored by MacLeod, Young, Weir and Co., one of Foothills' financial advisers. During his speech, Crowe made several remarks which could be interpreted as favouring the Alaska Highway pipeline over a Canadian Arctic Gas pipeline.

The following month, Crowe gave a talk to a lunch sponsored by Loeb, Rhoades and Co., the financial advisers to Northwest Pipeline, the American sponsor of the Alaska Highway pipeline.

Crowe has admitted to having been a dinner guest of Bob Blair's during the pipeline hearings.

After the pipeline decision and after leaving the NEB, Crowe became a director of a small exploration company controlled by Northwest, Energy Ventures, whose board of directors was dominated by Northwest employees, including John McMillian, Northwest's chairman. Energy Ventures cooperated with Alberta Gas Trunk in the latter's purchase of Husky shares on the American stock exchange in early 1978.

In 1978, Crowe also did some consulting work on the possible connection of Siberian gas fields to the Alaska Highway pipeline.

Although this is all circumstantial evidence, it had led Earle Gray, the former director of public affairs of Canadian Arctic Gas to argue in his book *Superpipe* (Griffin House, 1979, Toronto) that "it could hardly be expected that Crowe would freely offer the benefit of his personal observations to members of the financial community in both Canada and the United States, and at the same time withhold such views from government officials in Ottawa". Gray's argument has considerable merit. Crowe's behaviour after the Supreme Court ruling raises questions not only about the propriety of his conduct but indeed of the role he may have played in the pipeline decision.

17.*Oilweek*, October 15, 1973

18.J.G. Stabback: Notes for an address to a seminar on "Doing Business with Canada" held by the Law Schools of the University of Georgia and Emery University at Atlanta, February 28 to March 1, 1975

Chapter 5

1.Robert Pierce, executive vice-president, Alberta Gas Trunk Line, May 25, 1976, Federal Power Commission transcript pp 24, 625-6

2. Letter from Ed Phillips, president of Westcoast Gas Transmission, to Senator Ted Stevens, October 14, 1975

3. Letter to the author, August 7, 1978

4. Testimony submitted by S.R. Blair, president and chief executive officer of Alberta Gas Trunk Lines Ltd. for joint hearings of the Interior and Insular Affairs Committee and the Commerce Committee of the United States Senate, March 24, 1976

5. Much of the information on McMillian and Northwest's early years is based on two articles by Richard A. Fineberg which appeared in the *Alaska Advocate* on April 27 and May 11, 1978

6. *Forbes*, August 15, 1976

7. Earle Gray, *Superpipe* (Griffin House, 1979, Toronto), p 28

8. Katherine Govier, "Radical Sheik", in *Canadian Business*, February 1979

9. Federal Power Commission transcript, p 24, 266, May 24, 1976

10. *Oilweek*, July 26, 1976

11. Telegram to the Secretary of State, Washington, DC, September 29, 1976; reprinted in transcript of Subcommittee on Indian Affairs and Public Lands of the Committee on Internal and Insular Affairs, House of Representatives, Oversight hearing on transportation of Alaskan natural gas, serial number 95-4

12. Position brief of the Federal Power Commission staff, December 7, 1976

Chapter 6

1. Federal Power Commission, *Initial Decision on Proposed Alaska Natural Gas Transportation Systems*, February 1, 1977

2. Earle Gray, *Superpipe* (Griffin House, 1979, Toronto) pp 93-4

3. Interview with the author, June 23, 1978

4. Statement of John G. McMillian, chairman of Northwest Energy Company, before the House Interior and Insular Affairs Committee, Subcommittee on Indian Affairs and Public Lands, February 17, 1977.

5. *Ottawa Journal*, February 5, 1977

6. *Globe and Mail*, February 17, 1977

7. NEB transcript, page 17,070

8. NEB transcript, page 19,804

9. *Toronto Star*, February 27, 1976

10. *Globe and Mail*, February 23, 1977

11. Transcript of Prime Minister Trudeau's press conference at the National Press Club, Washington, DC, February 23, 1978

12. *Vancouver Sun*, February 1, 1977

13. *Financial Post*, August 5, 1978

14. TransCanada Pipelines, *Preliminary Report to Shareholders*, January 25, 1977

15. John Helliwell et al.: "An Integrated Simulation Approach to the Analysis of Canadian Energy Policies". Reprinted in the *Proceedings of the IASTED Simulation, Modelling and Decision in Energy Systems Symposium*, June 1978, Montreal.

16. CTV Question Period, May 22, 1977

17. See D.J. Gamble, "The Berger Inquiry: An Impact Assessment Process", in *Science*, Vol. 199, March 3, 1978

18. November 8, 1976. Transcript, page 15,993

19. August 8, 1976. Transcript, page 9,041

20. Memorandum to file from Alastair Gillespie, March 7, 1977

21. Ibid

Chapter 7

1. Thomas R. Berger, Corry Lecture at Queens University, Kingston, Ontario. Reprinted in *Queens Quarterly*, Vol 83, No. 1, spring, 1976

2. Martin O'Malley: *The Past and Future Land* (Peter Martin Assoc., 1976, Toronto)

3. Presentation by W.P. Wilder, chairman of Canadian Arctic Gas Pipeline Ltd., to the Genesis Club of Toronto, March 15, 1977

4. Martin O'Malley, *op. cit*[1], page 100

5. *Ibid*, page 14

6. D.J. Gamble: "The Berger Inquiry: An Impact Assessment Process" in *Science*, Vol. 199, March 3, 1978

7. Quoted from R. Guild Nichols, "Public Participation in Energy Policy in Canada", unpublished case study prepared for the Committee for Scientific and Technological Policy of OECD, Paris, December 1977.

8.O'Malley, *op.cit.*[1], p 170

9.Berger staff report

10.Thomas Enders, telegram to Secretary of State, September, 1976. See footnote 11, Chapter 5

11.See testimony of Father Fumoleau in O'Malley, *op. cit.* , pp 118 to 135.

12.T.R. Berger, *Northern Frontier, Northern Homeland*, Report of the Mackenzie Valley Pipeline Inquiry, Vol. 1 (Ministry of Supply and Services, 1977)

13.*Financial Times* , June 13, 1977

14.W.P. Wilder, "Risky to Deny a Mackenzie Gas Pipeline?", *Globe and Mail* May 9,1977

15.*Toronto Star* , May 10, 1977

16.The CBC National TV News, May 11, 1977

17.*Perspectives on a Northern Pipeline Decision: A Research Report for the Department of Energy, Mines and Resources,* (Goldfarb Consultants Ltd., June 1977).

18.Memorandum from N.E. MacMurchy to Economics Branch, Mackenzie Valley/ Yukon Hearing Group of the National Energy Board, March 25, 1977

19.National Energy Board, *Reasons for Decision: Northern Pipelines*, (Ministry of Supply and Services, June 1977)

20.*Ibid*, p. 1-168

21.In 1970, the NEB approved a fifty percent increase in gas exports; in 1971, the application of the same surplus formula used to justify the 1970 exports showed that domestic requirements were no longer fully protected; in 1974, the board licensed a petrochemical project in Alberta involving the export of ethane, a natural gas component, thereby establishing the first exportable surplus since 1970; in 1975, it found that a natural gas shortage had already begun; in 1977, the date of first shortfalls was pushed back to 1982.

22.See John Helliwell et al: "An Integrated Simulation Approach to the Analysis of Canadian Energy Policies". Paper presented to the Simulation, Modelling and Decision in Energy Systems Symposium in Montreal, June 1978.

Chapter 8

1.Letter to Dr. James Schlesinger from John C. Bennett, vice-president of El Paso (Alaska) Company, June 12, 1977

2.*Globe and Mail*, July 6, 1977

3. *Montreal Gazette*, August 16, 1977

4. Report of the Working Group on Supply, Demand and Energy Policy Impacts of Alaska Gas, July 1, 1977

5. Letter to Senator Ted Stevens from Douglas J. Bennet, assistant secretary for congressional relations, State Department, July 26, 1977

6. Press conference in Washington, DC, August 9, 1977

7. *Report of the Alaska Highway Pipeline Inquiry*, Ministry of Supply and Services, 1977

8. Press release from the Prime Minister's Office, "Northern Pipeline Statement", August 8, 1977

9. *Financial Post*, September 17, 1977

10. Statement of Hon. James R. Schlesinger, Secretary of the Department of Energy to Committee on Energy and Natural Resources of the United States Senate, September 26, 1977

11. Press release from the President of the Privy Council, "Canada-US Agreement on a Northern Pipeline", September 9, 1977

12. The considerable figure of $1 billion claimed by the government as a saving on the transportation of Canadian gas was reached by multiplying the proven reserves in the Mackenzie Delta (5.2 tcf) by the decrease in costs ($.21/mcf) attributable to the cost-sharing arrangement and the increase in pipeline capacity. The "reduction of approximately $1 billion in transportation costs" is therefore an aggregate figure which covers twenty years of pipeline operation; it also incorporates an annual rate of inflation of 5%. One obtains a more meaningful measure of Canada's potential saving by deflating the $1 billion to express it in today's dollars. Furthermore, it is necessary to discount this sum to calculate its present value. Dollars earned over a period of time are not directly comparable, as a dollar today is worth more than a dollar tomorrow because of the interest it can earn in the interim. Therefore, it follows that a flow of savings which would begin in 1985, the date a Dempster pipeline was assumed to deliver its first gas, is worth much less today than if that flow had started when the Pipeline Agreement was signed.

   Assuming that the present reserves in the Mackenzie Delta were delivered at a constant rate over a period of twenty years, the present value of the savings referred to by the Canadian government, discounted at 5% annually, would be 283.83 million (in 1975 dollars; 1975 was used as the reference year for most of the economic calculations done by the US and was adopted in this instance by the Canadian government). In other words, Canada would be indifferent if it were given the choice between receiving $283 million in 1977 or $520 million (the product on the present reserves in the Mackenzie Delta and the reduced transportation tariff expressed in constant dollars) over a period of twenty years starting in 1985.

   Should the construction of a Dempster pipeline, however, be delayed five years or more to reflect the improved domestic natural gas situation, the present value of these savings is reduced to slightly over $200 million.

13. In order to obtain a true measure of the value of this revenue flow, it is necessary to deflate and discount it to the present. Discounted at 5% annually, the Yukon Property Tax would have generated a benefit with a present value of $250 million in 1977. Since the pipeline's construction has been delayed, however, Canada will start collecting the Yukon Property Tax later and the present value of this benefit must be reduced correspondingly.

14. The Yukon Property Tax will yield more revenue than either of the plans proposed by the NEB and the Lysyk Commission. However, it by no means represents ... "more than twice the return under the arrangement proposed by the Lysyk Inquiry and three times that advocated by the NEB" as the government claimed at the conclusion of the negotiations. (The NEB proposal would have generated revenues with a present value of about $205 million). The reason behind the government's inflated claim is not difficult to surmise. It is ironic however that the United States should have objected so strenuously to the proposition that Foothills be charged for a compensation fund only to accept a more costly alternative. This, of course, was a cheap price to pay to avoid setting such a precedent.

15. See the testimony of H.L. Lepape and S. Orlosfsky on behalf of US gas companies supporting the Alcan project before the US Senate Committee on Energy and Natural Resources, October 11, 1977.

16. Alaskan gas has a net present value of over $24 billion according to US government calculations. See the calculations by the Federal Energy Regulatory Commission included in the response by James Schlesinger to the Senate Energy Committee questions, February 5, 1979.

Chapter 9

1. *Globe and Mail*, August 19, 1978

2. *Time Magazine*, September 11, 1978

3. *Globe and Mail*, November 17, 1978

4. *Globe and Mail*, March 1, 1979

5. *Canadian Business*, April 1979

6. Minutes of Proceedings and Evidence of the Standing Committee on Northern Pipelines, March 20, 1979

7. Northwest's admission is contained in the minutes of a meeting of Carter's Executive Policy Board, January 9, 1979

8. Quoted in Joseph M. Chomski and Richard G. Haggart, "Alaska Gas Pipeline Perspectives", a report to the Legislative Affairs Agency of the State of Alaska, February 15, 1979

9. I have relied extensively in the following discussion on two reports prepared by Arlon Tussing and Connie Barlow of the Institute of Social and Economic Re-

search at the University of Alaska for the Alaskan State Legislature. The first report, dated January 12, 1979, is entitled: "The Alaska Highway Gas Pipeline: A Look at the Current Impasse". The second report, dated April 1979, is entitled: "Financing the Alaska Highway Gas Pipeline: What is to be done?" Both reports provide an excellent overview of the financing issues the pipeline raises, the evolution in Northwest's and the Administration's position and the interests of all the parties involved.

10. Quoted in *Energy Daily*, November 4, 1977, Vol. 5, No. 214, Washington, DC

11. Quoted in Tussing and Barlow, "Financing the Alaska Highway Gas Pipeline: What is to be Done?" p. A-31

12. For an analysis of the views and percptions of major lenders, see ibid, pp. A-65-68

13. Discussed in ibid, pp A-50 and 51. Tussing and Barlow refer to studies by Foster, Associates, an economic consulting firm, and the Gas Requirements Committee which show considerable uncertainty on the marketability of Alaskan gas in the US in the 1980s.

14. "Financing the Alaska Highway Gas Pipeline: What is to be done?" p. 1

15. "Minutes of Proceedings and Evidence of the Standing Committee on Northern Pipelines", February 27, 1979

16. Testimony of James Schlesinger before the Congressional Joint Economic Committee, January 23, 1979

17. United States Senate Committee on Energy and Natural Resources, "To Approve the Presidential Decision on an Alaska Natural Gas Transportation System", Washington, October 1977, p 13

18. US House of Representatives, "Conference Report to Accompany HR 5289", Washington (October 10, 1978), p 103. Quoted in Tussing and Barlow: "The Alaska Highway Gas Pipeline: A Look at the Current Impasse", p 26

19. Richard Corigan: "Pipeline Company Pushes Congress to get Alaska Gas Rolling—and Rolled-in", *National Journal*, May 20, 1978

20. "The Alaska Highway Gas Pipeline: A Look at the Current Impasse", p 32

Chapter 10

1. See John N. McDougall: "Politics versus Regulation: Parliament and the Mackenzie Valley Pipeline". Paper presented to the annual meeting of the Canadian Political Science Association, Quebec City, May 1976

2. Argument of the Canadian Arctic Resources Committee to the Mackenzie Valley Pipeline Inquiry. Excerpted in *Northern Perspectives*, Vol. 4, No. 5 (1976, CARC)

3. Quoted in D. Lindhal, *Alaska Oil Surplus*, published by the Congressional Research Service of the Library of Congress Brief number 1B77082

4. Remarks of S.R. Blair "Gas Pipelines from the Arctic: A Canadian Perspective", March 1977

5. Remarks of S.R. Blair to a meeting of financial analysts, Montreal, January 15, 1975

6. *Toronto Star*, May 11, 1977

7. Summary of a speech by William E. Richards, president of Dome Petroleum Ltd. to the thirty-fifth annual dinner of the Canadian Shipbuilding and Ship Repairing Association, Ottawa, June 7, 1979

8. Testimony of S.R. Blair to the National Energy Board hearings on natural gas supply and demand, November 15, 1978, Ottawa. Transcript p 2,630

9. CTV Question Period, February 18, 1979

10. Remarks of S.R. Blair to the Petroleum Society of the CIM, Calgary Section, August 1977

Chapter 11

1. *Globe and Mail*, March 9, 1979. See also House of Commons Debates, July 16, 1980, p. 2955 and July 17, 1980, p. 2990.

2. The Ontario gas utilities which would have been expected to question vigorously the desirability of large new exports also own gas-producing interests in Alberta and stood to benefit therefore from the prebuild's approval. Both Consumer's Gas and Norcen were restrained by these conflicting internal pressures throughout the hearings. Another reason the case for new exports went largely unchallenged was that only one public interest group, the Canadian Arctic Resources Committee, participated in the hearings. As a result of the lack of effective opposition, Pan-Alberta's export application escaped the rigorous regulatory review its importance deserved.

3. The Board grants export licences on the basis of three tests, one being the deliverability that is available to support them. This deliverability is not transferable in full from year to year. The reason why the Board allowed the export of less gas than it had found surplus was that the export applications did not conform to the deliverability curve the Board had calculated.

4. Minutes of Proceedings and Evidence of the Standing Committee on Northern Pipelines, House of Commons, December 13, 1979, p. 9.

5. Quoted in National Energy Board *Findings* in the Matter of Phase IV(a) of a Public Hearing Respecting Tariffs and Tolls to be Changed, the Financing of the Pipeline, and Other Related Matters of Foothills Pipe Lines (Yukon) Ltd., March 1980, p. 11.

6. Minutes of Proceedings and Evidence of the Standing Committee on Northern Pipelines, House of Commons, November 22, 1980, p. 30.

7. *House of Commons Debates*, December 6, 1979, p. 2101.

8. Speech to the Winnipeg Chamber of Commerce, February 21, 1980.

9. Transcript of press conference, April 23, 1980.

10. Statement in the Matter of the Hearing with respect to Condition 12 (1) of the Northern Pipeline Act, May 1980, p. 5.

11. The Presidential Decision did not allow the pipeline to start charging a tariff for its services until it had been completed in its entirety. Foothills, however, which had already suffered the consequences of delays in the United States, insisted upon charging its tariff and repaying its debt immediately after the Canadian portions of the project had been completed — even if the American ones had not. Foothills therefore wanted the Presidential Decision amended to allow it to pass its costs on to its U.S. customers right away.

12. *House of Commons Debates*, July 14, 1980, p. 2852.

13. *Ibid.*

14. *Globe and Mail*, July 14, 1980.

15. *Financial Times*, July 14, 1980.

16. Minutes of Proceedings and Evidence of the Standing Committee on Northern Pipelines, House of Commons, June 26, 1980, p. 20.

17. *Globe and Mail*, August 11, 1980.

18. Minutes of Proceedings and Evidence of the Standing Committee on Northern Pipelines, House of Commons, June 3, 1980, p. 11.

INDEX